CALCULATED CHOICES IN POLICY-MAKING

Also by Michiel S. de Vries

DE ENTROPIE HYPOTHESE, INFORMATIE EN STRUCTUUR IN INTERNATIONALE SYSTEMEN

CALCULEREN MET BELEID

CULTURELE, DYNAMIEK EN BELEIDSONTWIKKELING
(*co-edited with O. van Heffen and P. J. Klok*)

Available from Michiel S. de Vries, Department of Politics and Administrative Sciences, Free University Amsterdam

SALOMO: Manual, Cases and Software for Impact Assessments

DISCARDED

First published in Great Britain 1999 by
MACMILLAN PRESS LTD
Houndmills, Basingstoke, Hampshire RG21 6XS and London
Companies and representatives throughout the world

A catalogue record for this book is available from the British Library.

ISBN 0–333–73182–4

 First published in the United States of America 1999 by
ST. MARTIN'S PRESS, INC.,
Scholarly and Reference Division,
175 Fifth Avenue, New York, N.Y. 10010

ISBN 0–312–21984–9

Library of Congress Cataloging-in-Publication Data
Vries, Michiel S. de.
Calculated choices in policy-making : the theory and practice of
impact assessment / Michiel S. de Vries.
  p.   cm.
Includes bibliographical references and index.
ISBN 0–312–21984–9 (cloth)
1. Policy sciences.   2. Decision making.   I. Title.
H97.V75   1998
658.4'03—dc21   98–38460
                                                                  CIP

© Michiel S. de Vries 1999

All rights reserved. No reproduction, copy or transmission of this publication may be made without written permission.

No paragraph of this publication may be reproduced, copied or transmitted save with written permission or in accordance with the provisions of the Copyright, Designs and Patents Act 1988, or under the terms of any licence permitting limited copying issued by the Copyright Licensing Agency, 90 Tottenham Court Road, London W1P 9HE.

Any person who does any unauthorised act in relation to this publication may be liable to criminal prosecution and civil claims for damages.

The author has asserted his right to be identified as the author of this work in accordance with the Copyright, Designs and Patents Act 1988.

This book is printed on paper suitable for recycling and made from fully managed and sustained forest sources.

10 9 8 7 6 5 4 3 2 1
08 07 06 05 04 03 02 01 00 99

Printed and bound in Great Britain by
Antony Rowe Ltd, Chippenham, Wiltshire

Calculated Choices in Policy-Making

The Theory and Practice of Impact Assessment

Michiel S. de Vries
Senior Lecturer
Department of Political and Administrative Sciences
Free University Amsterdam
Amsterdam

To Lies, Linda, Liza and Machteld

Contents

List of tables xi

List of figures xiii

List of formulae xiv

Preface xv

1 An introduction to making calculated choices 1

Introduction 1
1.1 An example 5
1.2 What does impact assessment look like? 7
1.3 Developments in the application of the methodology 8
1.4 Impact assessment as an advanced cost-benefit analysis 9
1.5 Impact assessment within the framework
of evaluation research 16
    1.5.1 User-oriented approach 18
    1.5.2 The independence of evaluation methodology 19
    1.5.3 Effect orientation 21
    1.5.4 Value-bound 26
1.6 A tactical approach 27
    1.6.1 Choices in policy-making 28
    1.6.2 Alternatives and criteria 29
    1.6.3 Test scores 29
    1.6.4 The importance of criteria 29
    1.6.5 Compilation 30
    1.6.6 Analysis 32
    1.6.7 Leave the decision to the decision maker 33
1.7 Structure of the book 33
1.8 Summary 34

2 The task is to make a well-thought-out choice   35

Introduction 35
- 2.1 The elements of policy-making 37
- 2.2 Merits of the tactical approach 40
  - 2.2.1 Problems with an intuitive choice process 41
  - 2.2.2 Advantages of the tactical approach 45
  - 2.2.3 Problems with the tactical approach 46
- 2.3 Conclusion 49

3 Alternatives and criteria   51

Introduction 51
- 3.1 The relationship between information and decision-making quality 53
  - 3.1.1 Incrementalists and synopticians 53
  - 3.1.2 Information theory and cybernetics 56
- 3.2 What determines information search behaviour? 59
  - 3.2.1 Factors related to the content of the choice problem 59
  - 3.2.2 Factors related to the characteristics of the Decision maker(s) 60
- 3.3 Does an optimum exist? 68
- 3.4 Types of criteria 69
- 3.5 Types of alternatives 72
- 3.6 Conclusion 74

4 Determining how well alternatives score on criteria   75

Introduction 75
- 4.1 Criteria and indicators 76
- 4.2 Methods for determining criterion scores 79
  - 4.2.1 Information from previous evaluations 79
  - 4.2.2 Information derived from performance indicators 88
  - 4.2.3 Ask the experts: the classic Delphi method 98
  - 4.2.4 The policy Delphi 100
  - 4.2.5 Comparative case studies 101
- 4.3 Environmental impact assessment in practice 107
  - 4.3.1 A meta evaluation 108
  - 4.3.2 The outcomes of content analysis 109
- 4.4 Conclusion 119

5 The weight of criteria 122

Introduction 122
5.1 The basic problems 124
5.2 Theories on prioritizing 124
5.3 Methodological aspects of weight determination 132
5.4 Transformation of weights 136
5.5 Attribution of weights in practice 142
5.6 Conclusion 147

6 Compilation into a ranking order 148

Introduction 148
6.1 Utility of alternatives 149
    6.1.1 Bentham 150
    6.1.2 John Stuart Mill 151
    6.1.3 The utility formula 152
6.2 Decision rules 153
6.3 The example 156
6.4 Various analytical techniques 156
6.5 Interpretation of ranking order 171
    6.5.1 Variation of outcomes with identical scores 171
    6.5.2 Input of scores in a new analysis 172
6.6 Conclusion 172

7 Analysing the outcomes 173

Introduction 173
7.1 Decision requirements 174
7.2 A simplified example 178
7.3 The analysis 180
    7.3.1 Adding bad alternatives 180
    7.3.2 Adding criteria 183
7.4 Stepwise and pairwise analysis 185
7.5 The 'locations for a nuclear power station' case 188
7.6 Conclusion 192

8 Leave the decision to the decision makers   195

Introduction 195
8.1 Advantages of impact assessment 197
8.2 Use of impact assessment in decision-making 197
8.3 Threatening information 198
8.4 The strategic nature of impact assessment 199
8.5 Conclusion 203

References   205

Subject Index   215

Author Index   219

Tables

1.1	Example of a scorecard	5
1.2	Costs and benefits of the construction of a highway	11
1.3	A fictuous example on cost-benefit analysis	13
1.4	A problem of choice with different solutions	15
1.5	H.Q. Patton's ten steps for arriving at unambiguous objectives	24
1.6	Example of the construction of a highway	25
1.7	A fictitious scorecard	30
2.1	Example of a policy problem	48
2.2	Differences and similarities between the tactical approach and the intuitive choice model	50
3.1	The synoptic and incrementalist approach	54
3.2	Typology based on belief system: dotted lines indicate intermediate positions	62
3.3	Janis' four questions	65
3.4	Recommendations regarding the number of alternatives	68
3.5	Example of a stepwise approach	70
4.1	Requirements for criteria indicators	76
4.2	Steps in ex post evaluation	81
4.3	Purposes for performance indicators	89
4.4	Eleven requirements for performance indicators	91
4.5	Characteristics of the classic Delphi method	98
4.6	Stages in a case study	106
5.1	Inverse qualiflex method	132
5.2	Recommendation concerning attribution of weights	135
5.3	Five weight transformation techniques	136
5.4	Ranking order weights	138
6.1	Bentham's criteria	150
6.2	Elaboration of decision rules	154
6.3	The input data	156
6.4	Differences between methods	157
6.5	The standardized scorecard	159
6.6	Ranking order of alternatives using the expected value method	161

Tables

6.7	Ranking order of alternatives using the concordance method	162
6.8	Ranking order of alternatives using the discordance method	163
6.9	Ranking order of alternatives using the con-discordance method	164
6.10	Consequences of different standardization techniques for con-discordance	164
6.11	Ranking order of alternatives using the regime method	165
6.12	Quantitative standardized scorecard	168
6.13	Qualitative standardized scorecard	168
6.14	Dominance-matrix quantitative	168
6.15	Dominance-matrix qualitative	168
6.16	All possible permutations given three alternatives	170
7.1	An example where both alternatives have equal dominance	178
7.2	Scorecard	180
7.3	Analysis of condition 2	183
7.4	Order of dominance	187
7.5	Order of dominance	188
7.6	Evaluation matrix of locations for a nuclear power station	189
7.7	Alternatives in ranking order of dominance	190
7.8	Pairwise analysis of five locations for a nuclear power station	191
8.1	Scorecard Lauwersmeer	200
8.2	Sets of weights Lauwersmeer	202
8.3	Strategic function of impact assessment	203

Figures

1.1	Elements of a Multi-criteria evaluation	7
1.2	A tactical approach to calculated choices	27
2.1	Interaction between the actor-, choice- and calculating system	37
3.1	The relation between quantity of information and quality of decision-making according to four theories	58
4.1	The connection between ex ante and ex post evaluations	84
4.2	Authoritarian argumentation	95
5.1	Weighing at two levels	130
7.1	Sensitivity of the expected value method	181
7.2	Dominance of alternatives I and J affected by an alternative K	182
7.3	The influence of adding irrelevant criteria	184

Formulae

1.1	Utility	32
5.1	Standardization of weights	137
5.2	Ranking order weights	139
5.3	Determination of standard weights from ranking order weights	139
5.4	Maximization of the first criterion	140
5.5	Maximization of the two most important criteria	140
6.1	Expected utility	152
6.2	Extended formula for expected utility	153
6.3	Standardization of weights	158
6.4	Standardization of scores	159
6.5	Standardization of scores according to evamix	159
6.6	Utility function	160
6.7	Standardization of scores according to evamix	166
6.8	Regime method	168
6.9	Utility in Evamix-method	169
6.10	Result of Evamix method	169
7.1	Calculation of dominance scores	179
7.2	Calculation of dominance scores using a third alternative	179
7.3	Discrimination factors	186

Preface

This is a book about making choices based on the evaluation of alternatives. Although primarily written for people having (to learn) to make policy decisions, the methods discussed are generally applicable. The starting point of the book is the notion that the outcomes of choices are often worse than people expect. To improve outcomes, an evaluation beforehand and a thorough deliberation of the advantages and disadvantages of various alternatives can be useful. Dealing with policies in a rational way without distorting the political context in which choices are made is a complex if not impossible matter. This book discusses the major problems and makes recommendations for decision makers who want to optimize the outcomes of their choices. In doing so, the subject matter of this book is at the crossroads of policy- and research methodology. How can information derived from empirical research benefit a policy maker or decision maker, and how should this information be incorporated in the decision-making process?

Acting rationally seems ideal, yet so many complications are inherent in the idea of rational choices that rationality - even when using rational methods - is often hard to find. In the real world, this lack of rationality is demonstrated by the implementation of policies determined on the basis of policy evaluation. The same can also be shown by critically analysing the inherent logic of the methods themselves. The aim of this book is therefore twofold: to clarify the theory of impact assessment and to make recommendations concerning the practical application of impact assessments.

This book is primarily intended for students at a higher professional or scientific level. Many people perceive a fundamental distinction between these types of education. In general, this idea is inaccurate. There are good, reasonable and bad academic training programmes, and there are good, reasonable and bad higher professional training programmes. If a choice has to be made based on differences of standards between these types of education, a problem of choice has arisen. Because such a choice involves a complex deliberation of positive and negative aspects, application of the methods dealt with in this book can be particularly useful.

Parts of this book have been published in various scientific journals. A section of Chapter 4 was published in Beleidswetenschap 1993/3, under the title 'Criteria voor milieu-effectrapporten'. A part of Chapter 6 appeared in International Review of Administrative Sciences, 1994 Vol 60, with the title 'Establishing Priorities: Technocratic policy-making in the Netherlands'. A section of Chapter 7 was published in Quality & Quantity Vol 26. 1992, and was titled 'Stepwise multiple-criteria evaluation'.

Amsterdam, July 1998

The software program SALOMO

The author has together with Ronald Groenink developed a software program called SALOMO, named after the Biblical king known for his wise decisions. Those who are interested in making impact assessments in practice, who want to evaluate impact assessments or want students to practice in making calculated choices, may find this software very useful.

It is a menu driven package, ranking alternatives on the basis of criteria, the scores of every alternative on each criterion and the criterion weights. The β-version which is now available, offers several standardization- and analysis techniques as well as several possibilities for doing sensitivity analyses. Salomo can handle up to 18 alternatives and 18 criteria. It has easy to use input and output possibilities and takes away the time-consuming mathematical analysis.

The aims of this program are educational, giving decision makers practical experience in making and checking decisions.

Its development was guided by simplicity and user-friendliness. The use of the software-program Salomo and applying the methodology to practical examples will not only enhance understanding of the theory, but will also prove to be useful in practice.

For further information about this software, which is accompanied by a user-manual and cases, one can contact the author directly.

Address: Dr Michiel S. de Vries
                Department of Political and Administrative Sciences
                Vrije Universiteit Amsterdam
                De Boelelaan 1081-c, 1081 HV Amsterdam,
                The Netherlands

1 An introduction to making calculated choices

> This chapter introduces the book and discusses the merits of impact assessments. After articulating the general objectives and discussing a simple example, a comparison will be made between the impact assessment model and classic cost-benefit analysis. In addition, the model will be positioned within the framework of evaluation research, given that impact assessments are in fact a form of multi-criteria evaluation. Finally, the steps of the model will be dealt with.

INTRODUCTION

A large number of expressions remind people of their responsibility concerning the negative consequences of their decisions: 'You have to bear the consequences and pay the penalty. This expression applies to individuals, managers, policy makers and politicians. Therefore, the starting point of this book is the notion that before taking decisions it is sensible to carefully reflect on the various possibilities. There is nothing new in this statement, and the number of expressions emphasizing this point is just as great. 'This possibility needs careful consideration', 'a moment's thought would show you it won't work', 'one has to weigh up the pros and cons', and 'think before you decide.' Moreover, the increasing importance of environmental impact assessments demonstrates that policy makers are becoming more aware of the subject. Yet, it appears that decision makers all too often regret their decisions later. Despite their efforts, the consequences of a decision may turn out to be more negative, i.e. it may appear to be more expensive, to take more time, or in case of something desirable, to be too short-lived. To quote a phrase from a poem by Judith Herzberg, 'It is always more expensive than you think it is, even when you think 'it will probably be more expensive than I think', it still is more expensive than you think.'

Impact assessments were developed in order to avoid as many unforeseen consequences of policy decisions as possible. The positive and negative effects of decisions about large-scale investments are made explicit beforehand so they can be taken into account during the decision-making process. In order to create a more rational decision-making process, an intended initiative is compared to other alternatives on the basis of expected consequences. Alternatives are put into ranking order of utility (the sum total of their positive and negative effects) and a calculated decision is made possible. This may seem simple, but later in this book we will see that in fact it is far from simple.

A well-known example of a problem of choice that had disastrous consequences is the story of King Priamos of Troy. About four thousand years ago, after a long siege of the city of Troy, the Greeks withdrew their troops leaving behind a giant wooden horse. Priamos was presented with the choice either to treat the horse as a trophy and bring it inside the city walls, or to leave the horse outside to save costs and energy. He took the wrong decision and brought not just the horse inside the city walls, but also the Greek soldiers that were hidden inside it. Consequently, the city was lost. In decision theory this still is an important example.

In the past and in the present, people were/are continuously choosing from various alternatives on the basis of deliberations about costs and benefits. Such deliberations can be made explicit, but can also remain implicit or intuitive. Moreover, although often a calculation may seem rational, it may just as often lead to irrationality if applied intuitively.

A second example, given by Sen, is about a husband and wife who have read a particular book review. Each holds a personal opinion about the book. The woman argues that although it is important for her to read the book, it is even more important for her husband to read it. Her husband argues that whereas it would be bad for him to read the book, it would be even worse for his wife to read it. Calculation results in the husband reading the book. In the eyes of the wife, this is the best choice; in the eyes of the man, it is the least undesirable choice. Yet in reality it turns out to be the wife who reads the book.

A more recent example concerns an experiment among students who are given pens and asked to swap them among themselves. Most of the students turn out to be willing to do so. However, if a lottery ticket is given to the same students, they are not willing to swap. Yet, these tickets represent exactly the same value, provided the draw has not taken place.

In this book the calculating approach towards taking decisions is central. Its possibilities and limitations will be discussed. The presupposition is that regrets afterwards about a choice can be reduced by carefully weighing advantages and disadvantages of the various alternatives before making a decision. This implies a tactical approach, making the possibilities more explicit and assessing each of these possibilities in accordance with a number of criteria that are also made explicit. Regardless of whether much or just little information is available, all rational choices are characterized by the inherent logic that results from an ideal-type model playing a part in every decision, be it implicit or explicit. It is the logic of this model that will be described in this book.

However, compliance with this decision model is no guarantee that choices will result in optimal outcomes. For decision makers who want to determine their policies in such a calculated way, this book will point out the possibilities as well as the consequences and pitfalls.

It cannot be emphasized enough that the attitude of a decision maker at the beginning of the decision process is crucial. In the case of a predetermined choice, a model or a rational approach is of no avail. Chances are high that the model will be followed in reverse order and that already fixed choices will merely be rationalized. Choices made in the model, concerning the consideration of alternatives on the basis of criteria, are likely to get distorted. The deliberation about alternatives can only be useful in cases where the decision maker is still susceptible to various options, i.e. where a priori all options have an equal chance of being selected.

This book is written from the perspective of a (future) decision maker, making choices at work, in the public or the private sector, or simply being a consumer. Although the majority of examples used in this book refer to policy-making in public office, other examples deal with consumer choices, research into business locations and SWOT analyses. All choices are based on the (alleged) value or utility of alternatives and on the sum total of expected positive and negative effects. Regardless of the amount of criticism of utility theories, people have good reason to try and make their plans as useful as possible, implicitly or explicitly. The allocation of means should lead to goal-attainment and bring about the intended outcomes. Possible side effects need to be minimized in case of negative appreciation, and maximized in case of positive appreciation. The argument here is that this can be achieved by deliberating upon effects prior to making a decision. It is precisely the lack of deliberation about alternatives on the basis of their possible effects that leads to choices that are regretted or criticized afterwards.

Information is not the only item decision makers need in order to arrive at good policy-making, as is often thought. They also need a model that allows them to use that information and make a well-deliberated decision. Information should not necessarily be collected by the decision maker. It can also be collected, analysed and communicated by external researchers and become a so-called black box for the decision maker. Consumer organizations collect information and regularly publish reports comparing consumer goods. Research organizations collect and analyse information for the public and the private sector. A problem arises when such information is unreservedly taken to be true or even to be objective. In this book, information is itself regarded as the result of a number of decisions that can be influenced by the decision maker. In this way the result can be made to fit the framework, the wishes, preferences and ideas of the decision maker, instead of being a ranking order reflecting the preferences of the provider of information.

The main objective of this book is *to add to the understanding of how to make well-deliberated choices in a policy-making process*. Calculating behaviour does not always lead to better outcomes. Its rationality depends on the way in which consecutive steps are taken according to the model and on avoiding the pitfalls discussed in this book.

The model that will be described originates from *multi-criteria evaluation* and *cost-benefit analysis*. The following sections of this chapter will compare these models with the impact assessment model. Alternatives will be evaluated on the basis of the sum total of all advantages and disadvantages, taking into account the weights of the criteria. The method distinguishes a number of phases that have to be considered explicitly by a calculating policy maker. Avoiding pitfalls in the different phases will be a recurring subject of this book. Although on the one hand we are concerned with pitfalls inherent in the methods of rational decision-making, on the other hand pitfalls can be a consequence of the way these methods are applied in practice.

The second perspective from which this book can be read is as a *critical reflection on the methodology*. Nowadays reports on impact assessment can be seen everywhere. Before a decision is taken it has to be made clear what the effects are of all alternatives. Well-known are environmental impact assessments where large-scale projects with possible environmental effects are investigated beforehand, i.e. the possible effects on flora and fauna, and of air, water and soil pollution, noise nuisance, etcetera are looked at. Following the success of environmental impact assessments, they have also been developed in the field of management and economics, e.g. emancipation- and age impact assessment for personnel departments, and youth- and safety impact assessments for government policies. The doctrine of Total Quality Management mentions a similar model called Quality Function Deployment. Here, alternative options are related to the strengths and weaknesses of the organization and of its competitors. In addition, for each alternative the criteria are compared to find out to what extent a more favourable score on one criterion (e.g. cost-efficiency) is at the expense of other criteria (e.g. output-quality).

So far a critical reflection on the methodology is lacking, that is, a reflection starting with the logic of the methodology and its application. The objective of such critical reflection is not to find arguments to reject the application of the model, but to result in recommendations. Using these recommendations, application of the model gives evidence not only of calculating behaviour, but also of rational behaviour.

The third part of this book is aimed at *offering guidelines for the evaluation or creation of impact assessment reports that make use of this methodology by following the steps of the model.*

1.1 AN EXAMPLE

Impact assessment implies evaluating alternative choices on the basis of several criteria, given the weights of those criteria. Such an evaluation results in a ranking order of alternatives. In a simplified model one might think of a ranking order based on price-quality ratios. When purchasing a product (for example, a washing machine), a choice can be made between several products, the alternatives. The products differ in purchase price, durability and after-sales service. These are the criteria.

	Miele	Philips	Zanussi
Price	$ 1200	$ 800	$ 1600
Lifespan	10 years	5 years	15 years
Service	excellent	good	reasonable

Table 1.1 *Example of a scorecard*

The differences are illustrated in Table 1.1. Such a table is called a *scorecard*. It is not easy to arrive at an unambiguous ranking order of alternatives on the basis of this information. Regarding price, the best choice is Philips, the cheapest. As far as durability is concerned, Zanussi is the best alternative. Miele is the best choice with regard to after-sales service. Which of the washing machines will be purchased also depends on the value given to the various criteria.

To a well-to-do buyer, the purchase price will be of less importance than durability and after-sales service, whereas to a less wealthy buyer the purchase price might be decisive. In other words, criteria can have different weights.

In essence, impact assessment is an 'objectivized' method which generates a ranking order of alternatives on the basis of explicit criterion scores and their weights. In our example, a choice has to be made between three washing machines. The higher the priority given by the buyer to a criterion on which a certain product scores best, the higher the probability that this product will be selected. This is the inherent logic of impact assessment. Determination of the optimal choice is based on the qualities attributed to alternatives and the importance attributed to these qualities.

People make such evaluations almost daily, either implicitly or explicitly. A consumer makes choices in a supermarket, when purchasing a television set, buying a house or deciding where to go on holiday. Parents make choices regarding the education of their children. Physicians choose when prescribing medication. Politicians make choices about their position on policy issues, and policy makers make choices about the allocation of funds for the renovation of residential areas, the construction of a bridge or a tunnel, the location of industrial activities, possibilities for extending an airport, and ways to process household garbage. Common to all these problems is the variety of ways to take or refrain from taking action, and also the variety of criteria on which to assess these possibilities. Impact assessment, therefore, is an instrument to be used when taking *relatively complex decisions*.

Impact assessment offers a general model that can be used to deal with any problem of choice. The value or utility of each alternative is determined by adding up the scores of criteria, each of which has its own weight. Utility scores determine the ranking of alternatives in order of preference.

1.2 WHAT DOES IMPACT ASSESSMENT LOOK LIKE?

In general, the structure of impact assessment is characterized by a number of stages. For example, an actor is faced with a problem. This means something needs to be done to bring the perceived situation closer to a desirable situation. The problem, for instance, is traffic congestion. Several means are available to deal with this. The alternatives are formulated, and to assess them, criteria are chosen. Using these criteria, the alternatives are evaluated. Then the scores of each alternative on the criteria are determined. Because an unequivocal ranking order is desired and because one alternative scoring best on all criteria is hardly ever the case, the criteria have to be weighed. Next, criterion scores and weights are adjusted to make them comparable and the ranking order of alternatives is calculated by way of a formula. The steps taken are presented in Figure 1.1.

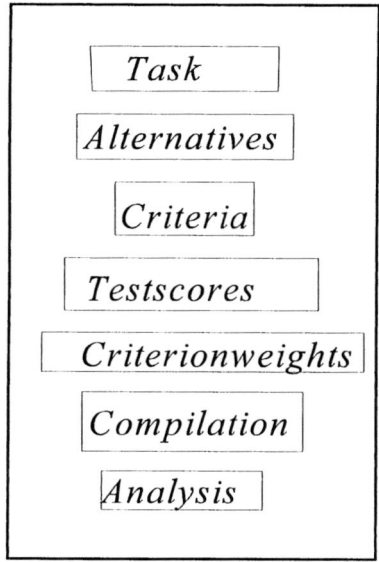

Figure 1.1 *Elements of a Multi-criteria evaluation*

1.3 DEVELOPMENTS IN THE APPLICATION OF THE METHODOLOGY

Impact assessments by way of multi-criteria evaluation are often carried out. They were first used after the Second World War by researchers at the Rand Corporation. After their successful application in social geography and geographical planning, the advantages of this approach were increasingly recognized. Applications on national, district and city levels are known in the fields of the environment, traffic and transportation, and business economics. What factors have led to the rise of impact assessment?

- First, the kind of problems that have been dealt with by means of the methodology. Complicated problems of choice, i.e. those involving a large number of factors, are tackled, using the method to arrive at an unequivocal ranking order of alternatives. The method serves as an *instrument* for finding the most preferred alternative.
- Second, impact assessment is considered to be an *objective method*. Taking into account the preferences of decision makers, a calculation of data determines an unequivocal ranking order of alternatives. This calculation is given; preferences of decision makers cannot alter the process. Such an objectivized choice appears to meet people's needs.
- Third, the method has an inherent logic that is recognized as such by decision makers. All aspects regarded as relevant by decision makers can be included in the analysis and can be presented in a clear way. The weights of all criteria, based on the opinion of the decision makers, are also taken into account. All criterion scores and weights are combined in a mathematical utility function, resulting in dominance scores with the highest utility given to the most dominant alternative.
- Fourth, impact assessment is associated with *rationality*. By using the method, it would be possible to determine the most effective and efficient choice.
- Fifth, deliberated criteria and priorities need to be made explicit for impact assessment. This way the decision-making process becomes *transparent and controllable*.
- Sixth, there is a wide range of *possible applications* for impact assessment. These possibilities are not limited by either the subject matter or the complexity of a problem.

An introduction to making calculated choices

- Seventh, multi-criteria analysis has *proved to be useful in practice*. Results do not differ from evaluations based on common sense. In particular, the Stunet study and research into the extension of the national airport have contributed to this development.
- Eighth, developments of the method itself can be pointed out. On the one hand, advanced solutions have been found for technical problems. On the other hand, various approaches have been tested extensively. Both developments have increased confidence in the outcomes of impact assessment.
- Ninth, developments in society can be referred to, where the call for alternatives has become louder and louder. For example, no bridge can be built or there has to be at least an investigation into the effectiveness of a tunnel. Every policy plan needs to contain alternatives, so that decision makers can choose from them. In recent years, in some areas, the indication and comparison of alternatives has even become legally compulsory. This applies to, for example, infrastructural measures where an environmental impact assessment is mandatory.
- Tenth, impact assessment can play an important role in public conflict resolution. One of the most important recommendations given in this area concerns the decomposition of problems by applying fact-finding (preferably joint fact-finding) and its appreciation. When decisions involve a lot of contrary interests, it is recommendable to divide the problem into its most elementary parts so that discussions can be more pragmatic and efficient. In this way, no lengthy arguments arise over aspects of a problem of choice that could have been avoided beforehand (Hammond et al. 1977, Kleindorfer et al. 1993, p.226). The model here described is characterized by the fact that a problem is divided into and made explicit in separate units that can be dealt with consecutively in order to arrive at an optimal choice.

1.4 IMPACT ASSESSMENT AS AN ADVANCED COST-BENEFIT ANALYSIS

Impact assessment as described here is an advanced version of the classic cost-benefit analysis. Typical of cost-benefit analysis is the fact that the scores of alternatives on all criteria are expressed in money terms. With this method, too, the central question is which alternative should be chosen. The answer cost-benefit analysis provides is fourfold. First, the preferred alternative will be the one where the cost-benefit ratio is most favourable. Second, nothing will be done (that is, the zero alternative will be chosen) if for any other alternative costs are higher than the benefits. Third, it is possible that costs may not rise above a predetermined limitation level. In that case, costs are called a veto criterion. Fourth, the plausibility of the outcomes may not become too uncertain.

The definition of a cost-benefit analysis can be broad or narrow. Looking at public cost-benefit analyses only, many definitions have been given. Prest and Turvey (1965), for example, defined cost-benefit analysis as 'A practical way of assessing the desirability of projects, where it is important to take a long view (in the sense of looking at repercussions in the further, as well as the nearer, future) and a wide view (in the sense of allowing for side effects of many kinds on many persons, industries, regions etc.), i.e. it implies the enumeration and evaluation of all the relevant costs and benefits.' Dasgupta and Pearce (1972: 19) use a somewhat narrower definition: 'Cost-benefit analysis purports to be a way of deciding what society prefers. Where only one option can be chosen from a series of options, CBA should inform the decision maker as to which option is socially most preferred.' Most economists use a straightforward definition: 'Cost-benefit analysis will indicate that the government should produce at the point where the marginal costs of the project equals the marginal gains or benefits derived from it.' (Gill 1973: 758)

Cost-benefit analysis is characterized by the fact that all costs and benefits are expressed in money terms. The advantages of an identical unit of measurement for all criteria are that scores do not need to be standardized and that the assignment of weights to criteria is not necessary. After all, one pound sterling is equal to any other pound sterling.

A limited, fictitious example of a cost-benefit analysis concerning the construction of a highway is given in Table 1.2 (from Newton, 1972: 39).

Obviously in practice such a cost-benefit analysis is much more extensive. The example serves to clarify the advantages and disadvantages of cost-benefit analysis. Because of the subject matter of the criteria, it may be called a solid method. All subjective elements, such as the assignment of weights to criteria, appear to have vanished. It provides a clear understanding of the pros and cons of the alternatives. Moreover, determination of cost and benefits of government policy has become easier because the number of statistical indices is increasing.

An introduction to making calculated choices

Questions that can be answered are, for example, what are the costs of giving subsidies, and how are efficiency and effectiveness influenced by using computers?

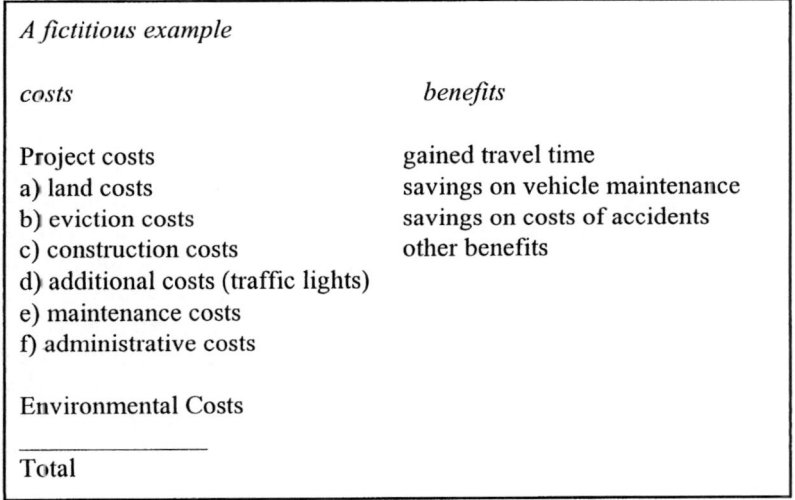

A fictitious example

costs	benefits
Project costs	gained travel time
a) land costs	savings on vehicle maintenance
b) eviction costs	savings on costs of accidents
c) construction costs	other benefits
d) additional costs (traffic lights)	
e) maintenance costs	
f) administrative costs	
Environmental Costs	
Total	

Table 1.2 *Costs and benefits of the construction of a highway*

From the perspective of a private company, such a cost-benefit analysis can be a sensible thing to carry out. After all, economic justification for investments lies in their potential for financial merits. Analysing investments aims at assessing those financial merits and serves to evaluate costs and benefits for the company.

With government investments and private decisions, this is a more complex matter. Economic justification of a government decision lies not merely in its potential for yielding financial returns, but also in its contribution to social prosperity. Therefore, government needs to determine societal costs and benefits, just as an individual needs to determine private costs and benefits. 'Societal' refers to the principle that the government institutions involved ought to take into account the 'external effects', as they are known by economists. These effects are costs and benefits that are not at the expense or in favour of the subject that undertakes a certain activity. Governments will have to take into consideration the distribution of costs and benefits among different groups. Who profits from a policy, and who pays the costs?

A disadvantage of cost-benefit analysis is that the distribution of costs and benefits among different actors is not incorporated in the analysis. However, when using impact assessment the costs for different groups can be considered as separate criteria with specific weights. When using cost-benefit analysis, it makes no difference who takes care of the costs and to whom an investment is advantageous. In the example, the question is raised which travellers are taken into consideration when determining travel time. In addition to local commuters, others will make use of the highway.

Whether a cost-benefit analysis is possible depends on the question whether all cost and benefit items can be expressed in money terms. Items that cannot are called imponderabilia. These are items for which prices cannot be given directly. Examples are pollution, human lives, traffic safety and a reduction in the area of a nature reserve. Sometimes in a cost-benefit analysis such items are referred to as PM items. Literally these are items to be kept in mind, but in reality they are usually insufficiently taken into account. How to deal with PM items is of course a problem of the choice system. From the perspective of the actor system, it is likely that less significance will be attached to a PM item than to a cost or benefit item expressed in money terms.

One of the questions is whether a certain item really belongs to the imponderabilia or whether perhaps indirectly value determination is possible after all. Discussion about this topic has been extensive. Weisbrod claims that measurability depends on the time period we live in. Whereas in the Middle Ages everybody would have believed that body temperature is unmeasurable, nowadays we are happy that Gabriel Fahrenheit did not agree (Weisbrod 1962). The possibility of measuring costs and/or benefits also depends on the amount of time one is prepared to invest in measurement.

Thirdly, the outcome of cost-benefit analysis depends on the way in which costs and benefits are calculated, and the way in which one is weighed against the other. These are problems inherent in the calculating system.

Some people maintain that cost-benefit analysis is a more reliable method than the more general impact assessment method, because all scores are expressed in the same quantitative unit of measurement. However, there are also problems with cost-benefit analysis, such as, for example, the incorporation of imponderabilia. In the past, five solutions to this problem have been suggested:

The first solution is, as already mentioned, to incorporate imponderabilia as PM items. Because this may distort the outcome of the analysis, however, this solution is problematic. Nevertheless, sometimes this is a necessary solution. In the analysis, the distortion can be partly undone. One way to do this is to calculate for which value of the imponderabilia costs become smaller, equal or higher than benefits. The decision maker can estimate how big chances are that this might happen. Suppose a cost-benefit analysis yields the following data:

Costs	20 million
Benefits	30 million
Pollution	[PM]

Table 1.3 *A fictuous example on cost-benefit analysis*

The solution here is to explicitly include in the conclusions that if the economic cost of pollution will be higher than 10 million the project will not be profitable.

The second solution is the use of so-called shadow prices. Determination of shadow prices is a way to indirectly calculate the market value of an item. This applies to items where direct determination of price is impossible, or to items whose direct monetary value differs from their market value. What is the value of a nature reserve that has to yield to a highway? One way to calculate this is to determine what it would cost to create a comparable nature reserve elsewhere.

Calculation of the value of gained travel time can be done by multiplying the average hourly wage of highway users, the number of highway users and the travel time gained. In this way, minutes can be converted into money terms. These shadow prices are always based on assumptions. In this case, for example, the assumption is that a certain number of minutes of leisure time represents an equal value as the same number of minutes working time. A third example is the value of human life. In determining this using shadow prices, total reproduction costs would be involved, i.e. the total investment in a person that has taken place in the past. Among others these are the costs of upbringing, training and experience. Consequently, the value of a person's life is higher if that person is older, more trained and has a longer working history.

The third solution is the use of so-called opportunity costs. The value of a nature reserve is determined by calculating the value it would have if it were used in the most profitable way, for example as agricultural land or as a residential area. The allocation of the area which would give it its highest value will be used to calculate the price for the area.

It will be immediately clear that this way of calculation decreases the chances of arriving at a positive cost-benefit balance. In this case, the value of human life is determined using the sum total of the expected or maximized future income. The assumption here is that the economic value of a person decreases as he or she grows older.

The fourth solution is to determine the *consumer surplus*; in other words, how much a user is willing to sacrifice in order to save a nature reserve, given that there are other nature reserves. It is the value added that counts, i.e. the marginal costs and benefits, and not the total value of the area. With regard to the economic value of human life, this involves the principle of insurance: the premium someone is willing to pay for life insurance determines the economic value attached to this persons life.

The fifth solution, the most rigorous but also most frequently applied method, is to consider an item to be an *external effect*. Any item whose value cannot be expressed in money terms is not taken into account when performing cost-benefit analysis. They are taken to be indirect effects of a choice, it is unclear whether their appreciation is positive or negative, to whom they are positive or negative, and whether they are a consequence of the choice (Misjan 1978: 87). Human lives do not count when using this solution. The (unrealistic) arguments used to justify this are that human lives are not the decision makers' problem, that it is unclear whether construction of a highway is the cause of loss of life, or that it is unclear whether this should be evaluated as a positive or a negative effect. (cf Misjan 1978: 101 ff)

The analysis of costs and benefits

When all costs and benefits are known, the decision maker has to make a choice to do or not to do something. The question then is which *decision rule* will be used. The decision maker's choice can be determined by a favourable cost-benefit ratio and the magnitude of the difference between costs and benefits. This is a matter of division or subtraction. Table 1.4 illustrates that this distinction is relevant. Which project should be chosen? In project 1 the difference between costs and benefits is greatest (5 million vs 0.9 million). In the second project the ratio of costs and benefits is much higher (1:2 vs 1:10). The decision maker determines the decision rule. Different decision rules can produce various outcomes under similar circumstances.

	project 1	*project 2*
Benefit	10 million	Benefit 1,0 million
Costs	5 million	Costs 0,1 million

Table 1.4 *A problem of choice with different solutions*

The second problem concerns the way in which raw data have already been processed. Should all costs and benefits be taken into consideration when analysing an investment problem, or is it permissible that benefits arising directly from certain costs are deducted beforehand? This problem is known as *balancing*. Balancing influences the cost-benefit ratio. This can be illustrated by a simple calculation, where x is the amount to be balanced $\{[10/5 < (10-x)/(5-x)]$ for any $x>0\}$. This way, the result of a balanced cost-benefit analysis suggests larger profit/loss margins. In some countries, this is obviated by demanding that in addition to project costs and benefits such analyses include all investment costs.

Possible choices and their consequences indicate that cost-benefit analysis, too, is subjective in nature. It will be clear also that each of the methods of taking imponderabilia into account is based on (usually implicit) assumptions. It is this disadvantage that eventually resulted in the development of impact assessment.

The above-mentioned leads to the conclusion that a cost-benefit analysis involves relatively many choices, and that the process of choice itself remains largely implicit. Impact assessment offers an improvement here because it makes deliberations explicit.

Conclusion

Cost-benefit analysis has advantages over multi-criteria evaluation. The main one is that all criterion scores are expressed in the same unit of measurement. At the same time, however, this can be a disadvantage when measurements are artificial or unrealistic. Additionally, the suggestion that cost-benefit analysis is more objective is unfounded. As it turns out, subjective choices have to be made in all phases of cost-benefit analysis, and many of the suppositions that play a part remain implicit. In the next chapter it will be argued that this is one of the causes of intuitive and irrational choices. Furthermore, cost-benefit analysis results in one criterion only, namely the financial criterion, whereas impact assessment has a much broader scope.

1.5 IMPACT ASSESSMENT WITHIN THE FRAMEWORK OF EVALUATION RESEARCH

Impact assessment as a multi-criteria evaluation to determine the utility of alternatives is a specific form of evaluation and a relatively new variant. The first applications in the area of policy-making can be traced back to the Rand Corporation. Later, applications followed in a large number of policy areas. Walker published about its application at the New York Fire Department, which was trying to improve its organization (Walker et al., 1979), and Heafele writes about using impact assessment when making strategic choices concerning future energy supply (Haefele, 1981). In fact, taking decisions in such a way is nothing else than evaluation ex ante. This puts the model within the framework of evaluation research. It then becomes important to know what distinguishes impact assessment from other evaluation research.

In recent years, two schools of thought have come to dominate the discussion about evaluation. The classic school aims at measuring goal-attainment (summative evaluation), whereas the modern school aims at giving advice (formative evaluation). The discussion focuses on the question whether evaluation research should only provide facts and relations concerning the evaluand (mainly interpreted as goal-attainment) and leave conclusions to policy makers and other interest groups, or whether the evaluator should also be allowed to have opinions about the goals themselves, its side effects, efficiency and possible improvements.

Nowadays this discussion is related to a more generally experienced dissatisfaction with classic evaluation research, in particular with its dominant methodology. By way of experiments and quasi-experiments, investigations were conducted into the effects of implemented policies on objectives formulated by policy makers, and into the question whether these effects were attributable to that policy or to other developments. In 1960 this model of evaluation was the ruling paradigm. Scriven even called it a *Zeitgeist*. 13

In the 1960s more room was given to other forms of evaluation. At times the inaccurate impression was given that the classic model was no longer dominant. Nevertheless, the majority of evaluations are summative, set up according to experimental design and quantitative in nature. In 1985 Mark Lipsey said that

> 'The dominant methodological approach to program evaluation research today is based on the experimental paradigm, that is quantitative measurement of dependent variables with controlled designs to establish cause and effect relationships.' (Lipsey, 1985: 7)

This involves finding differences in situations as a consequence of interventions. A goal variable Y can only be a consequence of intervention X when Y occurs after the occurrence of X, and if Y is absent X should also be absent. The power of the classic model - i.e. its inherent logic - has made it the dominant paradigm in evaluation research. Until the end of the 1960s, scientific evaluation was mainly considered to be a technical and descriptive enterprise, where the role of the evaluator was minimal and only the goals and means of the policy maker should be considered in the research. All judgements, unintentional effects and side effects found by the evaluator were left out of consideration because they were unscientific statements.

Based on the dissatisfaction with the existing dominating methodology, a broader conception of evaluation emerged in the late 1960s. Four aspects are characteristic of this development.

- The role of evaluation has changed. There is a tendency away from a knowledge orientation towards a practicability orientation.
- The role of evaluation methodology has changed. Next to classic experimental and quantitative methodology, more qualitative methods have emerged aimed at future action by policy makers. Expert methods, such as Delhi technology, scenario methods and decision support systems, have become more fashionable.
- The direction of evaluation research has changed. Evaluation research is no longer limited to formally fixed objectives of policy makers, but also uses a multitude of sources, among which are the objectives and effects as made explicit by the evaluator himself.
- The role of the evaluator has changed. The evaluator is seen as someone who not only describes and explains, but also evaluates and therefore has opinions. The discussion is concerned with the

question whether the scientific nature of research will be lost. The objectivity of evaluation research seems to be at stake. However, if the values/criteria that constitute the basis of those opinions are accurately specified, the research itself can be considered objective.

These four tendencies will be clarified below. The focus will be on the position of impact assessment in relation to the ruling paradigm in evaluation research.

1.5.1 User-oriented approach

Impact assessment methodology is characterized by its user orientation. Information is presented in an orderly fashion in order to allow for more rational choices. The main objection to the classic school is that only summative evaluations are made possible. These are evaluations that give a description a posteriori of the extent of goal-attainment and refrain from giving related conclusions. Critics point out the naivety of its ideal image, i.e. that evaluation research has positive effects on policy programmes. The dominant idea in the 1960s, mainly articulated by Suchman, was that *evaluative feedback* about the effectiveness of realized policies would have direct consequences for maintaining and extending effective programmes and radical changes or termination of ineffective programmes. The problem with summative evaluations, however, is their lack of user orientation. Usually they only indicate afterwards whether a programme has attained its goals or, as happens more often, has not attained them. What is not pointed out is how a programme can be made to attain its goals better, what the explanations are and what the consequences could be of the evaluation results. Evaluations are never completely convincing, and results lead more often to differences of opinion than to consensus. The termination of policies, according to critics, turned out to be rare and certainly did not happen because of evaluation results (Cook & Shadish, 1986: 200). In other words, policy programmes are hardly influenced by summative evaluations. The solution to this problem is to shift summative evaluations towards formative evaluations. Cronbach goes even further and rejects summative evaluations completely. His very narrow definition of evaluation research is:

'By the term evaluation we mean systematic examination of events occurring in and consequences of a contemporary program - an examination conducted to assist in improving this program and other programs having the same general purpose.' (Cronbach, 1982: 14)

This definition leaves no room for independent summative evaluations. Only evaluations that are helpful to a policy maker and serve to improve his policy can be called evaluations. Despite his preference for formative evaluations, Michael Scriven, another representative of the new school, calls this an 'extraordinary blunder' (Scriven, 1986: 101). In his opinion it remains necessary to indicate the extent of goal-attainment. He agrees that this is not enough, but that it still does not mean that such research is superfluous or useless. His claim is that summative evaluations are necessary input for formative evaluations. Experience and the measurement of experience contribute to the sensibility of a recommendation or an opinion about desirable future programmes.

1.5.2 The independence of evaluation methodology

A second characteristic of multi-criteria evaluation is the irrelevance to the methodology of the way in which data, i.e. scores of alternatives on criteria, are collected. Even though experimental design is the classic methodology and is very powerful, it is only one of the possible techniques to determine scores on evaluation criteria. This too is in accordance with the tendencies in the development of evaluation research. Aside from a wider opinion about the role of evaluation research, the 1970s also witnessed an increase of criticism of the experimental research design so characteristic of the classic paradigm.

Essential to the experimental design is the distinction of two or more equivalent groups. All groups have a characteristic that is measured at time t_0. The ideal case is when this measurement is identical for each group. One group is a control group, the others are experimental groups. The experimental groups are manipulated, i.e. an intervention is performed that is expected to alter the target variable. After the intervention, the value of the target variable is again determined for each group and an investigation is carried out into whether a change really has taken place. The ideal case is when the difference in changes between the various groups before and after measurement can be exclusively attributed to the manipulated variable. If it can, then the intervention has caused the effect. The experimental method in evaluation research is characterized by the comparison of two situations, one without and one with policy intervention. The difference of the goal variable in both situations can then be attributed to the policy intervention.

In reality, a lot of experimental research is carried out on the basis of designs that are deficient in terms of structure, sampling methodology, measuring instruments, underlying theory, and explanation of negative results. They are of hardly any value (Gordon & Morse 1975, Bernstein & Freeman 1975, and Lipsey 1985). Lipsey states (1985: 24): 'The conclusion emerging from analysis of the present sample of evaluation studies is that evaluation research under the experimental paradigm is largely conducted at a level of marginal methodological and conceptual quality. Inferentially weak designs predominated, and the reliability, validity and sensitivity of dependent measures were rarely demonstrated. Lack of statistical power compromised many studies, even if otherwise well designed, and precluded confident statements about program effects.'

Others criticized the use of the significance tests that are inherent in experimental research. Schneider and d'Arcy came to the conclusion that these tests are too strict. Small but substantial effects are neglected, the assumption of linearity of relations is often used wrongfully and in general there is a misrepresentation tending towards finding non-significant results. Another criticism is aimed at the comparison of situations with and without policy interventions. This is considered to be an unrealistic comparison. Usually a decision maker is not concerned with choices between doing nothing or doing something, but with choices between one policy or another (Scriven, 1972). A subsequent problem with experimental research and performing significance tests is the great difference between significance and relevance. The significance of a difference can be increased by performing a large number of observations, while the relevance of this difference does not increase. Besides, significance can be influenced by artificially changing the experimental design. Differences that are significant in a design with two groups become more or less significant when the design is extended, while the number of observations in the original groups does not change (De Vries, 1992c).

Nevertheless, it will be clear that it is because of their inherent logic and quantitative basis that the outcomes of well-structured experimental designs have a great cogency. Whether the outcomes of such currently fashionable methods as qualitative case studies, the Delphi technique, in-depth interviews and scenario methodology have the same cogency remains to be seen. Here, too, a fundamental criticism is possible (Choucri 1978, Wheelwright & Makridakis 1985, Chapters 15 and 16).

1.5.3 Effect orientation

With impact assessment, goals set by policy makers are only a part of all the effects of alternatives. Alternatives are evaluated on their intended and unintended effects, that is, on their direct and indirect effects. Classic evaluations are judgments and measurements only of the extent to which goals are attained. If these evaluations were to make one thing clear, it would be] whether a policy or a programme is (has been) goal-directed, and that evaluation of that policy should be directed at investigating to what extent these goals are attained. To arrive at a sound evaluation, it should be clear which objectives are intended and which standards are relevant (Modderkolk & Janssen, 1988: 70). The objective of an actor can be defined as a desirable, future situation or action, whose realization can be brought about or encouraged (G. Kuypers, 1980: 55). Conceivable objectives can be the maximization of profits, levelling of income differences by way of taxation, road safety, or students who can read and write. Then, the objective of the actor is given and it is up to the evaluator to investigate to what extent the objective has been attained.

What is problematic about this ideal-type conception is that although description of these objectives seems simple, it certainly is not. Insufficient clarity about policy objectives from which evaluation criteria can be derived is among the most frequently mentioned problems concerning policy evaluations (Hoogerwerf, 1988: 43, 1986: 269,273). Traditionally it is supposed that objectives should be clear, specific and measurable (Patton, 1982: 103). Problems concerning objectives arise when they do not comply with these criteria. According to a large number of contemporary evaluators, this is almost always the case.

- Objectives are often obscure, ambiguous, hard to trace or absent.
- Usually objectives are no more than common platitudes (Weiss, 1972: 25).
- Often there is a difference between formulated objectives and the actor's actual objectives.
- Objectives can change during a process (Herweijer, 1981).
- Often, objectives cannot be made sufficiently operational, because their formulation is too qualitative.

These problems, however, are not on the same level and do not have the same cause, consequences or solution.

Obscure and ambiguous objectives

Obscure and ambiguous objectives can be the consequence of a political negotiating process between various actors. Two or more departments may have a different opinion about the objective of a certain policy. The result of this difference, when persistent, may be that the policy will not be pursued; however, it can also be regulated by reformulating the objective in order to satisfy every department. The obscurity or abstraction of the objective is then the reflection of a compromise. The task of the evaluator in that case is to unravel the abstract objective, find the concrete objective of each of the departments involved and bypass the more general objective.

Objectives as platitudes

Objectives being nothing more than platitudes may be a consequence of two factors: 1) the extent to which the original objectives are controversial, and 2) the fear of actors that the original objectives may not be attained.

The first applies to the platitudes in the election programmes of political parties. To attract a large number of potential voters, the objectives mentioned are intended to appeal to an audience as wide as possible, and accordingly are hardly controversial. Voters may not be allowed to use the objectives as a reason not to vote for the party. Such objectives as reduction of unemployment, attention to the environment, priority for urban reconstruction, promotion of tourism and recreation, and the pursuit of administrative modernization are aimed to appeal to a very large audience and to antagonize as few people as possible.

In some situations, a personal appeal is made to the actors involved concerning the extent of goal-attainment. To reduce the chances of not attaining the objectives, not the means but the objectives themselves are adapted. This is also called the prevention of *post-decision surprise*. When the objectives are ambitious and the means with the highest cost-benefit ratio are selected, better results are more probable. On the other hand, however, the difference between what is actually achieved and what was intended to be achieved will be greater. To the policy actors, this implies a dilemma. Deliberation about achieving as much as possible coupled with a low level of goal-attainment is in fact making a choice between, on the one hand, optimal policy which has a great chance of being evaluated negatively because goals are only partially attained and, on the other hand, minimal policy which will probably be evaluated positively because goals are fully attained (Harrison & March, 1984).

Changed objectives

The next problem concerning objectives is that they change during a process. In terms of evaluation this means it remains unclear what is to be evaluated. If the policy effects of the original objectives are assessed, the evaluation will not be up to date and might be useless. If new objectives are selected, the chances are that means and goals will be brought together that were never meant to be brought together. Such changes can be brought about by, for example, the emergence of new ideas, new priorities, the change of problems and changing power relations. This sometimes leads to a zigzag policy and sometimes results in the continuation of a policy that is no longer goal-oriented: the policy instruments may not have disappeared yet, but the objectives will already have been completely adjusted.

Unmeasurable objectives

The last problem to be mentioned here concerning objectives is the fact that they cannot be made sufficiently operational. 'Increasing customer-orientation' or 'creating a livable society' are objectives for which it is very difficult to find indicators that measure what is meant to be measured (validity) and that produce data that allow for quantitative determination of differences or changes. Patton has indicated that objectives that cannot be made operational are not a problem regarding objectives but a problem of the evaluator.

Why should the formulation of objectives be restricted to those that can be measured by the evaluator in a quantitative way? The danger of a one-sided emphasis on the measurability criterion is that it is often detrimental to the relevance criterion. What use can a policy actor have for measurable but useless objectives? Measurable objectives are often directed at numbers and percentages, but can very well be pointless (Patton, 1982: 104).

Given these problems concerning objectives, two alternatives are possible: a *goal-free evaluation* and the formulation or *reformulation of objectives by the evaluator*. Both choices are possible and have a certain reputation (Guba, 1986 and Patton, 1982).

- Each goal and each objective should contain only one desirable outcome.
- Each statement should clarify what the actor wishes to achieve.
- Achievement of both absence and presence of a desirable situation should be conceivable.
- Formulation of objectives should be clear (no need to reread; positively rather than negatively formulated). E.g. 'stimulating employment' instead of 'reducing unemployment'.
- Nouns should specify products and verbs should be in the future tense. Active verbs are preferred.
- Adjectives should be used sparsely, and if used should express quality criteria and functional levels of nouns. Their purpose is to clarify.
- Specification of means to arrive at objectives should be disconnected from objectives.
- Write comprehensibly. Jargon should be avoided as much as possible.
- Objectives should reflect all important issues. Secondary objectives should be mentioned separately.
- Use text written by others as little as possible. Goals and objectives are specific and often express nuances that can hardly be borrowed by other actors.

Table 1.5 *Patton's ten steps for arriving at unambiguous objectives*

One possibility when objectives are obscure and unclear is reformulation. Among others this choice is made by Patton. Patton gives ten steps on the basis of which obscure, ambiguous objectives can be reformulated into clear, unambiguous objectives (Table 1.5). After the reformulation of objectives by the evaluator or the actor, a purposeful evaluation can be carried out.

An introduction to making calculated choices

The kindest argument for a goal-free evaluation is given by Scriven: 'You don't evaluate cars by checking if they turned out the way the design team or the board of directors intended, but in terms of whether they meet the needs of the consumers.' (Scriven, 1986: 99) When a goal-free evaluation is preferred, a criterion different from the objective of the policy actor has to become the focus of attention. For example, research questions. What is it the actor whose policy is being evaluated wants to know? The research focuses only on this question, regardless of the objectives of the policy.

A second possibility is when the evaluation focuses solely on *issues and interests* (Guba, 1986: 99), on policy theories (Sabatier, 1988), or on problem structuring.

A third possibility is when the evaluation focuses on effects, regardless of whether they are intended or unintended, important to the policy maker or others involved, or arise from a scientific theory (Guba 1986, Chen & Rossi 1981, Scriven 1967).

This is the point of reference in impact assessment. Whether the term goal-attainment is used or a term such as effect, subdivided into intended and unintended or main effects and side effects, is not of great importance. The scope of evaluation research is determined by incorporating the objectives of the policy maker or the wishes of other people involved; or in the case of scientific theory, by incorporating the hypothe-

---

The objectives of constructing a highway can be: stimulating mobility, improving infrastructure and reducing traffic congestion. The effects from the perspective of social scientific research are: new employment opportunities near the highway, pressure on the housing market near the highway, and a change of social economic structure in residential areas near the highway in terms of transport costs, prices, supply and demand of goods, land prices, land use and population. Sociological research proves that effects can also be expected in terms of lifestyle, local value systems, social patterns, racial composition, age distribution, social mobility, air pollution and noise nuisance.
According to the classic conception, an ex post evaluation should only consider goal-attainment. A more modern approach to evaluation also takes into account the other effects mentioned and judges on the basis of both intended and unintended effects.(After Chen & Rossi, 1980: 114)

Table 1.6 *Example of the construction of a highway*

sized policy effects, but not its scientific value (Table 1.6) Goal-free evaluations and - as Chen and Rossi claim - multi-goal evaluations only imply a more extended research design. And here nobody, except perhaps the financier of the research, will have objections. Whether they are called effects, targets or criteria makes no essential difference. What happens is that at a certain moment during analysis a deliberation has to be made. Which criterion, effect, objective is more and which is less important? This is why impact assessment is mainly effect-oriented. The actors' objectives, i.e. the intended effects, are part of all possible criteria.

1.5.4 Value-bound

Opinions about the role of the evaluator have also changed over the course of time. To Michael Scriven, the evaluator is mainly a kind of judge, keeping his measuring and describing function, who passes positive or negative judgement on policy programmes. Objectives are also regarded as problematic and are part of the evaluation. This is contradictory to the idea of value-free science. Even though evaluators were afraid of political vulnerability when making judgements and recommendations on the basis of their own research, they still did so because they considered judgement to be an essential part of evaluations and obviously regarded themselves as the most objective judges. Scriven's (1967) arguments for this development were given in a speech at the opening of a congress of the American Association for evaluation research:

> 'The correct formulation of the role of values in evaluation research is to say that the evaluator *must* draw evaluative conclusions (otherwise they are doing less than their job); that these conclusions *must* not be drawn from the evaluators personal values (whether or not those values coincide with the ones used); that the conclusions must be shown (or capable of being shown) to follow from objectively determined, demonstrably relevant and comprehensive facts by way of logically sound inferences; and that these conclusions will sometimes not reflect all of the values that will correctly enter into implementation decisions ... Evaluators are not decision makers, indeed; but it is a crude confusion to think that only the decision makers are entitled to

evaluate. Only they are entitled to *decide*, which is another matter entirely. The evaluator, on the other hand, is not entitled but required to evaluate.' (Scriven, 1986: 109-110)

The multi-criteria model also passes judgements. The methodology results in the presentation of a ranking order of alternatives according to their utility, indicating which choice is optimal to a decision maker given the criteria. The model does not take a decision but judges whether a choice is adequate.

1.6 A TACTICAL APPROACH

The model discussed in this book is based on the multi-criteria evaluation model. The term 'multi-criteria' is problematic because it does not distinguish between types of evaluation.

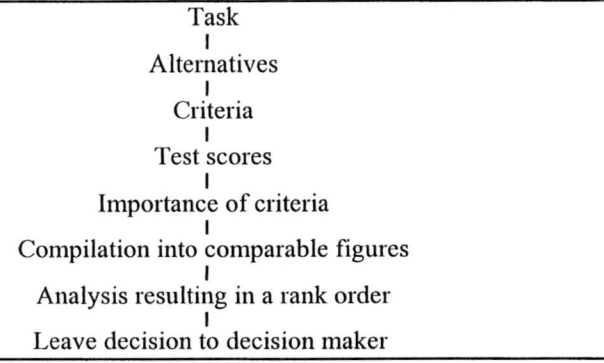

Figure 1.2 *A tactical approach to calculated choices*

After all, each evaluation is done on the basis of several criteria. The new term chosen here - 'tactical calculated choices' - is closely linked to the objective of the methodology, the steps taken and the content of the following chapters. A tactical approach is a model that serves to solve tasks involving the choice between alternatives on the basis of criteria, the test scores of alternatives on criteria, the importance of criteria and their compilation into comparable figures that constitute the input for analysis, leaving the actual decision to the decision maker.

1.6.1 Choices in policy-making

The starting point for the model is an arbitrary decision maker. The content of a choice is of secondary importance. The methodology here described is generally applicable to and usable by consumers, policy makers, politicians and managers. Choices can be made in a large number of ways. First, when the emphasis is put on the theoretical capacities of the policy actor, policy-making can be considered a thinking process. Secondly, when social skills are emphasized, policy-making can be considered a social or political process (e.g. Feldman, 1989). Thirdly, policy-making can be seen as a combination of both. In that case, political and theoretical factors together determine which alternative will be preferred. It is not inherent in the tactical approach to emphasize one of these factors. The strength of the methodology lies in the fact that both factors, along with any number of other factors, can be made explicit in the decision process.

It is the very goal of the methodology to serve to determine a ranking order of policy alternatives. However, the methodology can also be used as a strategic tool when analysing differences of opinion or when conflicts arise between parties concerning choices. When the scores of alternatives on the various criteria are known, it can be made clear which ranking order will be preferred by each of the participating actors by estimating the priorities they have set. This could serve to control a discussion or to stimulate reaching a compromise.

Making use of the tactical approach when making choices is possible, but use of this model is not vitally important. Obviously the essential question is what the merits are of using the methodology compared with an intuitive decision-making process. First, its explicitness is an advantage of the methodology. When using the methodology, policy alternatives, evaluation criteria, the scores of each of the alternatives on each of the criteria, and the weights of the criteria need to be made explicit. Secondly, an advantage of the methodology is that all kinds of irrelevant factors that could negatively influence policy-making have no impact on a choice. There are three main categories of relevant factors: those in the political-administrative context, those inherent in the way a problem of choice is presented, and those with regard to decision rules. Explicitness together with the exclusion of these three factors results in the avoidance of irrationality in policy-making. This topic will be extensively elaborated in Chapter 2.

1.6.2 Alternatives and criteria

A choice can only exist when alternatives and accompanying criteria are known. How many alternatives there should be will be the subject of Chapter 3. The relation between the quantity of information available and the quality of policy-making will be dealt with from the perspective of synoptics, incrementalism, cybernetics and information theory. Although it is irrelevant to the methodology itself whether more or less alternatives are compared regarding more or less criteria, it most certainly affects the quality of policy-making. Besides, the tactical approach will turn out to be more useful when the number of alternatives and/or criteria becomes larger. This means that the more complex the problem of choice, the more it is advisable to use the tactical approach model. The reason for this is human decision makers' level of comprehension, the implicit deliberation they make when choosing between alternatives and criteria, and the implicit shift of decision rules.

1.6.3 Test scores

Alternatives have a score for each criterion. In the example given in section 1, a Miele washing machine costs $f1200$. This is called a criterion score. Chapter 5 will discuss the possibilities for determining these scores of alternatives on criteria. Four methods of investigation are essential: the use of argumentation, case studies, performance indicators and experimentation. The merits of these methods will be discussed as will the question how the conclusion can be reached that a criterion score is unambiguously related to a policy alternative, and to what extent it is excluded that a score is wrongfully attributed to an alternative.

1.6.4 The importance of criteria

Chapter 5 will deal with the determination of the weights or priorities of criteria. The methodology will take this into account explicitly. Setting priorities influences the eventual ranking order of alternatives just as much as the actual scores on criteria. On the basis of criterion weights, the utility of an alternative can be lower than that of another alternative, while its effect (e.g. costs) can be twice as high. The possibilities and restraints in determining criterion weights will also be discussed.

1.6.5 Compilation

Because the methodology is able to take into account a multitude of possible scores on various criteria, it is necessary to make these scores comparable. When determining the utility of alternatives, apples and pears cannot be added just like that. Following the methodology, criterion scores are standardized. Chapter 6 discusses the various possibilities for standardizing criterion scores. This subject matter is somewhat mathematical, but necessary in order to arrive at the correct evaluation of the outcomes. After determining all scores and weights, a compilation is made of those scores and weights. A criterion measured in money terms needs to be made comparable with one measured in terms of e.g. time. Standardized scores have to be calculated and every criterion score needs

	Miele	Philips	Zanussi	Weigth
Price	ƒ 1200	ƒ 800	ƒ 1600	-10
Lifespan	10 years	5 years	15 years	30
Service	excellent(10)	good(8)	reasonable(6)	60
	Miele	Philips	Zanussi	
Price	1200/1600=0.75	0.50	1.0	-0.1
Lifespan	10/15 =0.67	0.33	1.0	0.3
Service	10/10 =1.0	0.80	0.6	0.6
U_{Miele} = [0.75*-0.1]	+ [0.67*0.3]	+ [1.0*0.6] = 0.73		
$U_{Philips}$ = [0.50*-0.1]	+ [0.33*0.3]	+ [0.8*0.6] = 0.53		
$U_{Zanussi}$ = [1.00*-0.1]	+ [1.00*0.3]	+ [0.6*0.6] = 0.56		

Table 1.7 *A fictitious scorecard*

to be transformed into a standardized score. This process is called standardization and is an essential step in impact assessment.

Standardization produces comparable criterion scores and comparable outcomes independent of measuring units. For example, it is conceivable that a criterion 'duration of procedures' will be measured in terms of weeks by one evaluator and in terms of months by another. By standardizing scores, the measuring unit used has no consequences for the outcomes of the analysis. One method used frequently to standardize scores is dividing the original criterion scores by the maximum score for that criterion. Weights too need to be standardized. This can be achieved by dividing each weight by the sum off all absolute weights. Table 1.7 shows that the sum of *absolute* weights of -0.1|0.3|0.6 equals 1.

The goal of the method is to indicate the relative utility of policy alternatives. This utility is determined by the evaluation of alternatives using criteria. The general characteristics of utility determination will be discussed in Chapter 6, as will the philosophical background to the utility concept. To a large extent, the tactical approach is in accordance with that of Michael Scriven (1980). To Scriven there are four major steps to be taken in evaluation research:

> 'First, justifiable criteria of merit have to be developed that specify what an evaluand has to influence as a condition for being labelled good;
> Second, justifiable standards of performance have to be selected for each criterion that specify how well the evaluand ought to perform in order to attain a specified level of merit;
> Third, performance has to be measured on each criterion so as to estimate whether specified standards of quality performance are reached;
> Finally ... the measured results have to be integrated into a single statement about the overall goodness or value of the evaluand.'

Scriven remains unclear about how to determine weights or priorities of criteria. Other researchers, however, do have explicit ideas on this topic. House, for example, adheres to Rawl's axiom of equity. The criteria derived from Rawl's theory are attributed high weights when formulating goal-attainment. Wholey emphasizes the objectives that have been formally formulated by policy makers. According to him the objective of evaluations is: 1) to assist managers and policy makers in clarifying programme goals, identifying the objectives and performance indicators on which the programme can realistically be held accountable, and developing evaluation/management options for changing programme activities in ways that will enhance performance; and 2) to assist government policy makers in developing and implementing systems that will create the incentives needed to stimulate managers and their staffs (a) to identify and get policy level agreement on appropriate objectives and performance indicators, and (b) to manage programme activities in order to achieve acceptable/improved performance (in: Levine, 1981: 104). The differences of opinion regarding these various paradigms turn out to be mainly a difference in set priorities.

To arrive at a ranking order of alternatives, the sum of all criterion scores needs to be calculated, taking into account the criterion weights. Chapter 7 discusses six methods (i.e. the weighed sum, regime, concordance, discordance, evamix and permutation methods) to determine the eventual ranking order.

1.6.6 Analysis

The next step in the tactical approach consists of analysing the ranking order and its unambiguity. The merits of each of these methods will be dealt with. They all result in a final ranking order of alternatives, based on their utility. The formula used to calculate utility is a variation of a general formula given in Formula 1.1.

$$U_i = \sum_{c=1}^{k} S_{ic} * G_c$$

Formula 1.1 *Utility*

In case of k criteria, the utility of alternative I, that is U_i, equals the sum of all weighed criterion scores. The weight of criterion c equals G_c and the score of alternative I on criterion c equals S_{ic}. Variants result from attaching higher/lower significance to either criterion scores S_{ic} or weights G_c.

In the most simple case, analysis consists of adding up all criterion scores for each alternative, taking into account the weights of criteria and their direction. This results in relative utility scores U_i for all criteria, as shown in Table 1.7. Given these scores and weights, the conclusion is that the Miele will be the best choice. However, the question remains how such a ranking order should be interpreted, i.e. whether the top ranking alternative is really the alternative to be preferred. Could the Miele be preferred to the Zanussi because a third alternative is present that distorts the ranking order between the Miele and the Zanussi? Is the resulting ranking order transitive? In other words, when the Miele is preferred to the Zanussi and the Zanussi is preferred to

An introduction to making calculated choices 33

the Philips, does that mean that the Miele is preferred to the Philips? These problems and their solution are discussed in Chapter 7.

1.6.7 Leave the decision to the decision maker

Finally, Chapter 8 will discuss the possible prescriptive character of impact assessments. It will be indicated that impact assessment can never be more than an instrument and that in the end those responsible for decisions have to take decisions themselves. Impact assessment is nothing more than an instrument that enables the making of well-thought-out decisions. This in itself is already a great advancement. However, it does not mean that decision makers are forced to make a choice because impact assessment claims that this choice is optimal. Certainly in cases where more decision makers are involved and responsible, a second-best solution may sometimes be preferred to the most 'optimal' alternative. Impact assessments, when reaching such a compromise, can have both a regulating and a catalytic effect/a regulating or a catalytic effect.

1.7 STRUCTURE OF THE BOOK

The steps mentioned earlier form the core of this book. Each chapter refers to these steps. Secondly, each chapter aims at a reflection on these steps. The methodology is not as simple as it may look at first sight. There are pitfalls and bottlenecks to each step that may influence the outcomes considerably. In each step, choices have to be made that can in themselves be subjected to the same tactical approach. This is why each chapter describes how a step should be taken in theory and what the accompanying theoretical and practical problems are. Recommendations are made on how to avoid irrationality and to improve the effectiveness of application of the method to choices being made in reality.

1.8 SUMMARY

This chapter introduced those that will follow. The objectives of the book have been formulated: i.e. increasing the understanding of how to make well-deliberated choices during a decision-making process, offering a critical reflection on the methodology, and giving guidance when judging evaluation reports that make use of this methodology or when making an evaluation yourself implementing the steps of the model. To do this, the tactical approach has been introduced. This methodology distinguishes itself from other evaluation methodologies because:

- evaluation takes place prior to a decision
- evaluation uses all relevant effects of a choice, not just the financial or desired ones
- evaluation does not depend on a specific research technique
- evaluation is value-bound in the sense that the optimal decision is indicated, given explicit alternatives and criteria and their importance.

These are positive distinctions compared to cost-benefit analysis, summative evaluations and ex post evaluations. The methodology aims to provide a decision-support model which will allow decision makers to improve their results.

2 The task is to make a well-thought-out choice

> The problems a policy maker faces when making an intuitive choice are discussed in this chapter. Three subsystems are essential: the actor system, the choice system and the calculating system. The discussion focuses on the question whether the problems that arise can be overcome using the model discussed in Chapter 1. Usually the assumption is that choices made using the model are more rational than intuitive choices and result in better outcomes. It will turn out that many of the problems regarding the choice system and the calculating system can be overcome by using the model. The actor system, however, remains a substantial factor when making choices. Because the actor system is closely related to the choice system and the calculating system, the model is not able to solve all problems concerning these systems.

Tasks
|
Alternatives
|
Criteria
|
Test scores
|
Importance of criteria
|
Compilation of data
|
Analysis of ranking order
|
Leave the decision to the decision maker

INTRODUCTION

Everyone knows examples of failing policy, i.e. policies whose outcomes turn out to be more negative than expected. Examples are a new highway that has not solved traffic congestion but instead has increased the number of car kilometres, a policy to improve awareness of the environment, or a positive action policy to help increase the participation of women and ethnic minorities in the labour process. Policy makers are inclined to explain failures by pointing at other people involved that have not been reacting as anticipated. Adversaries of policy makers then immediately claim that policy makers have been working thoughtlessly and did not have an overall view. Officials who did the preparatory work can stress the speed with which decisions had to be taken. Professional organizations in charge of enforcement can refer to the extremely complex problems that in fact prevented the possibility of making good choices. Finally, people politically responsible can indicate that they approved plans that were based on the information provided, emphasizing that the way the problem of choice was presented was decisive.

The above shows that policy-making can go wrong in various ways. Among other things, a suboptimal choice is indicated by the contentment of the actor afterwards. Looking back at his choice, he can see whether or not he has done well. If dissatisfied about the outcomes of his choice, the first factor that could have caused this is the way he reached his decision, e.g. thoughtlessly or shortsightedly. Secondly, the cause could be the nature of the problem in relation to the decision maker, e.g. too complicated a choice and too little time available or a lack of experience with regard to the problem. A third cause could be the nature of the problem itself, i.e. it is a problem that has no possible good solution (e.g. choosing between two evils, or a problem where every solution leads to insecure outcomes). Fourthly, part of the outcomes can be the result of choices made by other actors. Finally, the way in which the problem is presented could also be a factor.

The example also clarifies that there may be differences of interpretation between the people involved concerning the reasons why outcomes of a choice process are disappointing. One of the scientific answers is that a choice process can be improved by decomposing the process and using a standardized model. This chapter discusses the characteristics of a choice process with and without using the tactical approach. The main question dealt with is whether use of the standardized model has advantages and/or disadvantages compared to not using the tactical approach. The following questions will be answered:

- Which elements are characteristic of every choice process?
- What are the specific problems with intuitive choices?
- To what extent can using the tactical approach reduce problems and to what extent will new problems arise?

2.1 THE ELEMENTS OF POLICY-MAKING

Policy-making implies taking decisions about the content of policy, i.e. choosing and specifying objectives, means, time planning and activities. In a choice process there is always interaction between three systems: the actor or subject system, the choice or object system, and the calculating system.

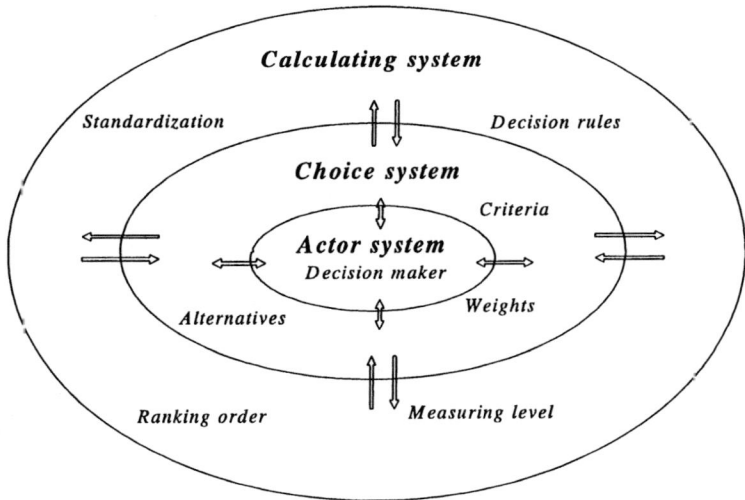

Figure 2.1 *Interaction between the actor-, choice- and calculating system*

First, there is an actor or a group of actors facing a decision. This is the *actor system*, which comprises the set of decision makers. Within this system, the eventual judgement is made about a diversity of (combinations of) outcomes. This is where decision-making takes place. Political decision-making, for example, is the realization of a plan made by (mainly but not solely) functionaries in the public sector to do or to refrain from doing something, thereby affecting the environment (Lebelle and Mulder, 1986: 132). But it is also concerned with the choice of a consumer or a manager. Although the content of the actor system is different for these groups, the actor system is still important regarding any choice.

The most used distinction between actor systems is whether decision-making is individual or collective. An individual is familiar with his own preferences and may, from a calculating perspective, arrive at an optimal choice. Collective decision-making is different. People involved have to take into account that wishes and claims may differ. The eventual choice may be collectively optimal while suboptimal to the individual decision makers.

The subject of choice is the *choice system*, i.e. what the decision is about. Within this system the alternatives are related to each other (White, 1975: 4). The choice system is the characterization of the problem. The first element of the choice system is, of course, that there has to be something to choose from. This means there must be different possibilities or *alternatives*. The content of choice may differ. It may concern the execution of system reforms in health care, the allocation among districts of city funds for urban renewal, the location of industrial activities, the recommendation of someone for nomination, or the choice between suppliers of an information system. The questions asked are, for example, has this been executed or not, and if so, to what extent, where, by whom and how.

The second element within the choice system concerns characteristics of the alternatives on the basis of which choices are made. There is at least one *criterion* on the basis of which a choice between alternatives can be made. Such a criterion can be, for example, cost, effect, policy objective or political feasibility. Where there are more criteria, their relative weights become important.

The calculating system contains the algorithm or decision rule on the basis of which an optimal ranking order can be computed. There are several decision rules conceivable, both for individual and for collective policy makers. With individuals the main concern is how a person arrives at a preference for a certain policy alternative based on criterion scores. Criterion scores can be added up linearly allowing weights to account for their importance; the most important criterion scores can be regarded as solely decisive, or polynomic or multiplicative utility functions can be used. Where collective policy-making is concerned, individual preferences have to be combined, using one of several possible decision rules, such as e.g. the unanimity rule or the majority rule. Within the calculating system, the construction of a ranking order takes place. Based on one or more criteria, the best alternative is determined and sometimes also the ranking order of the other alternatives.

The following comments illustrate that the distinction between the actor system, the choice system and the calculating system (Figure 2.1) is not always as unambiguous as it may seem.

It is not self-evident that there are alternatives and criteria. Dror, for example, calls policy-making *fuzzy gambling,* a process comparable to a treacherous casino: not playing also brings about high risks, the rules and outcomes of choices change continuously in an unpredictable direction, the game requires a combination of luck and skill, wild cards appear at random points in time, and issues are at stake that even the participants have no knowledge of. In those cases, outcomes cannot be predicted, the distribution of probabilities is unknown, and non-decisions (such as continuing existing policy) are just as dangerous as decisions because the effects of all the options are continuously changing. Values and goals lose their meaning and intelligence leads to the same results as ignorance (Dror, 1988: 168).

It is not necessary for all elements of the choice system and the calculating system to be dealt with explicitly during the choice process. Although a choice is based on information about scores of alternatives on criteria, given criterion weights, it is not imperative and perhaps even impossible for a decision maker to have exhaustive information at his disposal. In a choice process, more or fewer alternatives can come up, as can more or fewer criteria and a more or less complete ranking order. Only relevant information needs to be collected, analysed and related to a specific plan or decision (Wheelwright and Makridakis, 1985: 319). When a choice process is intuitive, the contribution of each of the elements to the eventual choice usually remains *implicit*. In that case, the actor cannot reconstruct how he arrived at a decision. The decision was taken ad hoc, he no longer knows which alternatives were deliberated, which criteria played a part and which decision rule was used. Another disadvantage of an intuitive choice process is that the various elements are often used in a mixed and *disorderly* way. This leads to a process of *limited transparency* and possibly to (sub)conscious distortion.

A third comment refers to the completeness of the elements mentioned (i.e. alternatives, criteria, weights and decision rules) that are part of the choice system and calculating system. Although these are the elements that are used in every choice process, they are only the necessary elements. Many choice processes take more issues into account, such as effects, criterion weights, measuring level of criterion scores, standardization and summation. If all these factors are not taken into account explicitly, it is probable that a *reduction* has taken place. The 'too complex' problem has been reduced to a solvable problem. The limited comprehension of human actors leads to a simplified representation of choices. It is the policy maker saying that in assessing policy alternatives only two criteria have been used, namely cost and feasibility. It is the organization that leaves alternatives out of consideration beforehand. With human actors, complete information-processing is not always possible.

Within the calculating system and the choice system, the elements are connected through the actor system. Choosing criteria, just like choosing alternatives, is a decision process. Making criteria and effects more explicit may result in extending the set of alternatives, and vice versa. There is a relation between including or not including criteria and consequences on the one hand, and considering or not considering alternatives in the actor system on the other hand.

Take, for instance, a project where the original choice is between the expansion of an industrial area in either location x or location y. By adding a criterion with a very negative score for both locations (e.g. the proximity of a housing area), further alternatives enter the picture. This means that the number of alternatives depends on the criteria chosen through the actor system. Including alternatives can also depend on the inclusion of other alternatives. In the discussion in Holland about building a second national airport, several alternative locations were suggested, i.e. Markerwaard, Noordoostpolder and Flevopolder. Because the Markerwaard was located nearest to the cities in the west of Holland and for the rest seemed to have identical advantages and disadvantages compared to the other two locations, the only alternative analysed was the Markerwaard. The moment it became clear that the Markermeer (a lake) was not to be turned into the Markerwaard (a polder) this alternative disappeared. With this, every analysis of the advantages and disadvantages of a national airport at the other locations also disappeared.

2.2 MERITS OF THE TACTICAL APPROACH

Chapter 1 presented a model where each element is made explicit, where complete information-processing takes place, and where every step in the decision-making procedure is followed. Adherent to the methodology, all alternatives are compared on the basis of the same criteria, after which the values of all alternatives are determined. This is policy-making based on policy evaluation. Such an evaluation is known as *multi-criteria evaluation*, and was called the *tactical approach* in the previous chapter.

The task is to make a well-thought-out choice

Using this standardized model has several advantages over the intuitive approach. To understand these advantages, the problems an actor faces when making an intuitive decision need to be clarified.

2.2.1 Problems with an intuitive choice process

When discussing problems in making choices, we focus on a choice that results in worse outcomes than could have been achieved by the actor. At some moment in time, after the choice has been made, the actor is less satisfied than he would have been had he opted for another policy alternative.

The many reasons for his phenomenon will be discussed below (after Tversky & Kahneman 1986; Wheelwright & Makridakis 1985; Bazerman 1990). To gain a good understanding of these problems, it should be made clear that the interpretation of each element in a choice process consists of again making choices - choices that have consequences with respect to the content of the outcomes of the analysis and that are not merely technical in nature, choices that depend on several factors that are mutually dependent too. Although in the following the three systems within which a choice is made will be distinguished, the separation between them will not be made so strict as to neglect the influences of one system on the other. Each of these three subsystems demarcates part of the problems. Once again they are called the actor system, the choice system and the calculating system (White 1975).

Problems originating from the actor system

First of all, suboptimal policy-making is the result of prejudice regarding the alternatives on the part of the actors involved. As a consequence of emotional, substantial or traditional rationality, an alternative is preferred beforehand irrespective of its effects. In the literature in question, several terms are given for this phenomenon. When referring to emotions and intuitions, the term 'affect referral' is used. The decision maker is not looking at the effects but immediately picks an alternative. This is reflected by, among other things, the search for criteria that will support exactly this alternative and by the neglect of criteria that are not supportive of the alternative. The term 'confirmation gap' is used to refer to merely considering supportive information (Bazerman, 1990: 7-8). Actors looking for criteria that support their prejudice is a more general phenomenon. This was demonstrated by an experiment carried out by

Wason, in which subjects were asked to state three numbers and were then given the task of finding out which calculating rule the researcher used to approve or disapprove of them. The researcher said 'yes' if the three numbers fitted the calculating rule and 'no' if they did not. The calculating rule was that numbers needed to be even and at intervals of 2. For example, 2, 4, 6 or 20, 22, 24. The series 3, 5, 7 was not correct. It appeared that people had an idea in advance, e.g. that the series should be at intervals of 2. After that they only mentioned series of numbers that supported their hypothesis. In other words, they failed to mention a series that did not comply with the calculating rule in order to verify the correctness of their idea about the calculating rule (Wheelwright & Makridakis, 1985: 319). People turn out to mainly apply verification rules and hardly any falsification rules.

Choices also prove to be dependent on the values from which the choice process has started. During the choice process it is difficult for individual or group actors to change the point of view from which a problem is looked at. The choice process is, as it were, anchored in the starting position. Often people turn out to be not very creative when solving problems, and can adapt to new problems only to a limited extent. Referring to the influence of starting positions, the terms 'anchoring' and 'adjustment' are used.

A second cause of suboptimal policy-making is overrating the amount of data. The value of decisions does not automatically increase as the quantity of data increases. Not every datum constitutes information relevant to the decision process. What does appear to increase along with the amount of data is confidence in a choice: actors seem to become more secure about the correctness of their choice when more data are collected.

A third cause can be found in the way in which group decisions are taken. A suboptimal solution becomes more likely when the group's unanimity increases, when room for nonconformity becomes smaller and when the isolation of the group from the outside world increases (Janis & Mann, 1977; Kleindorfer et al., 1993). This is called 'group think'. In such a situation, policy is not so much determined by the (expected) effects as by group norms and consensus.

Problems regarding framing

Human choices often depend on the way in which the problem of choice is presented. In this context the problem of so-called framing is well known. For example, people are presented with the following question: a few days before going to the cinema you buy a ticket for ten dollars, but when you get to the cinema it turns out you have lost it. Would you buy a new ticket or not? The majority of people interviewed would not buy a new ticket. The same people are then asked the following: you want to go to the cinema, a ticket to which costs ten dollars. When you get there, you discover you have lost ten dollars on the way. Would you buy a ticket or not? The majority of people interviewed would buy a ticket. The same goes for people buying trousers and a shirt. The shirt is 15 dollars, the trousers 125. If the shop assistant says the shirt is for sale down the street for 10 dollars, the majority would go to the other shop. If the assistant says the trousers can be bought down the street for 120 dollars, however, the same people would still buy the trouser for 125 dollars (Tversky, 1981). In both cases the deliberation is the same; namely, more walking for 5 dollars. The way in which this deliberation is made, however, turns out to depend on the way the choice is presented. This research has been replicated and confirmed for children, managers and consumers, and turns out to be a problem of categorization. People tend to think in other categories when the problem is presented differently. Whereas a large number of people who have lost their ticket and buy a new one do this mainly because they want to see the film, those who have lost the money usually claim that there is no relation between losing money and buying a ticket. Of the people who do not buy a ticket, the majority of those who had already bought one say that 20 dollars is too much to see the film, while the majority of those who had lost their money say they do not have that much money (Henderson, 1992). People change their criteria intuitively, varying the form of their problem regardless of changes in the actual content of their problem. The placing of alternatives in relation to each other also proves to have an influence on choice. An alternative hidden among a large number of other alternatives has less chance of being chosen than the alternative listed first or last, irrespective of their advantages and disadvantages. The opposite also occurs. During multiple choice examination, students prefer answers in categories b and c, and especially avoid those in d. Likewise, alternatives that are formulated positively have a bigger chance of being chosen. Research shows that people have a higher preference for a positive answer (yes, for) than for a negative answer (no, against) (Hoogstraten, 1979: 61).

The time allowed to make a choice also proves to play a part. The longer a choice process takes, the more dominant the importance attached to the most relevant criterion in relation to the importance of other criteria. In the end, the most important criterion becomes so dominant that the rest of the criteria are completely disregarded. In this case, the decision rule used is subconsciously changed. First, use is made of a so-called linear compensatory decision rule; that is, the decision rule where the value of an alternative is determined using all criterion scores weighed on their importance. After a while this changes into a *conjunctive decision rule*, where alternatives should satisfy minimum conditions for each criterion. Then the decision rule becomes *disjunctive*, where the only alternative considered is the one that sticks out on one criterion. In itself, each of these decision rules is legitimate. It is the subconscious change that is problematic when using decision rules. The same shift from a linear compensatory decision rule to a conjunctive decision rule takes place when a choice becomes more complex (Timmerman, 1991: 86).

Problems in handling data

An actor can make mistakes when collecting, processing, analysing or assessing data. Actors collecting data seem to have more confidence in their data if they are easier to get. Not only do they have more confidence in their data, they also remember them better and often weight them more heavily. They also tend to forget data that are not in accordance with their original ideas, to have more confidence in concrete than in abstract data, to construct relations between data based on first impressions without checking these relations, and to let themselves be misled by graphical presentations.

During data-processing, equivalent data may still be processed differently, or processing may be adapted to new data. This way data can be processed conservatively. New data are continuously considered to be less important than older data. Sometimes people attach more importance to data than is actually possible, or they assume that small amounts of data are representative of all data. Concerning the analysis of data, people tend to consider desirable outcomes more probable than undesirable ones. The term 'wishful thinking' is appropriate here. People sometimes assume relations between alternatives and criteria just because such an assumption takes away their insecurity, and thus give themselves the impression that the situation is under control.

When assessing data, actors sometimes wrongfully let the value of data depend on the extent to which these data were functional in the past. They are more confident about their data when the data have been used more often and no objections have been made to their use. In this way, someone may start to believe gossip that was started by himself, by repeating it often enough. When nobody reacts and claims the gossip is not true, the story becomes more and more trustworthy.

2.2.2 Advantages of the tactical approach

Use of the tactical approach has advantages for each of the three systems. First, its goal always is to create a ranking order of alternatives so that an optimal choice can be determined. In the intuitive model, the goal is sometimes to arrive at a compromise. Compromise is not often reached because the actual advantages and disadvantages of the alternatives remain implicit. Whereas with intuitive choices, emotional and traditional rationalities are sometimes decisive, the tactical approach is always based on functional rationality. What counts is the deliberation of all the effects of choices, whereas complying more or less with the requirements of fundamental values, traditions and sentiments is only partly relevant. In contrast to intuitive choices where group processes can play a significant role, with the tactical approach the content of the model is decisive.

Another advantage of this approach is that the outcomes are independent of framing. The chances that an alternative will end up at the top of the ranking order do not depend on the alternative's original positioning in the model. In accordance with the tactical approach, the utility of every alternative is determined, a value that is only dependent on criterion values and criterion weights.

A third advantage is the discipline the model introduces when dealing with complex problems. Without the model, orderliness will very soon be lost, and problems such as the incomplete processing of available information will arise. Although complete information is impossible, also with the impact assessment model, all available information will be completely processed. On top of this, the processing of information does not depend on characteristics of the actor: data-processing is standardized.

Using the intuitive choice model, there is a chance that a subconscious shift of decision rules will take place during the choice process. With the tactical approach model, this is out of the question: the decision rule is established beforehand and made explicit.

These advantages are supported by experimental research. The maturity of a decision turns out to increase because a larger number of criteria are actually used, the preparedness to change increases in relation to preferences articulated before, the complexity of problems decreases, and fewer alternatives are eliminated beforehand (Timmermans, 1991: 50,64,135).

2.2.3 Problems with the tactical approach

It may seem that policy-making based on policy evaluation is a logical model in itself, where a number of discrete steps are taken in order to arrive at optimal choices. Many of the problems mentioned regarding choice processes will be avoided by using impact assessment. Yet, essential to this book is that such an approach is not without problems and deserves critical reflection. The basic idea is that passing through every phase itself requires an impact assessment. Hidden behind every phase of the apparently rational, synoptic method are arguments, sometimes explicit but usually implicit. A researcher carrying out an evaluation might underline these arguments. However, the end user of the research (a policy maker or, more generally, a decision maker) very often fails to recognize them. In other words, problematic to the methodology is that a policy problem is unjustly presented as 'objective' and solvable without the subjective influences of decision makers. Researchers often present ranking orders of alternatives without knowing whether their approach corresponds with the preferences and ideas of policy makers. Likewise, consumer organizations produce ranking orders of products without making explicit the weights of price/quality criteria. This leads to problems with consumer research. Suppose you want to buy a car. Reading a comparative investigation issued by a consumers organization will give you information on such criteria as engine power, durability, purchase price, running costs, etc. However, if you happen to be two metres tall, you will have to choose a type of car with a lot of leg- and headroom, and disregard the ranking order of brands that are right according to the research. The same goes for policy choices.

In general, the longer it takes to make a decision, the less satisfaction (or consensus, in case of groups) there will be with that decision.

Problems with the actor system

One might wrongfully believe that by using the method the actor system no longer influences the choice process. There is a decrease in the influence of prejudice, primary affective reactions, overrating criteria on the basis of irrelevant attributes, and group think. After all, rationality, transparency and verifiability increase. Nevertheless, the actor system remains crucial and will always determine the evaluation to a high degree. The influence of subjective elements has changed but not disappeared. The arbitrary nature of subjective deliberations that affect policy-making refers to the following.

First, the formulation of the problem contains a subjective element. The problem - the subject of evaluation - always refers to the difference between a present situation as perceived and a desirable situation. There are subjective elements in both situations and in their definition.

Complete information about all alternatives, objectives and limitations is impossible. It is impossible to determine all effects of a certain policy afterwards (ex post), let alone beforehand (ex ante). This means that a choice has to be made that is open to 'subjectivity' with regard to the alternatives, criteria and effects to be incorporated.

The choice to include alternatives and criteria in order to solve a problem is a decision process in itself (Churchman, 1961). Alternatives may also be consciously neglected. Such an alternative may be considered to be unimportant a priori, the alternative may be taboo or unusual, or it may be in conflict with the dominant policy theory. At the Ministry of Justice, for example, it has for a long time been taboo to reward correct behaviour. The train of thought was focused on punishing lawbreakers.

The effect of the actor system on the choice system also has indirect consequences for the ranking order of alternatives; that is, on the calculating system. A change in the number of alternatives and criteria, for instance, has consequences for the ranking order of alternatives. Both the effects included in the model and the algorithm used to optimize it may be changed by selecting or not selecting alternatives.

The influence of the actor system on the choice system

With regard to the choice system, one may also assume that problems have disappeared. After all, the form and order in which a problem of choice is presented are insignificant when using the standardized model. The effect of framing the specific presentation of a problem of choice has been minimized. Nevertheless, also in the choice system some problems remain. These problems are briefly described below. Of course, here too the interaction with the actor system is essential.

> With the construction of a highway there will be several routes possible. These routes will differ in terms of construction costs, the quantity of land to be purchased, the quantity of traffic that will use the highway, the adverse consequences to the environment (stench, noise, poisonous exhaust), gained travel time, costs of procedures, construction time, and political and social feasibility.

Table 2.1 *Example of a policy problem*

Table 2.1 gives an example of a choice concerning a route for a highway to be constructed. This apparently simple assessment contains eleven criteria, about which it should be determined whether they are comprehensive or include the most important ones, what the scores are of alternatives on criteria, and how these scores should be compared. This example seems logical and solvable by using impact assessment.

But there are seven potential problems with impact assessment. These are:

- Unambiguous determination of the subject of the problem.
- Determination of the number of alternatives, answering such questions as whether all alternatives have been taken into account or whether some alternatives have been left out consciously or subconsciously.
- Determination of criteria, answering such questions as whether all criteria have been taken into account or whether all interests of the various groups in society have been fairly and proportionally dealt with.
- The importance of criteria, answering such questions as whether they are equally important, whether a ranking order of priorities can be established and if so, who will do it.
- Some research has to be done to determine the scores of the alternatives. Ranging from construction costs and construction time to social feasibility, the score of each alternative route has to be determined or estimated.
- Having overcome these problems, the next problem will be whether it is possible to compare the scores of alternatives on criteria and subsequently to establish a ranking order of alternatives according to preference. In addition to the number of

criteria, the diversity of units of measurement in which the various criteria are expressed is also problematic.
- It is often difficult to merge the effects of an alternative into one criterion/ranking order for one decision maker. On top of this, the factors of insecurity are often hard to formalize (White, 1975: 57).

2.3 CONCLUSION

This chapter discussed the method of impact assessment. The starting point was the problem that choices are sometimes based on irrelevant aspects of alternatives. It was stated that the impact assessment model provides a solution to this problem. Use of the model in policy practice has increased significantly because of its advantages. Table 2.2 gives a summary of the two models.

The advantage of using a standardized model lies mainly in making explicit every step that has to be taken. This prevents implicit shifts in the number of alternatives, in the criteria used and their importance, and in the use of decision rules. Nevertheless, this model turns out to have some problems of its own. The problems indicated concern characteristics typical of the decision maker and his surroundings, mutual dependency of the steps in the model, and the calculating system.

The most important disadvantage seems to be that using a standardized model suggests that the choice process, and with it the ranking order of alternatives, is a more rational process.

It is more rational because the synoptic ideal of extensive information-search behaviour would be largely satisfied. Consequently, choices made this way would be of higher quality. It is more rational also in the technocratic sense that a discussion about the outcomes of the decision-making process based on policy evaluation would not be useful. However, these suggestions are not undisputedly right, and even provide the model with a dash of ideology.

For that reason, let it be stated here that the outcomes of the methodology will never be of a prescriptive nature. The model will always be merely an instrument to be used at the discretion of the decision maker. The last step should also be made explicit; namely, always leave the decision to the decision maker.

Differences between two choice models

Intuitive choices	Tactical approach
Goal sometimes is compromise	Goal always is optimal choice
Choice is tied to group processes	Choice is bound only by its content
Chance of emotional rationality	Choice is always based on functional rationality
Choice usually depends on the the way the model is presented	More independent of the way the model is presented
Elements of the choice process usually remain implicit	Elements of the choice process are made explicit
Often too complex to comprehend	Complexity becomes transparent
Complete information processing often impossible	Complete information-processing
Less actual use of criteria	More actual use of criteria
Many alternatives eliminated beforehand	Fewer alternatives eliminated beforehand
Subjectively determined relation between number of data and their weights	Number of data and weights of data are independent elements
Compilation/processing of data is independent of actor	Compilation of data is standardized
Chance of shift in decision rules beforehand	Decision rule is established
Higher tendency to persist with original choice about choice	Higher tendency to change during choice proces
Higher subjective satisfaction	Less satisfaction about choice
Shorter duration of decision process	Longer duration of decision process

Similarities between two choice models

Complete information is impossible in both models
High importance of actor, choice and calculating system in both models
Relations exist between elements in both models.

Table 2.2 *Differences and similarities between the tactical approach and the intuitive choice model*

3 Alternatives and criteria

> Establishing alternatives and criteria is essential to multi-criteria evaluation. In this, the first question is: what knowledge can be derived from theory and research about an optimum number of alternatives and criteria? Does the quality of decision-making improve in relation to the amount of information used to solve a policy problem? What factors determine whether an actor collects more or less information relevant to his policy problem? What can be said about the optimum number of alternatives and criteria that should be used during an evaluation? To find some answers to these questions, the arguments exchanged in the discussion between adherents of a synoptic approach and adherents of incrementalism will be discussed. Subsequently, factors in the actor system that have an impact on information search behaviour will be discussed. Finally, some recommendations will be made concerning the desirable number of alternatives and criteria.

Tasks
|
Alternatives
|
Criteria
|
Test scores
|
Importance of criteria
|
Compilation of data
|
Analysis of ranking order
|
Leave the decision to the decision maker

INTRODUCTION

A civil servant once exclaimed: 'It drives me mad. Nowadays policy proposals can't be made without the council asking for alternatives. They always want to have a choice. Whereas it's clear that a tunnel under a road is necessary - everyone understands this is the best solution to our traffic problem - the city council wants a functionary costing 80 dollars an hour to keep himself busy for weeks on end working out a bridge alternative that we already know is going to be rejected.'

Thinking in terms of alternatives is fashionable. The shift from assessing existing policy to contemplating the assessment of alternatives is a clear trend in policy practice. Scientifically this is a very interesting development, because the theory of incrementalism has existed since the end of the 1950s. This theory indicates that government policy is mainly characterized by continuity, that new policy often diverges only slightly from existing policy, and that this 'strategy' also leads to better results (Lindblom, 1959, 1968, 1979). According to these theorists, policy is or should be less goal-oriented and more problem-oriented. By looking at the problems that accompany existing policy, it might be possible that changing a policy on one issue will cancel out the problems and bring about the same goal-attainment. Goal-attainment that has been proven, while a completely new policy may have so many unknown effects that it might be less effective because of its undesirable side effects. Striving for the impossible (i.e. completeness of information) Lindblom called this the system of preservation of information in contrast to the randomness of lacking information. Dror (1964) objected that if a defence policy was designed only on the basis of problems that originated from the previous war, the defence forces would be optimally prepared only for a war that had already been fought - in other words, a war that will never reoccur.

The synoptic method assumes that assessment of a policy afterwards will be more positive when more alternatives and criteria are incorporated in the policy analysis. Rationality of policy will increase when choices are made explicitly. When policy is designed more rationally the outcomes will be more explicit and unexpected outcomes will be sporadic. The degree of goal-attainment will be higher. This chapter focuses on devising, formulating and choosing policy alternatives using more or less criteria in the context of synoptic or incremental policy-making. The following three questions will be answered:

- What does theory say about the relationship between quantity of information and quality of decision-making?
- What can be said about the optimum number of criteria and alternatives?
- Which types of alternatives and criteria can be distinguished?

3.1 THE RELATIONSHIP BETWEEN INFORMATION AND DECISION-MAKING QUALITY

3.1.1 Incrementalists and synopticians

The question may be raised whether the model outlined in Chapters 1 and 2 is as general as claimed. The starting point for the model is an actor intensively looking for information, i.e. a synoptically-acting policy actor with enough capabilities to compare a multitude of alternatives using a multitude of criteria. According to Janis, acting synoptically complies with seven criteria, i.e. the policy actor:

- compares a wide spectrum of alternatives
- investigates a large number of objectives that have to be attained and all consequences of a choice made
- weighs for each alternative all his knowledge about costs and risks (negative effects) against the positive outcomes
- searches intensively for new information relevant to the assessment of alternatives
- incorporates and takes into account all new information or expert opinions, even if this is negative with regard to his preferred alternative
- reinvestigates all positive and negative effects of known alternatives (including the ones that were originally unacceptable) before reaching his final choice
- makes detailed arrangements for the implementation and enforcement of the alternative, and special arrangements for adaptations in case known risks become reality (Janis, 1982: 11).

The chances of unforseen negative consequences and later regrets are smaller to the extent that each of these seven criteria has been complied with. According to many people, the synoptic model is an ideal model that has hardly any explanatory power when actual choices are being made. The question is whether this model is an adequate representation of the policy design process as it takes place in reality. Is it not true that policy actors work incrementally, looking for an alternative that provides a satisfactory solution to a problem without looking any further for alternatives that might be a more optimum solution? This is the famous discussion between policy actors called 'optimizers' and those called 'satisfycers' (see e.g. Lindblom, 1979; Etzioni, 1984; Janis & Mann,

1977). Of course the answer to all these questions should be that policy actors more often act as 'satisfycers' than as optimizers. A crucial difference between incremental and synoptic policy-making is the intensity of information search behaviour. The more information search behaviour by a policy actor, the more synoptic the policy-making. The differences between actors acting synoptically and those acting incrementally are given in Table 3.1.

Incrementalism	Synoptics
Compare a limited number of alternatives that differ slightly from the status quo	Identify the problem
Limit the number of effects to be determined	Make all objectives explicit
Reformulate problems continuously during information-gathering	Make all alternative means explicit
Regard making choices as an interactive process, not as a single step	Make all effects explicit
	Compare all alternatives
Regulate problems, do not solve them	Choose the best alternative, given the
Share responsibilities with others	objectives

Table 3.1 *The synoptic and incrementalist approach*

The arguments in discussion

In reality, information search behaviour usually turns out to be limited. To many people this is the main point of criticism regarding the synoptic model, namely that it is hardly realistic to think that policy is made this way (Lindblom, 1979). Because the synoptic method does not take into account existing practices and developments, i.e. the acceptability of policy within government or administrative organizations, this methodology may lead to optimal but not very realistic policy designs. According to Dror, it is almost impossible to work synoptically. With regard to alternatives, he states: 'Having to list all alternatives (including doing nothing) is an impossible task, both quantitatively and qualitatively. There are often simply too many of them, and even the major alternatives may be so abundant that all of them cannot be considered. Quantitatively, it is even harder to imagine all relevant new alternatives for action, since this task requires amounts of creativity, initiative, time, knowledge, and energy, and a bias in favour of innovation, that cannot be mobilized.' (Dror, 1968: 138) Nevertheless, one of his recommendations is that looking for alternatives should be intensified and that the costs and benefits of each alternative should be well deliberated.

Other criticism concerns the issue that complete information (i.e. information about all alternatives, criteria and criterion scores) is impossible to attain. Thus searching for complete information involves not only a search for the impossible, but also a delay in policy-making.

According to the incrementalists, their method is also more pure. By changing existing policy only on one point, an experimental situation is created in which two situations in the same policy area can be compared. Ceteris paribus, differences between these situations are a consequence of the incremental change alone. This way it can be experimentally determined what the actual effect is of the incremental change. If a policy changes completely because of a synoptic way of policy design, then changes in the area of the policy involved cannot be explained. This is because the many changes in policy that occur simultaneously cannot be distinguished. The reply to this criticism is also acceptable.

First, the synoptic model has an inherent logic. It is self-evident that well-considered choices, after intensively investigating the advantages and disadvantages of the different options, lead to better policy results than choices that are not.

The fact that this model can hardly be discerned in reality is not sufficient reason for not striving for it. That would be justified only if failing policy does not occur and current policy results are optimal. This does not accord with reality. Policy outcomes are often disappointing. When an evaluation does take place, it usually turns out that the claimed objectives were not realized. This reality of incremental and failing policy is not an argument against but for the synoptic method.

It is theoretically correct to assert that complete information is impossible, but the question remains whether it matters with regard to policy-making that the policy maker has been informed completely or almost completely. Incomplete information having consequences for decision-making disputably assumes that every unit of extra information equally influences decision-making. The differences of opinion about this topic will be discussed later on.

The next point of criticism according to followers of the synoptic method is that incremental policy is only possible under very specific conditions. The quantity of policy resources, the situation in the policy area, and the dimensions of the policy problem need to be relatively stable. Such a stable situation is almost impossible in a dynamic society.

Smith and May claim that incrementalism is too conservative and anti-innovative, and that it encourages slowness (Smith & May, 1985: 119). According to synoptics, incremental policy results in inertia, a policy organization that is introverted and unable to bring about changes. The incrementalists object to this by claiming that many small steps can indeed lead to major changes, and that incrementalism does not lead to inertia; in fact, given the inertia in policy organizations, incrementalism is the only way to bring about changes. Lindblom calls this 'smuggling changes into the system'. Twenty years after his first article on incrementalism, Lindblom introduced 'disjointed incrementalism'. With this concept he positions himself in the middle of the discussion, a position that says that neither intensive information search behaviour nor complete incrementalism is desirable. According to Lindblom, every policy maker takes his own (middle) ground regarding 'strategic analysis' on a continuum ranging from 'ill considered often bumping incompleteness in analysis' to 'meeting all conventional theoretical requirements'. Synopsis is impossible and a complete incremental analysis is shortsighted. Politically policy may develop incrementally, which has considerable advantages, but the analysis of policy should certainly contain analysis of alternatives.

3.1.2 Information theory and cybernetics

Adherents of synoptics assume a positive relation between quantity of information and the chance of making optimal decisions. Based on both information theory and cybernetics, this assumption can be highly criticized (see Shannon 1948, 1954; Wiener 1958).

From information theory it can be deduced that usually the interpretation of information is unambiguous, even though that information is incomplete. The missing part is called redundant. Redundancy in language can be used as an example. Although it is true that a phrase without vowels does not provide complete information, the number of possible interpretations of such a phrase is limited.

th nmbr f pssbl ntrprttns f ths phrs s lmtd

It is almost certain that a person reading this sequence of letters will understand what the phrase means. This leads to the assumption that with much yet incomplete information an actor may be expected to act as though he is completely informed. This is a consequence of the fact that different interpretations have different probabilities. These unequal chances can be found in language itself. The chance of an 'e' occurring in a word is many times larger than that of a 'b'. The missing part of information does not matter to a well-informed actor. The difference between almost complete and complete information will most probably be redundant. Knowing that the lifespan of a washing machine is 8 to 10 years does not constitute complete information. To have complete information, the impossible should be known, i.e. it should be known that the lifespan will be e.g. 9 years, 3 months and 6 days. It is, however, unlikely that this difference between the two forms of information will lead to different decisions. Other examples of redundancy are when information is collected about irrelevant criteria or about criteria whose scores do not diverge. If the added information does not contribute to decision-making, it should not be called information. Naturally, it is hard to answer the question regarding when continuing to collect new information becomes redundant. This depends on a large number of factors.

The theory of cybernetics states that an increase of information can even have a negative effect on decision-making. This is the case when actors have more information than they are able to process, and is known as information *overload*. Deutsch (1963: 161-162) defines information overload as 'A decision system ... where either the collection, or the transmission, or the screening and evaluation of the information has broken down, or was never adequately developed. Such systems perform well on occasion, but in the long run the odds should be heavily against them.' It should be emphasized that this point of view is derived from a definition of information that differs from all others. To Deutsch, information can be found in coherences and regular patterns, and the purpose of information is to neutralize insecurity and disturbances in the system. His proposition is that when insecurity is high, there will be no comparable situation on which to base choices; when the problem-solving capacity of a system is low, the chances of information overload are high. In such a case, a lot of information is necessary but the decision maker is unable to process, analyse and assess all of it. A decision maker will select only the information that supports his intuitive choice and will ignore information that might refine his point of view.

This position is supported by experimental psychological research. The consequences of using too many alternatives and/or criteria are: a smaller chance of choosing the 'right' alternative, a decreasing level of agreement between the outcomes of impact assessment techniques (Voogd, 1983), and a higher chance of ranking order intransitivity. Higher chances of time pressure is also a consequence and usually results in actors giving too much weight to negative information about alternatives (Ben Zur & Bresnitz 1981; Wright 1974). Disagreement between actors about their decision will also increase (Tversky, 1972), but in spite of this disagreement confidence in a decision taken will (wrongfully) increase (Christensen-Szalanski 1978). The effects of information according to these four positions are graphically presented in Figure 3.1.

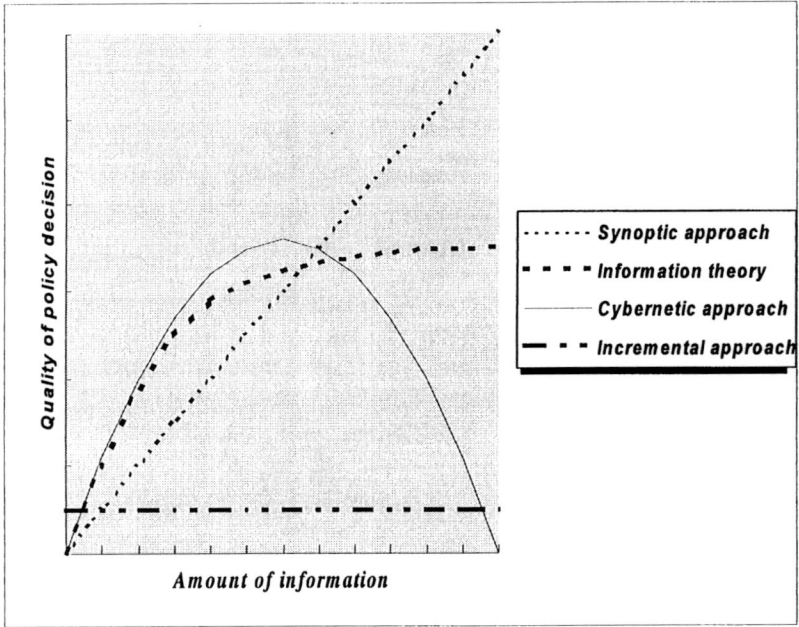

Figure 3.1 *The relation between quantity of information and quality of decision-making according to four theories*

Adopting the views from information theory or cybernetics indicates that it is certainly useful to strive for optimum information - 'optimum' meaning that most relevant information is present while at the same time its quantity is still manageable.

3.2 WHAT DETERMINES INFORMATION SEARCH BEHAVIOUR?

The question whether the perspective of incrementalism, synoptics, cybernetics or information theory should be preferred has, according to a number of people, degenerated into an academic discussion. Some even think that the discussion is artificial (Smith & May, 1985: 116). The differences are not fundamental but gradual. Research does not provide an unambiguous answer to the question whether the search for more and more information, following the synoptic approach, leads to better policy outcomes. Herek et al. claim that both forms of policy-making occur and that policy makers working more synoptically 'tend to make decisions that better meet their goals ... the quality of the decision-making process *is* related to the decisions outcome' (1987: 218). Although success is not guaranteed using the synoptic method, the authors claim success becomes more likely as unexpected outcomes become less likely. The questions then remaining are under which conditions will the synoptic model become more likely, and which conditions will encourage policy actors to opt for satisfying behaviour and the incremental model. These questions will be dealt with in this section. Without the pretension of completeness, the following factors will be discussed:

- Factors related to the content of the choice problem
- Factors related to the characteristics of the decision maker(s)

3.2.1 Factors related to the content of the choice problem

The first question is whether it is *sensible with respect to content* to include certain alternatives and criteria. The following factors play a role in this:

- The political and social feasibility of alternatives
- The robustness or uncertainty of effects
- The reliability, or the chance an alternative will actually generate the effects predicted
- The flexibility, or the extent to which an alternative can also be utilized for other problems
- Time barriers

Such decisions themselves deserve an evaluation research effort. There are two alternatives, namely including an alternative in the evaluation or not including it. This choice can be made on the basis of the five criteria mentioned. Secondly, *formal reasons* can be given not to include an alternative in the evaluation:

- Preconditions and limitations embedded in the objectives of decision makers, such as the time aspect. Is enough time available to discover new alternatives and to elaborate them?
- Preconditions and limitations embedded in legal provisions. Is it allowed to impose taxes in a way that redistributes income? The central government is free to do so, but the local government may do so only partially.

Thirdly, *technical or financial reasons* can play a role in excluding alternatives from impact assessment.

- A large number of alternatives makes an evaluation less transparent. With regard to decision makers, it does not seem sensible to present more than six to eight alternatives.
- The outcomes of impact assessment become more dubious to the extent that more alternatives are included simultaneously.
- Every alternative added makes an evaluation more costly. The determination of scores of alternatives costs time and money. Sometimes there is very little known about an alternative, making it difficult to include it in the evaluation. This applies, for example, to the zero alternative; that is, the alternative where the choice is to do nothing. Both its costs and its effects are often harder to determine than might be expected.

3.2.2 Factors related to the characteristics of the decision maker(s)

The theory of belief systems

One of the older theories explaining information search behaviour stems from political science and was elaborated by Converse in 1964. Later research on this subject was carried out by Rokeach, Klingemann, Barnes and Kaase. These authors make a distinction between actors according to the dominance of fundamental values in their individual mind frame. They distinguish so-called ideologues at one end of the continuum and non-ideologues at the other. Fundamental abstract values are crucial to the thinking of ideologues because they are capable of incorporating new information into their mind frame. However, they are less capable of adapting their values and standards to new information. The people concerned process information selectively, aiming to fit it into their value system. Non-ideologues are people who are hardly capable of thinking in terms of abstract values and standards. However, they are much more capable and prepared to process new information although they cannot process it consistently. Because they are affected by new information, their ideas about a certain subject change continuously. In between there are the 'near ideologues' who mainly think in terms of group perspective (e.g. 'What does my party think about this?') and the 'issue-oriented' who mainly think in terms of issues and fashion. The theory stems from political science and was first presented in 1960 in *The American Voter*. It was elaborated in 1964 by the political scientist Converse, and scrutinized at the end of the 1970s by Barnes and Kaase in *Political Action*.

The theory based on the concept of *belief systems* is the starting point of these theorists. The theory is significant because it clarifies that although values play a part in everyone's life, not everyone thinks in terms of abstract values. Only a small group of highly-educated people think systematically and consciously in terms of 'freedom', 'equality' or 'inner harmony'. A belief system is a conceptual framework allowing people to structure their thoughts and actions. Converse defines a belief system as 'a configuration of ideas and attitudes, in which the elements are bound together by some form of constraint or functional interdependence'.

Groups of people can be differentiated on the basis of the way they integrate new (political) information into their belief system. This happens in an ideological and a non-ideological way, depending on the centrality of ideological concepts in their way of thinking. 'Ideological' means that people use abstract and general theoretical concepts when interpreting, identifying or evaluating events. These concepts can be used more or less often, which indicates their centrality in the mind frame. Based on the level of conceptualization, there are four groups:

- People who continuously use abstract terms and values
- People who think that only associations with group concepts are relevant
- People who make associations with issue concepts
- People who do not make associations regarding content

The first group is characterized by trying to place new information in a wider perspective. These are people capable of abstracting and evaluating new information within their existing mind frame. This capability decreases from Group 1 to Group 4. People in Group 4 do not think in terms of abstract values and concepts. They lack the capability to integrate new information into their mind frame and are inclined to adapt their value system to new information. 'A meaningful integration of external stimuli and new information' does not take place (Klingemann, 1979:6). Research into this theory has indicated that there is a relation between level of education and the centrality of abstract values in a conceptual framework. To people of a high educational level, abstract values are more central than to people of a low educational level (Converse 1964; Klingemann 1979; Barnes & Kaase 1979). Furthermore, the group of people with an ideological mind frame turns out to be small. The largest group is that of the non-ideological people. Table 3.2 is a representation of this theoretical classification.

	Ideologues	--------	-------	Non-ideologues
Attracted to	abstract terms and concepts	group concepts	issue-concepts	no associations regarding content
Group size	small	------------	------------	largest
Education	high	------------	----------	low
Choice behaviour	stable			changeable
Sensibility to new information	hardly	somewhat by reference group	Very, with some durability	Very, but fading out by new information
Associations	post-materialists	-----------	-----------	materialists

Table 3.2 *Typology based on belief system: dotted lines indicate intermediate positions*

Types of leadership

The extent to which information is collected, processed, analysed and interpreted is also a function of the characteristics of the policy actor. Mulder differentiates between 'infozeros', 'infophiles' and 'infonates'.

The criterion on which this distinction is based is the affinity of someone to collect and process information. Infozeros are those who attach no value whatsoever to collecting and processing information. They are headstrong and self-determined. Infonates on the other hand are people constantly looking for new information, postponing decisions as long as possible until they are 'completely' informed. Infophiles are positioned somewhere in between these two extremes.

Mulder (1992: 24) claims that the personality of people - and here he is mainly referring to leaders - determines whether they are infozeros, infophiles or infonates. Distrustful actors are inclined to expose more infonate behaviour than credulous actors. Power-oriented actors would expose more infonate behaviour than people-oriented actors. Insecurity evaders show more infonate behaviour than gamblers. Mulder characterizes infozeros by their dramatic attitude, such as their need for grandeur and excitement and their stressing of the importance of intuition. These are mainly depressive and detached leaders. Suspicious and compelling leaders are infonates.

Cultural factors

Cultural factors are the third group of factors explaining the intensity of information search behaviour. Culture usually means values and standards that are dominant within organizations. Feldman and March claim that Western organization culture has strengthened the symbolic function of information. Organizations have a culture that shows high appreciation for information search behaviour regardless of whether this leads to better decision-making. To Western organization culture, rationalism and ready knowledge are important. Such knowledge represents authority and creates an image of competence and legitimacy. March claims:

> 'Thus the gathering and use of information in an organization trying to make decisions intelligently in a situation in which the verification of intelligence is heavily procedural and normative. A good decision maker is one who makes decisions in the way a good decision maker does, and decision makers and organizations establish their legitimacy by their use of information.' (Feldman & March, 1981: 186)

Making gathered information explicit leads to a more acceptable or accepted decision-making process. March calls this symbolic and ritual information because usually information-processing does not serve to make choices but to rationalize choices already made. According to March, within organizations the values and standards leading to information search behaviour are the result of implicit rewards or appreciations. This is demonstrated by the division of labour between the gathering and the use of information. Information search behaviour is placed in a monitor perspective and not in that of a decision maker. Information is used strategically and committed to the rational choice model. An explanatory model of information search behaviour has been formulated, claiming that this behaviour occurs more often when:

- The choice criteria are more ambiguous and/or vague. The quality of choices is relatively low and cannot be determined quickly. The outcomes of choices also depend on uncontrollable and unforeseen choices made by others, and other legitimating factors play a minor part. Examples are traditions and religion.
- The ideology of rationality within organizations is relatively important. 'Information is significant symbolically because a particular set of beliefs in a particular set of cultures ... As social norms change, the relevance of information as symbol, or signal, changes with them.' (March, 1981: 186)

There are also *cultural hindrances*. Some policy proposals are unacceptable in some cultures. Rewarding law-abiding people instead of punishing those who violate the law can be taboo in some cultures.

Social-psychological factors

Janis provides a social-psychological model to explain the way in which people deal with choice problems. The most important explanatory variable in his model is the extent to which a choice has consequences for the actor himself. According to Janis, the way in which choices are made largely depends on the actors' personal involvement regarding the effects of a choice. Interpretations of what defines a policy maker determine whether this theory is more or less applicable. Is a policy maker interested in his policy choices in the same way a citizen who wants to buy a house or select a school for his children is interested in his choices? In other words, do policy makers lie awake in bed trying to make decisions, and do they worry about that? Or is a policy choice more like an opinion about a political party or a political issue, i.e. a choice where one hardly needs to worry about the personal consequences of a position taken?

The following five propositions reflect the relation between stress and the choice problem (Janis, 1977: 50).

- The extent to which stress is generated by a choice problem is a direct consequence of the desired goals that, according to the decision maker, will not be attained. The fewer goals expected to be attainable and the more important they are, the bigger the stress.
- When a decision maker perceives new threats and chances motivating him to change policy, stress is a function of the extent to which he is committed to his present policy.
- When a problem of choice is more serious because all alternatives represent a threat, the absence of the expectation that a solution exists that is better than the least troublesome alternative will result in defensive avoidance of making choices.
- When a choice problem is serious, threats become real and the decision maker has little time to find and develop a better alternative, the stress level stays extremely high and 'hypervigilance' (panic) becomes probable.
- A low stress level in reaction to threats results in a tendency towards information search behaviour; new alternatives will be elaborated given the decision maker's expectation of the existence of alternatives that will solve the choice problem in a more satisfying way.

Are the risks high when my policy remains *unchanged*?
Are the risks high when I *do change* my policy?
Is it realistic to *hope for a better* alternative?
Is there enough *time* to continue search and consultation?

Table 3.3 *Janis' four questions*

About stress and the approach to problems of choice, Janis (1977: 52) claims that there is a curvilinear relation between the level of stress and the probability of acting synoptically:

'Extremely low stress and extremely high stress are likely to give rise to defective information processing, whereas intermediate levels of stress are more likely to be associated with vigilant information processing. These stress effects, of course, have to be evaluated against a baseline of the individual's usual level of information processing under conditions of little or no stress arousal.'

A synoptic strategy will be more probable when the four questions of Table 3.3 are answered positively. To a smoker having to choose between continuing or stopping his habit, the first question to be answered positively is whether continuing to smoke brings about risks (Janis, 1977). If the smoker does *not* perceive his behaviour as hazardous, he will continue smoking without being interested in the remaining questions. A smoker might say he is smoking filter cigarettes because they are not dangerous to his health, or that to stop smoking is useless because we will all die some day, or that he thinks statistics is a pack of lies. He is not looking for further information. Only if the first question is answered positively does information about the second question become relevant, i.e. are the risks high if he does stop smoking? He might think of nervousness, irritation, increased sweet consumption, etc. If the answer to this question is negative, his information search behaviour will cease and his behaviour will change. If the answer is positive, that is, risks are perceived following a policy/behavioural change, the following question needs to be answered. In answering question 3, the smoker asks himself whether it is realistic to think that he can stop smoking. If the answer is negative and he perceives no realistic alternative for his smoking behaviour, his information search behaviour will cease and he will stick to his old habit. Given the positive answer to the first question (namely, whether continuing his behaviour will bring about risks), the smoker is faced with a problem. This may lead to one of four kinds of behaviour: flight, the shifting of responsibilities, panic, or bolstering. In the first place, he can push the problem aside and stop thinking about it. He can also try to shift the responsibility to another person. Our smoker might say it is the job of the government to deal with the problem. In the third place, the smoker can become agitated. He tries to stop because he knows smoking is not healthy. But his failure to do so results in no longer accepting his own policy without having the option to change it. In the fourth place, he can put a higher value on the positive aspects of smoking, or minimize the negative aspects, in order to legitimize his behaviour. If, however, his answer to the third question is positive, he will arrive at question 4 and ask himself whether there is enough time to look for a better alternative. Our smoker will now gather information about smoking behaviour and health, and may reach the conclusion that he has been smoking for such a long time that it is too late to stop anyway. His behaviour is the consequence of answering each of the four questions either positively or negatively. Negative answers to the four questions lead to flight, incremental policy, avoidance of choices and panic, respectively. Positive answers in the proposed order to the four questions will lead to decreasingly incremental and increasingly synoptic policies. This way it becomes clear that a synoptic process does not necessarily lead to a change of policy or behaviour. Synoptic only means that a policy actor deliberates upon as many alternatives as possible on the basis of as many criteria as possible. The conclusion of a synoptic process can be that a policy change will result in worse outcomes than would a continuation of existing policy. A synoptic approach is reflected by information search behaviour, not by changing policy choices.

Structural factors

Structural factors that determine the way a problem of choice is approached are associated with power, dependency and interests. Policy actors do not independently determine whether they will work synoptically, but do so within a contextual structure. Characteristics of the context have an effect on the behaviour and the actions of actors. Following the structural approach, the outcomes/effects of alternatives are not just the consequence of an alternative but vary with the contextual characteristics. Structural variables also lead to more or less insecurity about these effects. The features of such a contextual structure are reflected by power structure, structure of interests and dependency structure.

All three structures determine the extent to which a policy actor can deal with a problem of choice independently and the extent to which he can determine the effects of his choice independently. All three also determine the maximum quantity of information an actor has to gather. These are the two fundamental relations. Furthermore, these factors can influence practical matters such as time and preconditions. It will be clear that power factors finally determine whether, among other things, an alternative gets a chance to be included in an impact assessment. Who determines the usefulness of including an alternative, and who determines the preconditions of an evaluation? Especially action groups and pressure groups need to invest a lot of energy in getting one of their preferred alternatives included in evaluation research.

3.3 DOES AN OPTIMUM EXIST?

Different scientific disciplines claim that an optimum number of alternatives and criteria exist. This optimum is supposed to be around seven. The more alternatives investigated, the better the decision-making. However, more than seven alternatives and seven criteria can hardly be managed by humans: unfortunately, people have a limited capacity to process information. In the 1950s, Miller mentioned the magical number seven in this context (Miller 1956; Voogd 1982: 201).

First analyse as many alternatives as possible on the basis of as many criteria as possible.
If the number of alternatives exceeds seven, limit the alternatives to seven plus or minus one.
Limit the number of criteria to seven plus or minus one.
If this restraint is impossible, try to merge (aggregate) alternatives or criteria and try a stepwise evaluation.
Make sure that alternatives and criteria are of the same level of aggregation

---

Table 3.4 *Recommendations regarding the number of alternatives*

Experimental research by Timmermans (1991) shows that individuals almost never use more than six alternatives and six criteria when making a choice, regardless of its complexity. Her research also showed that the number of actually used alternatives and criteria is smaller with intuitive choices than when using a decision support system. It turned out that when a problem of choice was made very complex (i.e. there were 5 - 12 criteria and 3 - 9 alternatives), individuals made the problem manageable by excluding alternatives and criteria beforehand. Furthermore, a negative relation was found between the number of alternatives and the number of actually used criteria. When the number of alternatives was increased, the number of actually used criteria decreased, and vice versa (Timmermans, 1991: 83).

It also appeared that the decision rule used changes according to the complexity of a problem of choice. The conjunctive decision rule is more often used with more than six alternatives and more than six criteria. This means alternatives are discarded because they score badly on one criterion, not taking into account the score of the alternatives on other criteria (Timmermans, 1991: 87). The effectiveness of decision-support systems, such as the multi-criteria model, also depends on the complexity of the problem of choice. Research by Timmermans and earlier by Chu & Elam (1988) resulted in the assumption that this relation is parabolic. Optimum effectiveness of such a system occurs when a problem is reasonably complex, and becomes less when problems are too complex.

Voogd (1983: 201) investigated the stability of choices, in particular stability in attributing scores to criteria and weights under conditions of increasing numbers of criteria and alternatives. He reached the conclusion that increasing the complexity of a choice problem has negative effects on stability. Individuals are hardly capable of attributing weights in a stable and substantiated way if the number of alternatives is too high. When the problem of choice is more complex, the choice becomes more arbitrary. The accordance between different analytical techniques of impact assessment also decreases when problems are more complex. Voogd too recommends limiting the number of criteria and alternatives.

However, it is not very pragmatic to limit the number of alternatives to 6 or 8. Sometimes there are simply 3 or 12 alternatives. When, for example, evaluating urban renewal in twelve different residential areas, it seems pointless to restrict that number to a recommended 6 or 8. The same goes for the number of criteria.

3.4 TYPES OF CRITERIA

In such a situation it is possible to perform a stepwise impact assessment. The alternatives are first evaluated using part of the criteria, and then by using the remaining criteria. The ranking order of alternatives that result from both analyses can then be used as input for a third overall analysis.

There is a major distinction between *optimizing* and *minimizing* criteria. Costs, disadvantages and negative effects are criteria to be minimized, and benefits, advantages and positive effects are criteria to be optimized. A stepwise evaluation can be designed in such a way that the criteria to be optimized are evaluated first, and the criteria to be minimized are evaluated second. The outcomes of both analyses can then be used as input for a third analysis. The two separate ranking orders of alternatives, and perhaps their utility scores, are the criterion scores to be used in the third analysis. The final ranking order of alternatives is determined on the basis of these *two* criteria.

A second distinction is between the *content* and the *level of aggregation* of criteria. For example, policy area can be used to differentiate between environmental, economic and administrative aspects. This is classification by sector. The criteria are an aggregation of more concrete indicators that are important to every aspect. Such an aggregation is significant because it may lead to a stepwise impact assessment. The first step is to evaluate by sector. The second is to aggregate the sectors where the outcomes of the first step are the input for the second step. Following the example of the construction and route of a highway, this could be elaborated as in Table 3.5.

	Alternatives
Economic criteria employment business growth construction costs	
Environmental criteria diversity fauna diversity flora	
Procedural criteria duration of procedures legal provisions subsidy possibilities political feasibility	

Table 3.5 *Example of a stepwise approach*

A third distinction between criteria is derived from Voogd (1980 and 1983: 58) and serves to characterize evaluations. Voogd distinguishes the following types of criteria:

Do the criteria indicate whether an alternative is feasible? These are, for example, criteria concerning finance, complexity of implementation and possible subsidies. They are called *attainability criteria*. An evaluation using only these criteria is called an *attainability evaluation*.

Do the criteria indicate whether certain minimum conditions for the alternatives are satisfied? These are, for example, criteria concerning exceeding marginal values or legal standards. They are called *veto criteria* because just one of them may lead to the unacceptability of an alternative. An evaluation using only these criteria is called a *sieve evaluation*.

Do the criteria indicate whether an alternative is desirable to various groups? These are, for example, criteria concerning efficiency, well-being, employment, economic growth and pollution. They are called *desirability criteria*. An evaluation using only these criteria is called a *desirability evaluation*.

By first comparing the alternatives using economic criteria, it can be analysed which alternative is preferred regarding this aspect. Then the environmental criteria and finally the procedural criteria are assessed. The results are three evaluations whose outcomes are used in an overall analysis to generate the ultimate ranking order of alternatives. The advantages of this procedure are:

The number of criteria per sector, and above all differences in numbers between sectors, no longer affects the outcome. In the final evaluation, the alternatives have been assessed by their sector scores.

The attribution of weights becomes more realistic. It is very difficult to indicate the relation between the weight of the criterion 'diversity of flora' and that of the criterion 'possible subsidies'. Furthermore, it is hard to explain why weights were chosen the way they were. This problem is reduced when both criteria are concerned with the same group of, for example, environmental aspects. There may be good reasons why in a particular region the importance of 'diversity of flora' is greater or less than the importance of 'diversity of fauna'. The same applies to economic and environmental criteria.

In turn, a comparison of the importance of economic, environmental and procedural aspects can also be very useful. Since the 1970s, the preferences of most populations in western democracies have been researched on a regular basis using survey techniques. In this, comparisons are based on criteria of the same level of aggregation.

3.5 TYPES OF ALTERNATIVES

A stepwise approach can also be useful with regard to alternatives. Eight types of alternatives are distinguished. It is recommendable to compare and to order alternatives within one evaluation only when they belong to the same type. By first analysing separately the alternatives concerning objectives, location, sector and implementation, followed by a comparison of the preferred options resulting from these analyses in a new analysis, the outcome of an impact assessment becomes simpler to interpret and less ambiguous.

Target alternatives   First of all, objectives may differ. The objective may vary from reducing demand by means of cost-cutting to satisfying demand by expanding production. Changes of priorities may be at stake. Should employment be stimulated at the expense of higher inflation, or should inflation decrease at the expense of higher unemployment?

Zero alternatives   Doing nothing is a possibility that is explicitly taken into account. The consequences of this alternative are weighed in the same way as the consequences of all other alternatives.

Zero-plus alternatives   These are alternatives that satisfy objectives, not by radical changes but by adjusting the present situation.

Sector alternatives   By focusing on a particular aspect, alternative means to attain an objective are adjusted in a way that optimally takes into account the interests of the sector. In this way, environmental, economic, legal or geographical aspects can be incorporated in each alternative.

Implementation alternatives   It is also possible that the objective has been established, but that the way in which the objective is to be attained

	varies. Increasing taxation is not the only way to reduce a government budget deficit; it can also be done by stimulating economic growth or reducing government expenditure.
Disaster alternatives	The effects of these alternatives are contrary to the established objectives.
Location alternatives	The location where something is to happen may vary even when objectives and means are established. It is clear that reliable energy facilities are necessary; it may also be clear that this will be done by building a nuclear power station, but the location of this power station may be debatable.
Time alternatives	This concerns the possibility of phasing the implementation of alternatives; that is, of delaying or expediting their implementation.

This classification of alternatives is also relevant to the discussion about incrementalism, because part of the discussion about designing policies incrementally is the result of failing to distinguish these types of alternatives (Etzioni, 1968). As far as alternative objectives are concerned, the views of Lindblom may be right. Often not all possible objectives of a certain policy are compared. Usually this is a subjective, perhaps even political choice that depends on the also subjectively-established problem definition, where many alternatives are excluded beforehand. In this respect, policy is usually incremental because objectives are often established to last for a longer period of time and change very gradually. As a rule, alternative objectives are part of strategic policy - policy that is almost irreversible and often established for a long period of time. There are, of course, exceptions, such as the change in Soviet military strategy in the 1980s from offensive to defensive policies, and the change of policies aimed at reducing inflation towards policies aimed at stimulating employment, and vice versa. However, this kind of change is less frequent than continuation of policy with regard to objectives. This is also somewhat true for sector, disaster and implementation alternatives, albeit to a lesser extent. Synoptic policies can frequently be found regarding location, time, zero and zero-plus alternatives. A company looking for a new location to build a factory and a city looking for a new location to set up an industrial zone will almost always look at more than one alternative, and perhaps at all possible ones. This strategy is known as 'mixed scanning', where intensity of information search behaviour is a function of the type of alternatives. When looking at the timing of policy implementation, it is also true that different alternatives are almost always considered. This concerns tactical or even operational decisions. As opposed to strategic policies, tactical choices are reversible and are usually short term. In general, the timing of an announcement of budget cuts or a budget windfall, of tax raises or tax cuts, is strategically determined. Government agencies try to control and plan as much as possible the disclosure of positive or negative messages about their policies in order to maximize acceptability. Likewise, government policy analysts are aware that their reports will be published only when it is strategically convenient to policy makers.

3.6 CONCLUSION

The question discussed in this chapter was how many alternatives and criteria should be included in an impact assessment. With regard to the discussion about the synoptic and the incrementalist approach, it was concluded that both ways of determining policies are undesirable if used exclusively. The characteristics of policy actors and the context in which they work were described as factors explaining the probability of synoptic or incremental policy-making. Five factors were considered: mind frame, type of leadership, social psychological factors, cultural factors and structural factors. Although systematic empirical research into the way in which these factors affect information search behaviour does not exist, they do indicate the direction where explanations might be found.

Finally, recommendations about the number of alternatives and criteria to be included in an evaluation were discussed. If the number exceeds seven, a stepwise impact assessment is desirable.

4 Determining how well alternatives score on criteria

> This chapter examines the requirements criterion scores have to satisfy theoretically, which methods are available to do so, and how they are dealt with in practice. This last aspect is investigated on the basis of content analysis of environmental assessment reports.
> First we will focus on measuring criteria in a general sense and the standards for assessment that are involved. Then we will deal with the problems people may encounter in practice, and finally with the possibilities of entering scores in the Salomo computer program.

Tasks
|
Alternatives
|
Criteria
|
Test scores
|
Importance of criteria
|
Compilation of data
|
Analysis of ranking order
|
Leave decisions to the decision maker

INTRODUCTION

This chapter is concerned with determining test- or criterion scores in a multi-criteria evaluation. Four research techniques are distinguished: argumentation, the use of indicators and monitoring, comparative case studies, and experimental design. The objective, the internal logic and the steps a user has to take in using it and the problems a user is confronted with will be discussed below. It will be concluded that each technique has its own advantages and disadvantages, and that a preference a priori for one or the other technique cannot be justified.

4.1 CRITERIA AND INDICATORS

What standards are used to evaluate criteria indicators? In general there are six requirements that indicators for a variable have to satisfy; these are given in Table 4.1.

Validity
Unambiguity / reliable measurement
Sensitivity to change
Comparability over time and in space
Accuracy
Applicability
Availability

Table 4.1 *Requirements for criteria indicators*

The *validity* of an indicator is a self-evident requirement. There must be conformity between what is actually measured and what is meant to be measured. Nevertheless, the validity of indicators turns out to be an important but often underestimated problem. An example of measuring discrimination will illustrate this.

The answer given to an item in a questionnaire, such as 'Do you sometimes discriminate?', indicates whether discrimination occurs. However, this question does not lead to valid answers. Somewhat more intelligent is the application of the Bogardus scale. Here respondents are asked to reply to consecutive questions, such as: do you or do you not approve of immigrants being in your country, your province, your city, your street, the house next door, or marrying your daughter? Nowadays also the number of immigrants approved of should be recorded. But the question remains whether honest answers will be given and whether these answers measure what they are intended to measure. A second method is to ask immigrants themselves: 'Are you being discriminated against?' Here too it is questionable whether the answers measure what they are intended to measure. After all, it is true of many immigrants that they have nothing to base a comparison on and therefore cannot know whether they are being discriminated against. It is also true that immigrants avoid places where they stand a relatively high chance of being discriminated against. A third method is to gather statistics, such as the number of reported acts of discrimination. Here too there can be doubt about the picture that will be discovered. This picture depends on the readiness to report and the news value. It is still possible that only the tip of the iceberg will be measured. A fourth method is to analyse existing statistics, comparing e.g. unemployment percentages and different levels of work and education between immigrants and original inhabitants. This seems to be a valid instrument, but it is very often hard to find arguments supporting the idea that the differences established indicate discrimination. Often, possible competing explanations for the differences found cannot be excluded sufficiently (Brunt 1977: 127).

This example only serves to illustrate that the validity of an indicator is often a problem and that assessment of indicators is a crucial step in assessing (evaluation) research.

The second requirement is concerned with the *reliability* of measurement. There are two types of reliability. In the first place, the indicator should provide reliable data, meaning there should be as few errors as possible. Errors can be a consequence of a faulty source, the faulty extraction of data from a source, faulty data-processing or faulty data-analysis. Data in the population register sometimes are very obsolete and contain many errors. Using these data as input for an impact assessment may lead to (typing) errors and allows for analyses that are inadequate with regard to the type of data in terms of e.g. the level of measurement or the level of aggregation.

The second type of reliability focuses on the fact that the value of data should be independent of the collector of data. With regard to the value of the indicator, it should make no difference whether it has been determined by one researcher or the other. This point should be emphasized if researchers have an interest in the outcomes of the research, or if the research deviates from existing rules for scientific investigation.

The third requirement regards the *sensitivity* of indicators to change. Research into the problems of residential areas may serve as an example. The city would like to know how its funds for city renewal or its welfare efforts should be distributed among residential areas. To satisfy such requirements as availability and applicability, indicators are used, e.g. number of immigrants, level of mutation, and percentage of unemployment. It will be immediately clear that these indicators differ strongly with regard to sensitivity. The sensitivity of indicators to city policies varies strongly. Regardless of the city policies concerning deployment of city means, the number of immigrants will hardly change. This is a variable that cannot be manipulated by city renewal budgets or the distribution of welfare funds. As far as policy is concerned, this is a constant. The level of mutation varies with the policy pursued, but its direction is more difficult to manipulate. The level of mutation does not necessarily correspond to the extent that policy has been successful. Certainly in the short term, it can either rise or decline when the quality of a residential area improves. In contrast, unemployment can indeed be influenced in accordance with city policy and serves as a good indicator for the criterion 'quality of a residential area'. Thus the sensitivity of indicators is strongly connected with the content of a policy choice. The percentage of immigrants can be a good indicator in one policy area (e.g. housing) for the quality of a residential area, and a bad indicator with regard to another policy area (e.g. welfare).

The fourth requirement is the *comparability* of indicators over time and in space. The indicator for a criterion should be the same for all alternatives. This concerns the source of the data, the way they are extracted from that source, the processing of the data and their analysis. This criterion too is not always satisfied. Comparability may not be attained because, for example, data are missing or have not been stored in a comparable way. This is a problem on the level of, among others, national comparative research. Criminality is defined and measured differently in different countries, thus making comparative studies almost always debatable. But also at the city level such problems arise. Different services and departments may have their own geographical classification (e.g. area code, block or street) on the basis of which they determine their registrations and levels of aggregation. Also the definition of policy areas may differ from department to department. Over time, changes can also occur which make data no longer comparable, or which make data useless that at an earlier stage served to operationalize indicators. The introduction of rules of accountability has had comparable consequences for city finances. The accountability these rules refer to includes the accounts and annual accounts as well as the budget (Mol, 1988: 33).

The fifth requirement of indicators is their easy *applicability*. In this respect, compound indicators are less suitable than simple indicators. It is argued that assessing the merits of an evaluation is complicated when the merits are based on criteria and indicators of these criteria that can hardly be controlled. When that is the case, evaluations lose credibility and therefore also practicability.

The *availability* of data is an obvious requirement. If data are not available, the value of an indicator cannot be determined. Missing data and the removal for that reason of criteria from an impact assessment may have consequences for the resulting ranking order. Besides, the measurement problem is but a very simple argument for leaving out certain (e.g. environmental) criteria that are unattractive to the decision maker. The criterion is completely left out of consideration, having a weight equal to zero. Of course this may lead to suboptimal ranking orders. For example, when buying a domestic appliance, a missing price tag may have far-reaching consequences with regard to making the optimal decision.

4.2 METHODS FOR DETERMINING CRITERION SCORES

4.2.1 Information from previous evaluations

The simplest and therefore most preferable method is, of course, to find out whether certain alternatives have already been put into practice elsewhere and whether their effects have been evaluated. The question is whether much information concerning certain options is already available. In practice, little use is made of this possibility. The results of evaluation research are often shredded, and often a lot of time, money and energy is invested in research into the possible effects of alternatives that are already known. A problem here is that evaluations do not always use the method or produce the results that a decision maker currently considers necessary in order to take a decision.

Quality of ex post evaluations

Meta research shows that the quality of evaluation research is often disappointing, little use is made of its results, and its usefulness is low. As a result of their meta research, Hoogerwerf and Zoutendijk strongly criticize evaluation research. They claim that 'Considering the formulated requirements there is a lot missing in the investigated reports. The most important drawback in the reports that were investigated was the lack of explicitly formulated standards.' (Bressers et al., 1991: 246) Reussing (1990) came to a similar conclusion based on his research: 'This assessment shows that evaluation research is open to a large number of improvements. This goes for both scientific quality (methodological requirements) and policy relevance (praxeological requirements) of the research.' (1990: 79,80)

According to Reussing, the following weak points can be listed regarding *methodological requirements*:

- the research objective is not indicated concretely
- assessment standards are not given
- assessment standards are not conceptualized
- assessment standards are not operationalized
- research design is not convincing
- only one explanation strategy is used instead of several
- only one reliability test is used instead of several
- no statistical analysis is made
- assessment of the effect of intervention does not comply with standards formulated earlier.

The following weak points can be listed regarding *praxeological requirements*:

- there is no link with a concrete policy decision
- the intermediate objectives of the policy programme are not mentioned
- the policy assumptions of the programme are not specified
- the research does not give information about reaching intermediate objectives
- results of research are not confronted with other results
- results of research are not presented in an accessible way
- no possible alternative choices are offered.

In addition to the familiar causes, such as quality of research design, quality of the researcher and the relation between policy maker and researcher (Patton, 1978; Weiss and Buchuvalas, 1977; Mulder and Walraven, 1991), the cause may also be the link between science and practice. Scientific classification of different types of evaluation research and the accompanying recommendations about the way such research should be carried out is less useful if these types cannot be found in practice. The strict distinction made by science between ex ante and ex post evaluations serves as an example (Chen & Rossi 1980; Scriven 1980; Cronbach 1982). Here the main issue is a comparison of advantages and disadvantages of the different types; the linking elements are not or hardly discussed.

In practice, the structure of evaluation research is usually as follows: first, a check is carried out on the content of existing policy, its (intended) effects, what has and what has not been realized, and what causes to this effect are conceivable. Then a decision is made and recommendations are formulated to adjust, continue or end a certain policy. This structure has both ex post, summative, formative and ex ante elements. Such a combination is beneficial to all parties involved, provided the research gets the best elements of each type of evaluation. Sometimes this turns out not to be the case. Some research may have all the disadvantages of ex ante and all the disadvantages of ex post evaluation, instead of all the advantages of both.

Expectations of effects are central in ex ante evaluations. Will the result of this alternative be ...? To what extent will this be the case? Will another alternative be more effective? When will the effects be noticeable? Do implementation problems play a part, and if so how should they be estimated?

The crucial term in this description is the word 'estimation'. There is no certainty about the effects of a policy alternative. This is a disadvantage as well as a reason to carry out ex ante evaluation. It is precisely in a situation where there is much uncertainty that an investigation of the assessment of effects will be useful. When there is still a choice between alternative policy measures, it is important to know what can be expected of these measures. Then it is also important to know in what respect, i.e. with regard to which criteria, one alternative is better than the other.

Steps in ex post evaluation

The objective of ex post evaluation is to determine afterwards whether intended objectives have actually been satisfied, and if so whether this is a consequence of pursued policy. 'Did the policy affect developments in

•   Determine whether and if so how policy is implemented
•   Determine objectives
•   Determine indicators for goal-attainment
•   Operationalize indicators
•   Determine the level of goal-attainment
•   Find possible competing explanations for the outcomes
•   Evaluate the effectiveness of pursued policy

Table 4.2 *Steps in ex post evaluation*

the policy area?' is a question typical of ex post evaluations. One characteristic of these evaluations is the abundance of information about effects, because they have already occurred. So the starting point of this method is policy that has already been implemented. However, this assumption is not always justified and is frequently neglected. In 1984 Reiss stated that 'Most evaluation studies fail to monitor whether or not the experimental or intervention condition actually occurred; hence it is entirely possible that either it did not take place or that it was altered in significant ways so as to blunt its effect.' (in McCall & Weber, 1984: 33)

As a rule, ex post evaluations are carried out according to the principle of the modus operandi method. Starting with the original policy objectives, it is investigated to what extent goal-attainment has been achieved. This is usually done by determining changes in the policy area (Scriven, 1967; Bressers & Hoogerwerf, 1991: 107). The next step is to investigate the extent to which the level of goal-attainment found can be attributed to policy and to what extent results can be accounted for by competing explanations. Like the first step, this step is sometimes omitted (Metselaar, 1991). The final step is concerned with evaluation of the effectiveness of policy based on these results.

Advantages of ex post evaluation

Compared to ex ante, ex post evaluation has the advantage of complying largely with the conception people usually have of evaluations: an assessment of policy pursued based on available data, which determines changes in the policy area as a result of policy pursued. This advantage is concerned with the actor system. Furthermore, the policy has been implemented, and given some restrictions the level of goal-attainment can be empirically determined. This is an advantage concerning the calculating system. On the basis of a comparison of a zero measurement and a measurement afterwards, differences in the policy area that are attributable to policy can be determined. It is also possible to evaluate effectiveness, goal-attainment or efficiency of policy on the basis of actual experience. Conjecture is less important with ex post than with ex ante evaluations. A much more substantial relation with policy can be established, and the actual course of the implementation process can be better described.

Disadvantages of ex post evaluation

There are, however, also important problems with this type of evaluation. Usually the disadvantages of ex ante evaluation concern the same issues as the advantages of ex post evaluation, and vice versa. It will be clear that data in an ex post evaluation can also be based on conjecture. Changes may be wrongly seen as effects attributable to policy, and even then not all possible alternatives may be known. The first three disadvantages listed below concern the choice system, the second three the actor system.

- During ex post evaluation, policy objectives may have shifted and criteria may have changed (Herweijer, 1981). Sometimes this is related to effects that have actually occurred. Because an effect has occurred as a consequence of policy, it could be called a policy objective afterwards.
- Ex post evaluations do not pay or pay only insufficiently attention to side effects and long-term effects.
- It is not always clear whether the changes found are a consequence of pursued policy.
- Decision makers are often not prepared to initiate ex post evaluation research, let alone cooperate with it. Few administrators like to be audited, assessed and possibly condemned for policies they have pursued. In other words, ex post evaluations can be perceived by decision makers as threatening.
- The outcomes of ex post evaluations are often presented too late to be able to influence policy. The duration of an evaluation project is in general at least one year. Sometimes it is debatable whether the outcomes after such a long period of time has elapsed are still useful.
- It is clear that ex post evaluations are expensive operations. Often a supervisory committee is installed and one or more researchers are appointed for a longer period of time. Also the research itself, depending on its design, can be very costly.

Use of ex post evaluations

Ex post evaluations have a long tradition. Parliamentary committees, for instance, are good examples of such evaluations. On a smaller scale, almost everyone carries out ex post evaluations. In meetings, usually the first questions asked are 'Have the agreements been observed?' and 'What has been attained and what has not been attained?' Consumers may ask themselves 'Is the product purchased satisfactory?' or 'Do we like the new car?' Examples on a larger scale are the evaluation of the university administration reform act and other acts. In the end, ex post evaluation is concerned with the assessment of developments observed on the basis of existing knowledge after policy has been implemented.

Interdependence of ex ante and ex post evaluations

The preceding sections discussed the differences between ex ante and ex post evaluations. From the perspective of utility determination, however, there are no fundamental but only gradual differences. Both ex ante and ex post evaluations are concerned with determining the value of policy. Research practice also shows that ex ante and ex post evaluations have differences as well as similarities. Chapter 1 dealt with the relation between purpose and effect orientation, the user and value orientation that is increasingly characteristic of evaluations, and the possibility of using information derived from ex post evaluations as input for ex ante evaluations.

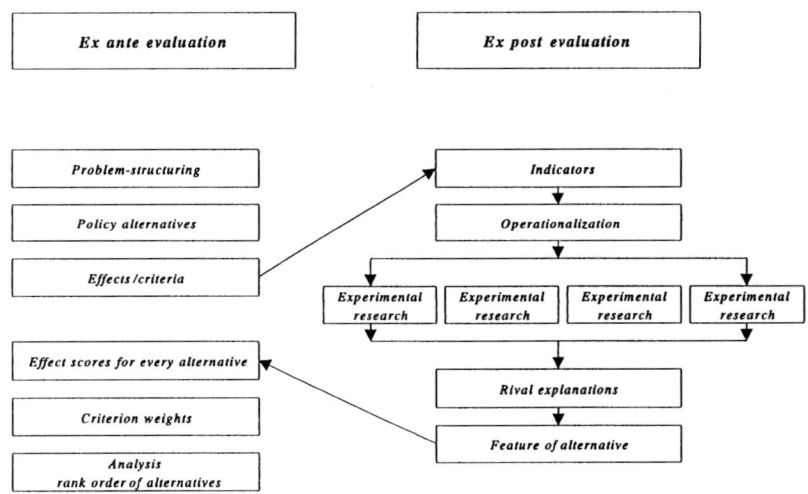

Figure 4.1   *The connection between ex ante and ex post evaluations*

The following discusses the improvement of policy evaluation that occurs when the mutual dependency of both types of evaluation is made explicit. Figure 4.1 presents a schematic representation of this. The criteria as formulated in an ex ante evaluation serve as input for ex post evaluation, and the outcomes of ex post evaluation serve as input for ex ante evaluation. Because the policy criteria have been made explicit beforehand, the criteria that will be used to evaluate this policy afterwards are also known. This assessment in itself produces the input for the list of effects that is necessary to arrive at a new policy choice.

The expected policy effects are made explicit beforehand, thus enabling these effects to be evaluated ex post. Suppose, for example, that the criteria for a policy choice are the expected costs of a project, the expected level of goal-attainment and the side effects. In such a case, the criteria on which to carry out an evaluation afterwards have been established. The questions will be: 'Has the budget been exceeded or not?' and 'To what extent have the objectives been reached and to what extent did the side effects actually occur?' In fact, the difference from evaluations as they are done nowadays is not that great. It is, however, different from the classic approach to evaluation where both the aspect of costs and the side effects remain outside the evaluation. The crucial question is how the effects that have not been anticipated by policy makers are found. Chen and Rossi (1981) mention the following sources:

- social scientific theory and knowledge
- implicit objectives
- target group research into effects on different groups
- the way of policy implementation in relation to communication with target groups and their anticipations
- specific effects resulting from interaction between the programme and its context.

The outcomes of such ex post evaluation again serves as input for new, ex ante evaluation. However, it is not the case that ex post evaluations are the only source of input, or that a complete ex ante evaluation can only be made after ex post evaluation has taken place. Other data can be useful, depending on the nature of the criteria. Besides, the results of an ex post evaluation may be missing at the time of ex ante evaluation. Primarily the idea is that a combination of ex ante and ex post evaluations may lead to improved policy-making.

When policy choices are made on the basis of such an approach and all steps are observed, this may be called policy-making based on policy evaluation in a strict sense. In practice, however, policy-making is usually based on merely partial application of the steps given in Figure 4.1. Some explanation for this practice can be found in the emphasis that until now has been put on the differences between ex ante and ex post evaluations.

Have all disadvantages been avoided?

The aim of the model given above is to underline the mutual dependency of the two forms of evaluation. Because of this dependency, the disadvantages of both methods can be decreased or eliminated, provided all steps are observed. It will now be discussed to what extent the disadvantages of ex-ante evaluations can be eliminated by this combined method.

The danger of self-fulfilling and self-denying prophesies is reduced because the core of the evaluation consists of data concerning pursued policy, its alternatives and the effects the policy has had. The effect should discriminate between alternatives, but self-fulfilling prophesies do not do this. They count regardless of policy choice and will play no part in winding up the evaluation.

The fact that changes of political preferences may occur as the implementation of policy progresses cannot be avoided. However, this information can be gathered partially because the combined method also considers already pursued policy and because changes may have taken place regarding the objectives of this policy and the policy itself.

By including the effects of alternative policies and by indicating how futile or useful they are compared to the pursued policy, a technocratic decision-making process cannot be entirely prevented. It does, however, clarify the extra advantages and disadvantages of a policy change. Besides, the possibility of qualitative argumentations has been explicitly included in the model. These are not necessarily limited to the technical aspects of alternatives, but can also arise from political preferences. As far as they discriminate between alternatives, political preferences and their weights can be included in order to produce a ranking order. Participants in the decision-making process may even control the outcomes of the evaluation by choosing their own criterion weights.

Data used for ex ante evaluation contain much less uncertainty. They are computed on the basis of harder or softer empirical data. Of course, data may be included that are based on guesses. This, however, is no longer a problem typical of evaluation research but one of quality standards regarding the researcher.

The tendency to attribute effects to a policy is reduced by mentioning competing explanations explicitly and checking their relation to policy, as in ex post evaluation. The intermediate step 'competing explanations' in ex post evaluation is explicitly included in ex ante evaluation. The criterion scores (intended and unintended effects) are therefore investigated to see whether they are actually a consequence of the alternative or whether they can be explained by other causes. This is a necessary but often neglected step in ex ante evaluation. Its omission results in criticisms about effects being attributed to policy retrospectively. This step is necessary because a criterion can only discriminate between alternatives if it actually is a consequence of one policy alternative and not of the other alternatives.

Changes in political preferences and missing information about all relevant alternatives cannot be avoided. The combined method of evaluation too proceeds on the basis of available information. Obviously, if information is unavailable, it cannot be incorporated.

In reference to the avoidance of disadvantages of ex post evaluation mentioned in section 3.2.2, the following remarks should be made:

Enabled by this phased approach, changes of policy objectives as criteria can be included in the evaluation, insofar as the new objectives as criteria play a part in the new decision-making. Our approach does not exclude new objectives next to the original ones. It also does not exclude the investigation of each alternative in terms of goal-attainment. The only restrictions are the discriminating capacity of objectives and their relevance. If a certain objective can be reached by using any of the alternatives, this objective should be removed from the analysis that produces a ranking order of alternatives. The main advantage of the combined approach is that non-discriminatory objectives no longer play a part in determining policy choice. Nowadays, it still is often the case that a choice is made on the basis of criteria on which all alternatives score equally.

This means that with this approach there is room to include side effects and long-term effects. Here too they can be incorporated in the analysis insofar as they discriminate between alternatives and are sufficiently relevant.

By focussing evaluation research not only on the effects of pursued policy but also on the extent to which these effects can be attained by other policy alternatives, the relation between policy and effect can be clarified.

With a combined approach, the preparedness to initiate such research will increase. The main objective is no longer judgement or condemnation, but rather the control and adjustment of existing policy. This way the threat produced by this kind of research is reduced. On the other hand, the preparedness to evaluate may also decrease because the costs of research will rise.

Obviously, two problems seem to increase in magnitude when applying the presented model: the duration and therefore the costs of evaluation research will rise.

It may not always be expected that data from ex post evaluations are available regarding all alternatives to be deliberated, nor that all criterion scores can be derived from such research. In such cases, new research needs to be carried out into the effects of individual alternatives. Known methods for doing so are the development of performance indicators, interrogating experts, and comparative case studies. These three methods will be discussed in the following sections.

4.2.2 Information derived from performance indicators

The goal

This section will discuss the use of performance indicators and monitoring as tools in determining criterion scores (see e.g. Maine & Zapico Goni, 1996). The increased presence of performance indicators in organisations is striking. Also in government agencies, performance measurement is attracting more and more attention. According to Carter (1992: 166), this is the result of the *value for money* principle, i.e. the wish to increase control over expenses, the wish to improve the competence of management in government, and the increase of responsibility and accountability as a part of the decentralization process. A second characteristic of performance indicators is that the information they contain is at a quantitative level. Calculations are possible and they can serve to make comparisons. It is mainly this possibility that makes performance indicators appropriate when evaluating policy. *Performance indicators* are nothing but numerical quantities which provide a concrete representation of a concrete (policy) situation, relevant to choices, policy

Determining how well alternatives score on criteria

or management. This is in conformance with the definition of a performance indicator, i.e. the characteristic essence of a phenomenon expressed in a figure (Baltus, 1987). Some people think performance indicators only include ratios. However, such data as 'unemployment in this neighbourhood is 20 percent' or 'in 1980 this agency completed 800 applications for rent subsidies' or 'the tax rate for keeping dogs in this city amounts to 100 dollars per dog' are actually performance indicators. To a consumer, the price and lifespan of an article are performance indicators for that article. To a producer, output and profit figures are performance indicators. To a stockholder, price and expected dividend are performance indicators. A *monitor* is a series of performance indicators which enable a comparison to be made over time or by place.

A third characteristic of performance indicators is that their source of data lies in observation and not so much in prejudice. The fourth characteristic is the simplicity of getting them. Precisely because such concrete data are concerned and because public authorities increasingly acknowledge the value of using performance indicators, their quantity and availability has increased considerably in recent past. Using performance indicators has opened up a lot of possibilities for government policy. Some of these are listed below.

Instrument for controlling policy processes
Process complies with objectives
Adjustment of processes
Detect differences between standards and facts
Make agreements
Clarity of responsibilities
Transparency of effectiveness and efficiency
Tool for task definitions
Symbol of rational decision-making

Table 4.3 *Purposes for performance indicators*

The main purpose of performance indicators is, of course, to provide information about events. They create clarity, for example, about the number of staff in an organization, or how many men, women, immigrants or handicapped people there are in a certain area. They clarify the number of means allocated to perform a certain task and the amount of money involved. This is all information about the input for policy.

Performance indicators can also provide information about the *output* of policy. How many services are provided? How many permits are granted, how many questions answered? With this kind of information it is possible to gain insight into and subsequently to control the policy process. The policy process will be better understood by comparing its input with its output. How much time does it take to finish an activity? How many people are necessary to achieve this?

The second question that performance indicators can help answer is whether *objectives* are attained. How long do clients have to wait before being served? How does this compare to the waiting time in the past? Are more cases being dealt with than in the past, and has efficiency increased?

The third feature of performance indicators is its signal function. How great is the problem? How many overtime hours have been worked? How many people are eligible for a rent subsidy? How high are taxes in our city? How strong are we financially? How much interest has been received on our earmarked funds, and how free are we to spend this interest? In these cases, performance indicators measure what has actually been realized. Performance indicators also have a signal function regarding standards and facts. It could, for example, be a legal requirement that the fire brigade should arrive at the scene of a fire within eight minutes, while the average turns out to be twelve minutes. A legal requirement that the police should be at the scene of a crime within 15 minutes of it being reported might not be complied with in densely populated areas.

Fourthly, information derived from performance indicators enables the (policy) process to be controlled. The process can be managed and the people involved can be checked regarding whether they are actually doing what they are expected to do. Information derived from performance indicators also clarifies the effectiveness and efficiency of the policy process. What is the output, and what is the relation between that output and standard output and input, respectively? Performance indicators themselves may also serve as standards. For instance, they can indicate the minimum output that should be produced in terms of service per unit of time by a policy staff member, an agency, a department or an organization in its entirety. The performance indicator serves as the minimum standard, indicating a minimum level such as the number of services per day.

Performance indicators may serve as a guideline by indicating the normally expected number of services provided. How many services should be provided per day in order for the organization to be said to be functioning optimally?

Finally, performance indicators can be used as the basic input for a comparative analysis of the efficiency, effectiveness and productivity of departments, agencies or private sector organizations, and also over time. On the output side (which is the input side of impact assessment), it enables comparisons to be made of problems in different residential areas,

• Relation to observable matters
• Controllable
• Appeal to people involved
• Embedded in a clear responsibility structure
• Conformity with objectives of the organization
• Reference to goods or services leaving the organization
• Quantifiable
• Sufficient level of homogeneity
• Stability
• Exclusivity (no duplicate scores)
• Simplicity

Table 4.4 *Eleven requirements for performance indicators*

or of the strengths and weaknesses of cities as a location for setting up industrial activities. As said before, a few performance indicators may not be enough to do so and sometimes a monitor is necessary. This concerns performance indicators enabling a comparison over time to be made.

The logic

In the context of impact assessment, performance indicators provide a quantitative operationalization of concrete indicators that are characteristic of an alternative. Its power lies in the simplicity of operationalization and the absence of prejudice and dubious assumptions. The numerical value of a performance indicator can be relatively unambiguous and can be determined through consultation with the people directly involved. According to Van de Kar, the ideal performance indicator satisfies eleven requirements (in: Mol 1988). These are presented in Table 4.4. If a performance indicator meets these requirements, it becomes an instrument that enables a standardized comparison to be made, e.g a comparison over time, between organizations or, more generally, between alternatives.

Problems with performance indicators

Section 2.1.1 lists eleven requirements that an ideal performance indicator has to meet. Below, some causes for not achieving this ideal will be discussed. The abundant presence of performance indicators seems to be a great advantage. Although this is true, they are not always available. Particularly in the case of government agencies, performance indicators are measured differently. Moreover, existing performance indicators are sometimes hard to obtain, above all when the distribution of means among various units is problematic. Also, it often turns out that there is hardly any standardization. Units of measurement are different, formulas are different and sometimes it is even unclear what the figures are based on.

The fact that performance indicators have been made to serve a purpose different from making comparisons can make them difficult to compare. It might be the case that a performance indicator is simply not right for an impact assessment, or that the necessary data are not available. What has been measured by a performance indicator may not be relevant, because what is relevant is not measurable.

A solution to this problem is to save elementary registrations (which form the basis of performance indicators) for as long as possible. Not just the ratio should be saved, but also the figures in the numerator and the denominator of that ratio. When these elementary data are not preserved in their rough form, the question what has caused the change of a ratio may arise. Was it mainly a change of the numerator or was it a change of the denominator that resulted in the change of the performance indicator?

In the development of performance indicators, nowadays the emphasis is put on input and output data. Insofar as they are being related to each other, they produce the performance indicators of a process. However, what is usually lacking are performance indicators concerning outcomes (Smith, 1996), i.e. the effects in the long run, the more abstract objectives, the sense of safety instead of the number of burglaries. It is exactly this type of performance indicator that is usually relevant to an impact assessment. This is not to say that process indicators are always secondary to outcome indicators, or that process indicators become redundant once outcome indicators are available. 'Developing outcome measures is, at best, very difficult and may, in some cases, turn out to be a search for the chimera. Moreover, in some circumstances process indicators may actually be more relevant and more significant: the outcome of long-stay geriatric care is almost always death - and what really matters is the quality of the process leading up to it.' (Carter et al., 1992: 177)

Another problem with performance indicators is the obscurity of the way the link has been established between changes of performance indicators and change of policy. Precisely this method pays hardly any attention to 'competing' explanations. In other words, when comparing performance indicators over time or in space the question is whether changes are a consequence of changes in policy itself or of competing factors. Directly related is the question what to do with factors influencing the performance indicator that cannot be controlled.

The fifth problem a user of performance indicators is confronted with is the corrupting capacity of performance indicators. This capacity expresses itself in four ways (Ridgeway, 1956: 252). If some standard or norm has been incorporated in the performance indicator, the people involved could show adaptation to the norm. This may express itself in functioning faster or better than has been set by the norm in order to acquire more means. An agency dealing with rent subsidies may, for instance, settle only the more simple cases in order to demonstrate that it is working very efficiently, whereas in fact it is in need of extra personnel and means. The side effect of using performance indicators may then in some cases be inefficiency and loss. The use of performance indicators emphasizes quantity at the expense of quality. The number of settled applications for rent subsidy may become more important than the correctness of settlement.

The use of performance indicators may also lead to people behaving exactly according to standards. This is indicated by minimalism and the manipulation of time reports in order to satisfy the standard. Some students who get an assignment to write a paper of about 30 pages produce one of 25 to 30 pages. They comply exactly with the standard set without being worried about the content of their paper.

The corrupting capacity of performance indicators may also take the form of people making agreements not to satisfy the standard set. Employees may agree to work below a certain standard. Fast workers should slow down to keep slow workers acceptable to the organization and prevent standards from rising. This is the opposite of efficiency.

Another possible form of corruption is when people try to manipulate the outcome of a performance indicator in an improper way. Of course, this poses problems with respect to content, and to the use of performance indicators in a comparative analysis. After all, the content of a performance indicator is also determined by this kind of factor and it remains unclear whether each of the comparative groups has shifted in the same direction, the same way or to the same extent.

To this type of problem, too, solutions have been thought out. One solution is to complicate performance indicators to the extent that they can no longer be manipulated. A way to do this is not to use one limited indicator to compute the performance indicator, but to use several indicators to create a compound score. The disadvantage of one indicator is that it often creates merely a partial image of the situation, and that its value either cannot be influenced or can be influenced strongly but in an improper way. It is also probable that the value of a performance indicator will become less dependent on the way it is measured, as that value is based on more indicators conjointly (Ridgeway, 1956).

Another problem concerning performance indicators, although it falls outside this framework, needs to be mentioned here. The culture of an organization may change due to the use of performance indicators. Sometimes when a standard is met frequently, the standard is adjusted. This may lead to antagonism, apathy, low moral, tension, breakdown in communication, altered power relations and a culture less susceptible to integration and with a greater emphasis on individualism.

Finally, an additional and possibly most important problem is the frequent underestimation of the problems mentioned above. Too often performance indicators are presented as technical data without political, cultural or organizational consequences with respect to content. In doing so, the question what is being measured and how often remains unanswered and is kept outside the scope of political responsibilities.

Argumentation

> 'Argumentation is a language-oriented action consisting of a constellation of assertions to justify or invalidate an opinion, aimed at convincing a reasonable critic of a certain position concerning the acceptability or unacceptability of this opinion.' (Pröpper 1987: 118)

Determining how well alternatives score on criteria

Toulmin and then Dunn have given a number of elements that formally are always part of an argumentation. These elements are: policy-relevant information, the premise or the idea behind it and its support (so-called backing), the conclusion or claim, and the qualifier. Each argumentation leads to a conclusion, suggesting that, for example, the effects of alternative A will be better than those of alternative B. The qualifier indicates how certain one is about the conclusion, i.e. it is certain, likely or has a 95% probability. Policy-relevant information provides empirical understanding of the actual data that are the basis on which 'normative' conclusions are reached. In order to reach a conclusion based on empirical information, this information needs to be related to a normative presupposition. This is called the support of the argumentation. An example of argumentation is given in Figure 4.2.

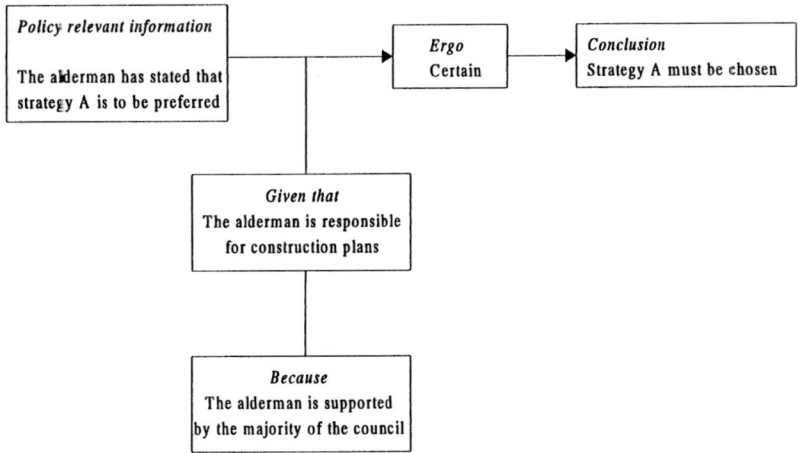

Figure 4.2 *Authoritarian argumentation*

The empirical observation is: 'The alderman for housing says that with strategy A the chances that local residents will stop resisting the city's plans for construction will be higher than with strategy B.' This is an empirical observation on which a normative statement is based, i.e. the conclusion that, given this criterion, strategy A is to be preferred to strategy B. However, by itself the empirical information has no significance to the correctness of the conclusion. Who does this alderman think he is, assuming his conclusion is right? This is reflected in the premise which, in this case, could be 'The alderman has a clear understanding of this matter', 'He is creative', 'He acts intuitively and has many years of experience in this policy area', or 'The alderman is in control and his statements should not be questioned.' This could be supported even further by indicating that the alderman is very well aware of the motivation of the local residents.

Argumentation like this is exposed to objections. Because the personal qualities of the alderman are central in the example given, the objection to this type of argument could be that the alderman has made mistakes before, that his intuition is weak, and that others who have better qualities are claiming exactly the opposite of what he is claiming. This kind of objection leads either to weakening the strength of the conclusion (i.e. it becomes less probable) or to the opposite conclusion (i.e. strategy B is to preferred). Obviously, which objective is relevant depends on the content of the premise of the argumentation. When support mainly lies in the personal qualities of the person making the assertion, a useful discussion will focus on those qualities. When the argumentation focuses on the position of the person making the claim, the objection too should have the same aim. There could be, for example, someone of a similar or higher position claiming the opposite. It is, for example, less meaningful to reject an argumentation that focuses on the dubious personal qualities of a person by pointing at this person's position. The issue here is not whether the objection is true or false, but whether it is relevant. Someone focusing his argumentation on the personal qualities of a person will consider this person's position irrelevant.

The strength of the Toulmin-Dunn model lies in the distinction between several types of argumentation: it can be authoritarian, statistical, classifying, intuitive, analycentric, explanatory, pragmatic or value-critical. This distinction clarifies whether an argumentation, in particular its objection, is relevant or irrelevant. An objection based on authority ('this university professor claims that ....') is not very convincing compared to ethical or explanatory argumentation. The argumentation persists and in such cases we say that the discussion is characterized by level differences. Participants in the discussion are not at the same level.

The Toulmin-Dunn model has been criticized by several authors who claim the differences between the types of argumentation are not always as clear as they should be. Supplementary to and following Schellens, Pröpper distinguishes five types of argumentation, i.e. argumentation based on regularity, rules, pragmatism, authority and examples. Argumentation based on regularity mainly serves predictions

(Pröpper 1989: 124). That based on rules comprises valuation- and behavioural rules that indicate whether a certain behaviour, a measure or an intervention is or is not appropriate. Pragmatic argumentation focuses on the assessment of events on the basis of their consequences, i.e. whether they are desirable or undesirable. Argumentation based on authority supports assertions by pointing out that they are endorsed by an authoritative actor (Pröpper, 1989: 135). This authority can be based on position, understanding or intuition. The strength of the entire argumentation and counter-argumentation indicates the certainty about the claim or conclusion, that is, the content of the qualifier. This is the last step. The claim has been established as more or less probable.

Problems

A number of problems regarding argumentations can be mentioned. The first is that this method is not so much concerned about the fact that policy-relevant information, the argumentation and its support should be sufficient to draw a conclusion following the rules of logic; instead, the main issue is the cogency of argumentation. To the people involved, authoritarian argumentation can be just as convincing as analytical argumentation. So it is the rationality of the decision process that is at issue here. After all, what is so rational about a decision based on the criterion that it is the will of an alderman? Such use of the multi-criteria model does not result in better chances of optimum outcomes.

The second problem is that criterion scores based on such argumentations can be at the most of ordinal measuring level. The claim could be, for example, 'this measure results in a greater effect than other measures'. It remains unknown how much greater the effect will be. This imposes restrictions on the possibilities for determining a ranking order of alternatives using these criterion scores.

The third problem is that in a social process objections are not always made, although they are possible and useful. One of the reasons for this could be differences in status between the actors involved. The higher the status, power or authority of an actor, the less likely that someone else will object, while the cogency of argumentation could be minimal.

The fourth problem is the actors' tendency to persist in argumentation already given, even though the objections are convincing. There will be no consensus and standpoints will remain opposed to one another.

4.2.3 Ask the experts: the classic Delphi method

A solution to these problems is to use the Delphi method. This method for determining policy effects was developed in 1948 by employees of the Rand Corporation in the United States of America. Its name is derived from the oracle of Delphi in ancient Greece. The priestess at the altar of Apollo predicted the future and articulated this in such ambiguous terms that, with hindsight, the predictions were always right. As a research method, the researchers at Rand Corporation used the Delphi technique primarily for military purposes; later, however, it was applied successfully to many other areas. A Delphi is defined as follows: Delphi is an interactive, time-dependent and consensus-oriented research instrument for eliciting future-oriented information from anonymous experts about probable or possible developments regarding an unstructured problem (Van Houten et al. 1988: 2). The aim of the method is to bring standpoints and argumen-tation into accordance by interrogating anonymous experts.

Interrogation of experts
Anonymity of respondents
The arguments, not the standpoints, are central to the research
Feedback of the results to the experts, enabling reactions to each - other's standpoint (interaction)
Repetition over several rounds
Increasing congruency of standpoints

Table 4.5 *Characteristics of the classic Delphi method*

The following elements are characteristic of the classic Delphi method:

The *interrogation of experts*. The basic idea behind this is that if the effects of a policy alternative are unknown then 'the people that might know' (i.e. the experts) should be asked. If they come up with a unanimous point of view, we may assume this to be correct. The viewpoint on which consensus exists is taken to be true. In the case of effect determination, experts are asked to indicate what in their opinion are the relevant effects. Usually a questionnaire is given to a limited number (15) of experts focusing on the following two questions:

Determining how well alternatives score on criteria

- What do you think ...? How likely do you believe that it will be ...? What will be the consequences of ...? To what extent will ... occur, under condition ..., at that point of time?
- What is your argumentation to support this standpoint?

Obviously, at this stage the selection of experts is a critical element. The question to be answered is whether an adequate selection has taken place, i.e. whether certain standpoints have been over- or underexposed. Experts need to be from different organizations in the policy area and should have an overview, one that is as wide as possible, of the spectrum of the policy area. This way, any possible bias in the various standpoints is made explicit. It becomes clear whether an opinion is the reflection of an expert in a certain area or the reflection of someone giving strategic information related to his position in the policy area.

Protecting the *anonymity of experts* is a necessary condition when using the Delphi method to attain the objective, namely a unanimous, well-argumented standpoint about the effects that are to be expected. The consequence of anonymity is that standpoints are not related to a person taking a position. This means that respondents can express themselves freely without having to fear loss of face, and without having to take into account strategic issues (such as their position in the policy area) or the opinions of other experts. This separation of standpoint and the person taking it is also important because it reduces the tendency to stick to standpoints already given. The assumption here is that someone will be more open to changing his opinion if this change is unknown to others. During a workshop or forum, there can be no anonymity because standpoints are related to a person. This is seen as the most important reason why during such occasions standpoints remain opposed to each other and no convergence occurs during the course of the discussions. Obviously, anonymity poses a problem in real life. Experts in the policy area usually know one another because theirs is a small world. This may mean that standpoints can be related to a person anyway, despite his anonymity. The result of the Delphi method may then be hampered to the extent that no convergence will occur.

Emphasis on arguments. Certainly during the early stages of a Delphi research, the arguments about standpoints are emphasized. The reasoning of an opinion is crucial in order to achieve consensus between experts at later stages of the research. These arguments together with the opinions are fed back to the respondents. Convergence has to originate from the strength of arguments.

Feedback of results. After the experts have been interrogated about their opinions and their supporting arguments, the results are analysed by the researcher. Simple statistics are produced and the disagreement about (sub)issues between respondents are investigated. The results including the arguments for and against are then given to the experts along with the request to redetermine their standpoint. The results from the previous round are central in this new questionnaire. Now, typical questions are: 'From the previous questionnaire, it appeared that ..% held the opinion that this effect is probable as a consequence of measure ... The supporting arguments used were as follows: ... ..% thinks this effect is improbable. Their arguments were as follows: ... Could you give arguments that substantiate whether you think this effect is likely to occur as a result of that measure?'

Repetition of several rounds. The results of the first questionnaire result in a number of new arguments for or against. After being analysed, they can be fed back to the respondents. Steps two to four are repeated several times.

Generally, after two or three rounds agreement is reached to such an extent that the Delphi can be concluded. The end result is a series of assertions about the effects of measures that all experts in the area largely agree on. The assumption is that these effects will actually occur because the people interrogated were experts.

4.2.4 The policy Delphi

Over the course of time, there has been a lot of criticism of the classic Delphi model. This criticism concerns the supposition that there is no difference between actual effects and estimated effects. Experts are just as vulnerable as other people to the limitations of human behaviour (see Chapter 2). Secondly, congruency of viewpoints does not always occur. Conflict or disagreement can also be seen as a normal phenomenon of the policy process. The third point of criticism is that pushing anonymity too far can be needlessly time-consuming and may hinder the course of the Delphi investigation (Turoff, 1970). As a result, the 1980s gave rise to the policy Delphi as an alternative to the classic Delphi. Policy Delphi starts off with anonymity during the first or the first two rounds. During the following rounds, discussion is public. No consensus is expected from the policy Delphi. Opposing opinions may result that are held by several clusters of experts. Statistics when analysing the results of each round has to do more than merely measure consensus. Data to be analysed need to be presented by decomposing variance into inner- and between-variance. Within the clusters of opinions, Delphi then results in a minimization of variance; between the clusters, it results in maximization of variance. The objective of policy Delphi is to create different scenarios. The idea behind policy Delphi is that the future is no longer seen as measurable or knowable, but as producible. Because the future is producible, different scenarios are possible. Delphi does not predict the future but provides designs of the future. Its desirability, of course, depends on the political and social position of the experts. Unlike classic Delphi where the expertise of experts is central, policy Delphi emphasizes the political and social positions of the people involved (Van Houten 1988: 56).

4.2.5 Comparative case studies

The objective

The rationale behind case studies is that when expertise about different alternatives is lacking, the situation should be thoroughly investigated through field research, using several data-gathering techniques simultaneously. The case study methodology may serve well when dealing with problems such as choice of location or priorities concerning the distribution of city reconstruction funds among several residential areas. By literally going into the field and observing the situation, and by analysing documents concerning the situation in the field and interviewing the people involved, it becomes possible to gain a thorough insight into the differences between several locations.

Ideas diverge as to the question how a case study is defined and what is characteristic of a case study. There seem to be just as many definitions of case study as there are cases. There are hardly any methodological rules a researcher opting for this research strategy has to comply with. There are no standards for case studies. They can be called case studies based on quantitative research, case surveys, case studies as a qualitative research method, comparative case studies based on the logic of sampling, or comparative case studies based on the logic of replication. There is no common frame of reference about how to deal with such an investigation. There is a difference between those who, working more intuitively, perceive such research as 'state of the art', and those who proceed from classifications and general patterns. The first group supposes that, phenomenologically, reality does not exist and that all knowledge is superfluous because it only exists by the grace of the person claiming to know it. According to these researchers, the necessity of strict methodological rules and the principle to make research findings explicit does not apply.

All case study researchers emphasize the preservation of complexity when analysing a case. This distinguishes case studies from, for example, surveys, where the number of research elements is usually large and the number of variables small. According to adherents of case study methodology, such a quantitative approach results in too great a reduction of complexity, i.e. more information is lost than won. Qualitative relevance is therefore preferred to quantitative rigour. Case study would mean a more profound research methodology. Processes are described in more detail without selecting the relevant variables beforehand. The most famous and cited work in the Netherlands about case studies is by Yin. According to him:

> 'A case study is an empirical inquiry that:
> -investigates a contemporary phenomenon within its real life context;
> -when the boundaries between phenomenon and context are not clearly evident;
> -and in which multiple sources of evidence are used.'
> (Yin 1984: 23)

Case studies can be applied in many ways. Bryman (1989: 174-175) mentions exploration, testing and confirmative use. Herweijer (1988) mentions the use of case studies in evaluation research. The contribution of case studies to the understanding of phenomena is almost undisputed. This understanding is not so much the determination of the dimensions of a phenomenon (problem, process, structure) but rather its explanation, *'das Verstehen'*. Mainly the 'how and why' questions can be answered using case study. For this reason, many adherents of case study methodology mention its theory building capacity. Case studies clarify not only the relatedness of two variables, but first and foremost the logic behind this relation. Mitchell (1983: 198) states: 'The inference about the logical relation between two characteristics is ... based ... upon the plausibility or upon the logic of the nexus between the two characteristics.' Huizenga (1993) calls this the generative principle. Cook and Campbell (1979: 32) call it the micromediation of social processes. To Yin, the support and explanation of theories and relations between variables are a distinguishing characteristic of case studies in comparison to other research techniques.

> 'Whether the case survey of case comparison approach is used, the case study researcher must preserve a chain of evidence as each analytical step is conducted. The chain of evidence consists of the explicit citation of particular pieces of evidence as one shifts from data collection to within case analysis to cross case analysis and overall findings and conclusions.'

To Miles and Huberman (1984: 151), following Glaser and Strauss (1967), the specific contribution of comparative case studies to the understanding of a phenomenon is that they enable social structures to be identified in which a particular theory can be applied. According to them, the use of comparative case studies enlarges the scope of a research project. This enables a wider generalization of results to be made, as well as an analysis of the conditions under which a theory is tenable. Rosenthal (1984: 70) claims that when using case studies, plausibility is preferred over falsification. Regarding the use of case studies in determining criterion scores, this opinion implies clarifying not only which effects are brought about by different alternatives but, and above all, how and why these effects are realized. This understanding enables assertions to be made about the question whether effects are indeed a consequence of a policy alternative or whether they have been attributed wrongfully to a policy alternative.

In this way, case studies can serve to answer the question whether a theory about a policy alternative being the cause of a certain effect is tenable, in what way such a theory can be further specified and under which conditions the theory is tenable. The purpose of such efforts is primarily to generate new insights that are useful for building theory (Burgelman, 1985: 42; Mitchell, 1983; Yin, 1984). Miles and Huberman considered this to be the main goal of case studies.

This goal is reached because a researcher using case studies will place the phenomena to be researched within their context. This is the ancient idea that events do not take place haphazardly but can be (partly) explained by the specific, almost unique characteristics of their context. In other words, there is no a priori separation between what happens within the context and the context itself. Unlike experimental design, an understanding of the actual situation by using case studies is not reached by creating an artificial laboratory situation where certain variables are manipulated and others are held constant. Case studies focus on *research of a particular object within its natural environment.* Case studies are specifically characterized by their starting point being an uncontrollable situation that cannot be manipulated.

Case study is also significant to testing theories because of what Yin has called the *replication logic* behind it. Comparative case studies do not involve the logic of sampling that is based on the law of large numbers. A case does not necessarily represent a large number of cases, and the objective of case studies cannot be to generalize the outcomes of cases to a population. 'The aim is not to infer the findings from a sample to a population, but to engender patterns and linkages of theoretical importance' (Bryman, 1989: 173). According to Yin (1984: 48) the logic involved is also the one that constitutes the foundation of the repetition of experiments. A case is taken as a separate experiment, and therefore the analysis should be according to intermediary experimental design and intermediary experimental logic and not follow the logic of experimental design. Just as equal outcomes of a repeated experiment enhance the level of corroboration of the conclusions, the comparison of case studies enhances the tenability of corresponding conclusions from each separate case. This is important when determining the effects of policy alternatives, because by means of case studies it can be analysed whether there are differences between alternatives (cases). The question can be answered whether the allocation of city renewal funds to a certain residential area has the same effects as their allocation to some other residential area. It can be investigated whether a criterion is useful in determining the merits of an alternative.

A fifth asset of case study methodology is that this research strategy allows for the use of several methods and techniques. Yin (1984: 90) calls this the 'major strength of case studies' and makes a comparison with the argumentation of a criminal case in court. The public prosecutor uses several sources to clarify the argumentation on the basis of which a suspect should be declared guilty. Each step in the chain of evidence becomes more convincing when it is substantiated by different sources. In Popper's sense, this is the corroboration of the validity of conclusions. By *triangulating research* the chances that a researcher is misled by one particular source of information are reduced. It also reduces the chances that the results are an artificial consequence of the type of research method. Triangulation enables converging lines of support to develop and stimulates critical reflection and interpretation of information from each separate source. On top of this, triangulation may lead to understanding relations that otherwise would have remained unrevealed (Campbell, 1959; Runkel, 1972; Crano, 1973). However, according to Yin one condition is that the researcher is well informed and has much experience with the whole gamut of research techniques. Therefore, research can only be called a case study when several research methods have been used to arrive at a conclusion. Possible methods are: document analysis, archive research, interviews, (participatory) observation and research into physical matters. The latter is also called analysis of accretion and erosion. To investigate the interest shown in museums, answers are sought by simultaneously studying the accounts, interviewing employees of the museums, observing the behaviour of visitors and examining the wear and tear of the carpets (erosion). In this way, a multitude of information is created about the interest shown in museums, enabling assertions to be made that are better founded than they would be if they were based on each of the indicators separately.

This triangulation is possible because with case studies one or more phenomena are thoroughly investigated. This implies that in such investigations the number of variables is and can always be larger than the number of research elements. This qualitative profundity does, however, have negative consequences for the possibility of quantitative analysis. Because of the small number of research elements and the large number of variables, Yin concludes that statistical analyses are not justified. He also claims that statistical analyses are superfluous because they do not do justice to the complexity of relations.

> 'The number of factors worthy of examinations is often large relative to the number of case studies available, producing a shortage of sampling points for identifying any statistical interaction effects. Second, the extraction of single factors from a case study unduly simplifies the phenomenon being studied. Third, the approach treats case studies as if they were data points ... For these reasons, the case survey method should be used in highly selective situations, where for instance a critical factor or two appear to be of enormous importance. In contrast, the case comparison approach is relatively new but is likely to prove more fruitful for cross case analysis.' (Yin, 1981: 62-63)

If we accept that the distinction between qualitative and quantitative research is useful, then case studies should be classified as qualitative research. This is no limitation. On the contrary, the number of different data-collection techniques that can be used simultaneously in a case study is variable and usually larger than in the case of survey or experimental research. Also, within cases quantitative analyses are indeed possible.

The stages

Yin recently formulated the main stages of case study methodology in evaluation research. The first stage is to develop a theoretical framework within which a policy programme can be understood. The aim is to arrive at a thorough understanding of the functioning and the intended objectives of a policy, given its context. He distinguishes two options: first, the development of a causal model connecting the outcomes of policy with the policy itself; and second, the development of a taxonomy of contextual conditions within which policy takes place.

The second stage is to broaden these insights by connecting them with outcomes of previous research. Competing hypotheses also need to be formulated and investigated in order to determine the tenability of the assumptions that form the basis of a policy. The objectives are threefold: clarification, structuring and enlarging the generalizing capacity of the research.

Developing of theoretical insights
Extending insight using previous research outcomes
Defining research element(s)
Making a feedback protocol
Defining and testing of measuring instruments
Collecting and analysing data
Creating a database
Analysing evidence
Writing a report

Table 4.6 *Stages in a case study*

The third stage consists of defining, for the time being, the research elements. In most cases, this is the policy programme and possibly its alternatives. During this stage the replication design can also be taken into consideration. Usually after this stage, feedback to stages one and two and extension of the theoretical instruments will take place.

During stage four, a plan is made and a procedure is established to make one or more intermediate and final reports. Case studies enable results to be continuously fed back to the people involved; however, in order to make maximum use of this possibility, a plan is necessary.

In stage five, the research instruments, the protocol and the procedures are defined and tested. This is necessary because case studies are characterized by the simultaneous use of several methods and techniques. The instruments and protocol serve to structure and control observations in order to avoid irrelevant matters.

Stage six comprises data collection, -analysis and -interpretation based on triangulation. Here it is important to pay attention to any possible bias of observations and to understanding the relevance of each observation.

In stage seven, a case study database is created comprising all collected observations in a formal and systematic way. This stage too often results in the researcher going back to the first stage because the first insights turned out to be incomplete.

In stage eight, the evidence is concluded, to use Yin's terms. Using a multitude of possible analytical techniques, an effort is made to create a consistent image of the process or policy described.

The final stage consists of writing a case study report. There are two conditions for this: first, it should be independent of the database, and secondly the basis of the crucial parts of the argumentation should be clear.

4.3 ENVIRONMENTAL IMPACT ASSESSMENT IN PRACTICE

Whereas the previous section dealt with the possibilities for finding criterion scores, the important question remains how criterion scores are determined in practice. Below, the determination of criterion scores will be discussed on the basis of ten environmental impact assessments. The objective is to clarify the possible difference between quality as it is desired theoretically and quality as it can be found in practice. Environmental impact assessments normally are high quality, very technical reports investigating the environmental effects of large investments preceding the decision to actually invest. A Dutch ministry once stated:

'Knowledge and influence are the pillars of environmental impact assessment ... The need for environmental impact assessments is learned the hard way and arises from decision-making in the past not paying sufficient attention to environmental aspects ... From experience we know that environmental impact assessment is worthwhile; not just from an environmental point of view but also because it enables better decision-making, better policy design and better implementation.' (Ministries of VROM and LNV, 1987: 3)

The basic idea is simple and logical. In order to prevent the environmental interests from being neglected during the decision-making process, a list of the consequences for the environment should be made before decisions are taken. In this way it becomes clear, from an environmental point of view, whether or not a certain decision should be taken. This list is called an environmental impact assessment. The idea is so simple and so logical that the number of environmental impact assessments has risen sharply since its introduction. At the moment other policy areas are following.

4.3.1 A meta evaluation

We will restrict ourselves to a meta evaluation concerning three aspects of impact assessment: the determination of criteria and of criterion scores, and their interpretation. A comparable investigation of American environmental impact assessments has been carried out by Culhane, Friesema and Beecher (1987).

The requirements often mentioned in literature with regard to research outcomes here result in concrete desiderata for environmental impact assessment. They emphasize unambiguity (criterion 1), impartiality (criterion 2), validity (criterion 3), accuracy (criterion 4), sensitivity (criterion 5) and applicability/correspondence to the question under investigation (criterion 6). The issues of argumentation, comparability and availability will return when discussing the criteria below. The six criteria used to evaluate environmental impact assessments (EIAs) are:

- *Unambiguity*: the interpretation of measured environmental effects needs to be unambiguous.
- *Impartiality*: the operationalization of environmental effects needs to be impartial, i.e. the values determined must be independent of the person or body determining them.
- *Validity*: the nature of the criteria to be measured need to do justice to the merits of the alternatives given. The objective of alternatives needs to be taken into account when determining the criteria. If an environmentally-friendly alternative pretends to have certain effects, those effects have to be included as criteria and the value of each alternative for this criterion needs to determined.
- *Accuracy*: the value of the same alternatives on the same criteria in different tables needs to correspond. Among other things this implies the following. The ranking order of interpreted data has to correspond with the ranking order of the original data. The summary of a report needs to contain information in such a way that justice is done to the information in the report itself. Combining alternatives can only result in unambiguous criterion scores if these scores are completely or almost completely identical.
- *Sensitivity*: criteria need to discriminate between alternatives. One and the same criterion may not occur several times in a list of effects.
- *Applicability*: environmental impact assessments should compare alternatives only in respect of their environmental impact.

4.3.2 The outcomes of content analysis

In this section, ten cases will be discussed showing that the aforementioned criteria are not always satisfied in environmental impact assessments. The focus here is on reports that describe the environmental consequences of an activity that is in its policy development phase. This investigation could be characterized as a comparative case study. There is hardly any pretension regarding generalization of the outcomes. Using examples, it will be argued that the ten EIAs conflict with the desiderata and that these conflicts are in favour of a positive assessment of the intended activity.

Unambiguity of interpretation

The unambiguity of the interpretation of the environmental effects found is the first requirement that has to be met by an EIA. The question here is whether an effect is considered to be more or less serious. The aspect 'noise nuisance' will be used to illustrate this.

Suppose that a number of activities are subjected to an environmental impact assessment, and that noise nuisance for alternatives has to be determined. Noise in itself is a concept that can be determined quite unambiguously, namely in terms of decibels produced. There are, however, large differences between EIAs regarding both the measurement and the interpretation of the number of decibels. Usually noise nuisance up to 50 dB is regarded as acceptable. In the EIA concerning high-speed trains, 70 dB is considered a normal noise level. The rationale for this interpretation can be found in the same EIA: 'At maximum speed the high velocity train has a noise level of 70 dB(A)' (p. 19). In terms of the interpretation given, this means a normal noise level.

Other EIAs show that this can be and in fact is interpreted differently. The most extended methodology can be found in the EIA concerning the construction of the Westrandweg (a road) by the Ministry of Waterways and Public Works.

First, the number of houses where noise nuisance would be experienced at a certain level (50-55, 56-60, 61-65, 66-70, 70+ dB) is determined. This number is multiplied by a subjective valuation index (0.9, 1.1, 1.6, 1.9, 2.6). The outcomes are added up, producing a total score indicating subjective noise perception. The final scores for 3,000 houses that would be subjected to noise nuisance varying between 50 and 70 dB are 8,900 and 9,400.

A third possibility is to investigate the distance in metres from the planned activity at which noise nuisance would exceed 50 dB. A fourth possibility is to investigate how many houses would experience noise nuisance between 70 and 57 dB, or between 75 and 50 dB, and how many silent areas would be disturbed. Of course, it is also possible to deal with the noise nuisance of an activity in the last section of an EIA and to categorize it as 'lacking knowledge'.

What is important is that there seems to be no accordance between researchers with regard to the measurement of noise nuisance. This would not be very serious if accordance existed about the interpretation of differences in noise nuisance. However, this is also lacking. The report about the construction of the Westrandweg uses intervals of 5 dB, implicitly assuming that a difference smaller than 5 dB is hardly noticeable. When analysing the results, it turns out that there is a difference of 500 between the most favourable and the most unfavourable alternative. This means that an increased noise nuisance of 10 dB would be experienced in 500 houses. In the report, this is considered to be an increase. A difference of 5 dB in 100 houses is considered to be hardly any increase. Now let us compare this with an EIA about a thermal power station in Diemen. Here, a cooling tower is included as an environmentally-friendly alternative because it would reduce the burdening of surface water. However, the average increase of noise nuisance by using a cooling tower is 1 to 3 dB. The summary of the EIA report states that this is one of the reasons this environmentally-friendly alternative is to be rejected. The conclusion must be that there is hardly any standardization of the way measurements are interpreted.

Unambiguity of indicators

The second criterion EIAs are subjected to is the operationalization of environmental effects. The question here is how abstract environmental aspects are measured in different reports. This is illustrated by the environmental aspect 'landscape effects'. It turns out that this environmental aspect can be measured in different ways. One report considers the space that would be occupied by the activity, another considers the landscape that would be preserved from the consequences of the activity, and a third considers the perception of landscape after completion of the activity.

  The EIA about the high-speed train paid attention only to the space that would occupied by the activity and to all facilities that might be necessary. The advantage of such a measurement is that all criteria can be expressed in a limited number of unambiguous units of measurement, such as kilometres, numbers and hectares. The disadvantage is that any benefit from environmental facilities (e.g. sound barriers) is automatically left out. After all, the space to be occupied will not be reduced by constructing sound barriers, wind screens and coverings. Because these facilities take up space they seem more likely to have a negative effect. The positive effects of environmental facilities would be discriminating if instead of considering the area that will be affected, the dimensions of the area that is preserved from negative effects (e.g. in terms of noise and vibrations) were to be considered. Besides it is clear beforehand, when using the chosen operationalizations, which routes would be most environmentally-friendly, namely the shortest ones. This actually turns out to be the case (p. 340).

The Green Space Structural Scheme (an EIA carried out by the Ministry of Agriculture, Environment and Fishery concerning the concentration or dispersion of recreational areas) emphasizes the dimensions of preserved landscape. In this case, the indicator turns out to be more favourable to the intended activity, that is concentration. The argumentation itself is very interesting:

> 'By realizing alternative 1, 2 or 3 (variants of concentration) recreation is concentrated in a limited number of places. This concentration brings about a number of positive environmental aspects that do not differ by area type, such as:
> - increase of the perceptual value of landscape resulting from the possibilities of experiencing peacefulness and nature in the remaining part of the area type
> - relief of the cultural historical and geological values outside the RGS area
> - reduction of dispersed burdening of the soil, ground water, surface water and air in those parts of an area type where no RGS projects are realized, and reduction of noise nuisance resulting from the concentration of recreation
> - increase of the possibilities for natural development outside the RGS projects resulting from concentration of recreation.' (pp. 141-142)

The different measurements of the same concept in different reports involves not only low reliability; as is shown here, the validity of measurements is also debatable. The four points are mentioned under the heading 'consequences for recreational use' and the conclusion is that the concentration of recreational areas will increase the perceptual value of the area. This may be questioned. Determination of the criteria focuses on the effects on the areas where recreation will be barred. The summarizing table, however, indicates that the perceptual value of the most concentrated variants is higher than the perceptual value of the dispersed variant.

Perceptual value is defined in a very specific way, namely in terms of diversity (preservation and reinforcement of landscape diversity) and information value (the contribution to not damaging the connection with the historic origin of the landscape) (p. 94).

A comparison with other EIAs shows this is no standard definition. Perceptual value is also defined in terms of landscape disruption and practical value of the same landscape.

The EIA concerning the construction of a thermal power station states that constructing a cooling tower in order to avoid negative environmental effects would have a negative effect on the landscape because of the tower's dominance. This involves the direct visual effect to the damaged landscape.

It may be concluded that identical environmental effects in different EIAs are operationalized in various ways. It is striking to note that the investigated cases indicate that the outcome of operationalization is that the environmentally-friendly alternative appears to be less environmentally friendly than the intended activity. The unambiguity of the interpretation of criterion scores involves not only the magnitude but also the direction of the interpretation of effects. It may be expected that comparable effects in different EIAs are invariably considered to be either positive or negative. When a negative effect is interpreted positively, or a positive effect is interpreted negatively, the term 'bolstering' can be used, meaning artificially persisting in one's own opinion.

The quotation given earlier may serve as an example. Alternatives are not rejected because of their negative effects, which are to be proven, but because they do not correspond to the intended activity. The arguments referred to in the above-mentioned Green Space Structural Scheme can be regarded as typical of bolstering. The effects, formulated in a comparable way, can also be valued negatively. To recreation there is no advantage because people will be barred from those areas where they might find peace and quiet, which is lacking in concentrated recreational areas. Also recreation does not benefit from cultural historic and geological values in areas where people are not allowed.

Another issue in which there is bolstering is when a negative effect is presented as being positive, or vice versa. In the Green Space Structural Scheme the following sentence can be found, which makes it very easy for investigators to give their own interpretation of the outcomes:

> 'The perceptual space of the area between cities is determined by the kaleidoscopic image arising from

mixing many different forms of land use. This may lead to variation and surprise. In cases where the existing landscape structure has become highly fragmented and torn up without new structuring patterns taking its place, chaos and disorientation may be the case.' (p. 69)

The report about the high-speed train states: 'A high velocity train does disrupt the landscape structure but at the same time brings a clear line into a presently somewhat unstructured landscape.'

A good example of bolstering can also be found in another EIA concerning the environmental consequences of the construction of a new housing complex. The following is stated regarding the perceptual aspects of the construction of a connecting waterway: 'The construction of a connecting waterway may increase the perceptual value of the polder, if watersides are well shaped. On the other hand, separation of the polder by water may also be perceived as a barrier.' (p. 482) Although in this case possible interpretations of the effects have been made explicit, an alternative can acquire a completely different, even negative effect by the choice of words when such criteria as perception are concerned. In practice, this problem is solved by asserting that there is a high uncertainty about the effects. Sometimes the researcher himself indicates whether an aspect should be assessed positively or negatively. Obviously the distortion by each of these interpretations is considerable.

The validity of criterion scores

The fourth criterion EIAs are subjected to is that the criteria used should measure what they are intended to measure, namely the effects of alternatives. There are two aspects to this: the focus is on effects, i.e. consequences and not characteristics, and the effects should be about alternatives, i.e. alternatives are compared using criteria that are expected to produce these effects. Some examples are given below of the violation of both these aspects.

The third point of the Green Space Structural Scheme quoted above mentions dispersed burdening of the environment as a disadvantage of dispersed recreational areas. Such an argument should be rejected because the issue here is not a criterion used to assess alternatives, but something inherent in the definition of the alternative. An alternative is considered good or bad while it is not demonstrated that

Determining how well alternatives score on criteria 115

it has negative effects. The question that should be asked is what could demonstrate these negative effects of dispersed burdening.

The Committee for Environmental Impact Assessment, considering the inclusion or exclusion of alternatives, states in its 1993 annual report that 'only useful alternatives should be included in the comparison' (p. 32). However, in practice EIAs do not satisfy this condition. The EIA about a thermal power station gives a disputable argumentation for rejecting the zero-alternative and persisting in the intended activity:

> 'In due course (after 1995) the zero-alternative will score more favourable than the intended activity with regard to the local effects in and near the IJmeer and the surrounding area. However, in both cases the objective of the intended activity - *The construction and separately placed WK-STEG, simultaneously generating electricity and heat with electrical and total proceeds as high as possible at the 'Diemen' location* - will not be realized. This implicates that the main objective of the policy intended cannot be satisfied.' (p. 34 summary, italics in the report)

This argumentation is self-evident; after all, we are dealing with a zero-alternative. It turns out that a zero-alternative in an EIA can serve two purposes. Sometimes the existing situation is considered to be the zero-alternative. In other cases, the zero-alternative is considered to be an autonomous development that stems from the existing situation. The first purpose of zero-alternatives is to indicate that environmental effects necessitate the intended activity. The zero-alternative itself should not be considered seriously but should serve as a reference situation. The second purpose is to indicate a realistic alternative that should be part of the decision-making process. The objective of an EIA in that case is to include in the investigation the environmental effects of maintaining the existing situation. In many EIAs, a zero-alternative is included in order to serve the first purpose. Usually the criteria included in the analysis are in favour of the intended activity. Problems with the existing situation are used to substantiate a preference for an intended activity.

The choices this leads to are surprising. In the EIA about the Green Space Structural Scheme, the intended activity and its alternatives are compared to the zero-alternative when there are relatively positive effects, but not when the zero-alternative has a more positive effect on a criterion. A quotation from the report (p. 150) might serve to clarify this: 'As stated, the consequences to the environment of the zero-alternative of construction at the abstraction level of this EIA are considered to be irrelevant. Also, the zero-alternative is not included in the assessment of the consequences of construction.' Of course, it is correct to claim that the zero-alternative is characterized by the absence of construction, but this also happens to be the alternative with no negative effects as a result of that construction, which is the case with all the other alternatives. The EIA about a thermal power station included the environmentally-friendly variant of building a cooling tower. This would reduce emissions of damaging substances and the warming up of surface water. The EIA, however, assesses this alternative on its effects on the landscape (the cooling tower will dominate the landscape) and on its effects regarding noise (the cooling tower will produce a certain number of decibels). In the comparison of alternatives, we find very little about the effects the cooling tower is intended to have.

Distortion of criterion scores from report to summary

Every EIA should conclude with a comparison of alternatives using the criteria that have been investigated. Usually this comparison is presented in the form of a table in order to clarify what exactly the problems are. The Committee for Environmental Impact Assessment in its 1993 annual report gives two clear guidelines:

> 'The table presenting the comparison of alternatives should be a clearly organized and controllable summary of the outcomes of the EIA. Information should only be edited or adjusted for purposes of clarity and organization. A balance should be found between on the one hand the advantages of clarity and on the other hand the loss of information and risk of diminished objectivity.' (p.35)

The summarizing process is as follows. First, for each criterion the score of each alternative is investigated. Then a table of comparison (the scorecard) is produced, presenting the scores of alternatives on the criteria. These scores are summarized in a summary table. The information required for the table of comparison is derived from the original, more technical analyses. The table itself is reproduced in the summary preceding the report.

The fifth desideratum of this process requires a correspondence between the original data, the table of comparison and its reproduction in the summary. A very remarkable impression arises when this desideratum is imposed on EIAs. Quantitative differences that are reported in the technical part are sometimes omitted from the table of comparison: the terminology of the table of comparison can thus be strikingly different from that of the summary table. This can be illustrated by an example from the report by the Dutch Ministry of Agriculture, Environment and Fishery about the Green Space Structural Scheme. While the original data about the effects of concentrated recreational areas indicate minimal negative effects on water quality, this is presented as 'the least negative' in the comparison with other alternatives. In the table of comparison, this is replaced by the symbol '++', whereas the summary table presents the symbol '*****'. At the bottom of the summary table '*****' is explained as 'very positive effects on the environmental aspect concerned' (p. 155). The empirical observation 'minimal negative effects' is changed into 'least negative' and finally becomes 'very positive effects'.

Another report states that the environmental effects to be expected of restructuring with regard to fragmentation of habitat and migration routes are ambiguous in the case of sandy areas (p. 144). The summary, however, translates this into a '+' which the legend interprets as 'the instrument is contributing to reducing the environmental problem' (p. 37).

Sometimes differences are considered negligible, just like that. The table of comparison appears to be unambiguous: a deliberation of pros and cons is no longer necessary because one alternative sticks out with regard to the majority of criteria. It also happens that criteria are combined regardless of the question whether the scores do correspond.

Although this does not mean that the preferred alternative may not be preferred, it does mean that to prefer an alternative the weights need to be made explicit. The practical examples show that this is often not the case.

The discriminatory capacity of criteria

The sixth question is to what extent criteria should discriminate between alternatives. The desideratum claims that the usefulness of criteria depends on the extent to which they are discriminatory. The EIAs show that differences between alternatives are sometimes defined away in the final table of comparison. This implies that a number of alternatives (and sometimes all alternatives) score equally well on such a criterion. When all alternatives score equally well or badly on a criterion, such a criterion may be expected to play no part in the decision-making and might as well be left out. However, there may be a good reason to include the criterion after all; namely, in order to reduce uncertainty about the scores of the alternatives on that aspect. A disadvantage is that this may also influence the preference for an alternative. The more non-discriminatory the criteria, the smaller the differences between alternatives appear to become, and the more freedom there seems to be to choose a certain alternative on other grounds after all (see Chapter 7). In some of the analysed EIAs, all alternatives actually score identically on eight out of ten environmental criteria. Implicitly, this results in a distortion of the outcomes.

Each of the criteria should measure a certain environmental aspect. It is useless to include one criterion several times in a table. Yet, in reality this occurs when a criterion is divided into several subcriteria, or when a criterion refers to several environmental aspects and for that reason the same criterion is presented under different headings.

Including criteria that are not related to the environment

The objective of an environmental impact assessment is, as the name implies, to investigate the environmental effects of intended activities and their alternatives. This is in accordance with the recommendations of the Committee for Environmental Impact Assessment (1993: 33). The sixth desideratum states the undesirability of EIAs comparing alternatives on the basis of effects that are unrelated to the environment. Nevertheless, in reality a number of cases include in their analysis economic, transportation and geographical criteria. Such criteria appear explicitly in reports when, based on environmental criteria, consequences of the intended activity are significantly negative compared to the consequences of more environmentally-friendly alternatives. In two out of ten EIAs there are alternatives that score more favourably than the intended activity on environmental effects. The difference, however, is defined away by including effects concerning cost-effectiveness, transportation and planning.

There are two conceivable strategies for selecting the effects on which to compare alternatives. Either the analysis is restricted to the

Determining how well alternatives score on criteria 119

environmental effects in order to determine which alternative is best for the environment, or the analysis compares environmental effects with other effects in order to produce a kind of summarizing overview of all relevant effects. The last approach, called integral impact assessment (Stichting Natuur en Milieu, 1979), brings about two problems. First, it is almost impossible to fulfil the pretension that all relevant effects are accounted for. Secondly, it is rather difficult to make a cost-benefit deliberation when effects are integrated that are qualitatively very different, which is after all the whole purpose of such an integral comparison of effects. In order to prevent environmental impact assessments appearing as integral impact assessments, making them disproportionately important to decision-making, it is recommendable to assume that only environmental effects are described.

4.4 CONCLUSION

This chapter discussed the requirements for determining criterion scores. Four methods were given for determining criterion scores in cases where they are unavailable. Ten EIAs were investigated in order to find out to what extent these desiderata are satisfied in practice. Despite the fact that the technical quality of these reports appears to be high, it turns out that none of the reports fully complies with the six requirements.

EIAs often include effects that are not or are hardly discriminating. Frequently there are differences between the report and its summary. Half of the reports lacked an unambiguous interpretation of landscape effects. Sometimes the interpretation of effects is different for each alternative. Problems with reliability and validity cannot be evaluated for each report separately; they are indicated by the differences between reports. It turns out there is little correspondence with regard to the operationalization and interpretation of data (measurement of noise nuisance and landscape effects).

Sometimes there is no correspondence between tables and text. The impression is distorted by adding or omitting adjectives. The correspondence between reports of the interpretation of 'hard' data is lacking. Often there is a shift from the original data to data in tables to summarizing data. This shift mainly involves replacing quantitative data by qualitative data. Another finding is that environmentally-friendly alternatives are only slightly tested by the criteria they are intended for.

It is striking that desiderata are not complied with, because the requirements are not exceptionally demanding. This is all the more striking because the violation of desiderata usually turns out to favour the initiators' intended activity.

Therefore, these outcomes can be seen primarily as a consequence of bolstering. In other words, a choice has been established before an EIA is carried out. The EIA only provides information to artificially support a choice already made. A policy choice has already been made and is subsequently rationalized. This adaptation of information, aimed at getting one's own alternative to the top of the list beforehand, is called bolstering (Festinger, 1957, 1964; Janis & Mann, 1977). Next to the problems discussed, there are six other techniques that could be applied:

- Exaggerating positive effects.
- Minimizing negative effects.
- Denying negative effects. Problems can be defined away. This can be done by defining problems in such a way that the desired situation no longer differs from the existing situation. Defining an unemployed person as someone registered at the job centre, writing at least ten job-application letters a week, appearing on the steps of an employment agency every day, taking several retraining courses and doing voluntary work, results in a drastic reduction of the unemployment problem. The problem of ageing and the increased cost of pensions can be reduced by raising the age limit of those entitled to a pension. It is also possible to present something negative as being positive. This can be done by choice of words, such as changing the term 'bureaucratic discretion' into 'creativity' or 'scope for policy-making', or changing the term 'incomplete information' into 'strategic distribution of information'.
- Exaggerating the time it takes for negative effects to occur, so that these negative consequences can be forgotten. 'Oh, those consequences are only noticeable in the long run. We don't need to worry about that now.'
- Concealing negative consequences.
- Minimizing personal responsibility. The importance of negative consequences is reduced because the policy maker claims he does not make the choice himself, but that the choice is forced upon him.

In other words, no matter how many desiderata are given, no matter how well methods are developed and refined, it seems to depend mainly on the attitude of the researcher and the interests at stake whether and if so to what extent choices based on criterion scores are optimal. This chapter has tried to create an understanding of the possibilities for identifying pitfalls that may be encountered in this process.

5 The weight of criteria

> This chapter will discuss the setting of priorities, both theoretically and practically. After a theoretical exploration, twenty-one impact assessments will be analysed. The deliberation process will be explicitly dealt with. Analysis will show that policy makers and evaluation researchers do not pay enough attention to prioritizing. The determination of relative importance (weights) seems to be rather arbitrary. Weights, although meant to be used during the decision-making process, only marginally represent the opinions of decision makers. As it turns out in practice, it is evaluation researchers who determine what should be considered more and what less important. Consequently, policy based on the conclusions of research reflects the priorities of researchers rather than those of policy makers.

Tasks
|
Alternatives
|
Criteria
|
Test scores
|
Importance of criteria
|
Compilation of data
|
Analysis of ranking order
|
Leave decisions to the decision maker

INTRODUCTION

In 1990 an average sized city commissioned research into the optimal distribution of urban renewal funds among residential areas. This distribution should depend on the housing and living conditions in the various districts. Districts in 'bad shape' should be entitled to more money. There are several criteria on which housing and living conditions are judged: the technical condition of houses, infrastructure, crime rate, mobility and social economic status of inhabitants. However, figures concerning these criteria did not result in an unambiguous ranking order of districts. Although some problems were common to all districts, it still appeared that in one district problems were mainly in the area of infrastructure, while in another the technical condition of houses was most problematic. In other words, to arrive at a ranking order of districts the importance of the various criteria needed to be established.

The deliberation this brings about - the setting of priorities - is the focus of this chapter. In the case just mentioned, the deliberation process was (implicitly) left to the research bureau. Hence, the research bureau determined what stakeholders should consider important. Whether the priorities set by researchers showed any conformity with those of policy actors remained unclear. Nevertheless, based on their deliberations the researchers concluded that 'The combination of these factors indicate the proposed priority of each district regarding improvement and renewal measures by the city, housing corporations, private landlords and other parties involved.' (Werkgroep 2000, 1990)

The main issue raised in this chapter is whether this example is an isolated case, or whether neglecting priority-setting is a widespread phenomenon in the policy-making process. Three questions will be addressed.

First, what is the theoretical solution to the problem of setting priorities? Is it theoretically possible to have an external research bureau determine priorities objectively, or is priority-setting subjective and liable to political influences?

Second, with regard to the methodological aspects of setting priorities, is it possible to measure the priorities of policy makers? If so, which methods and techniques are particularly appropriate for this purpose? The sources of weights are derived and the individual determination of weights will be discussed.

Third, with regard to setting priorities in practice, how does the determination of weights take place in policy research practice? Is this accounted for? Which techniques are being used? Who decides on the importance of each criterion when comparing alternatives?

These questions will be answered on the basis of the results of an investigation - a comparative content analysis - of twenty-one impact assessments.

5.1 THE BASIC PROBLEMS

The first problem concerning weights is the difficulty of arriving at consensus when setting priorities. Several theoretical approaches suggest solutions to this problem. The objective approach provides criteria to 'objectively' determine the importance of problems. The subjective and political approach claims that consensus on priorities is unlikely and that setting priorities objectively does not solve but merely displaces the problem.
    The second problem is the almost impossible attribution of useful relative values, although it may be possible to create a ranking order of importance concerning goals, problems, effects or criteria in general. The proportionate value of different weights is more difficult to determine than a simple ranking order of criteria according to their weights. The methods for determining priorities that will be discussed will also deal with this issue.
    Because of these two unsolvable problems, some researchers hold the opinion that all evaluation of policy pursued or to be pursued in the future is unproductive in cases where more than one criterion is used. They conclude that the necessity of weights in so-called impact assessments is also an insurmountable difficulty (Blommenstein & Mol, 1991: 191). If the conclusion that impact assessments are useless is correct, given the irrational determination of weights, this also applies to all evaluation research. The evaluation of the success or failure of a policy will always be based on criteria. It will always be the case that some criteria are not taken into consideration. In terms of priorities, skipped criteria have been implicitly attributed a zero weight.
    Nevertheless a lot of (mainly complex) policies are based on ex ante evaluations. Policy makers seem to be all too willing to base their choices on external research, producing a ranking order of policy alternatives based on several criteria. Sometimes this is a way to legitimize policy proposals, but often this is also seen as a way to optimize policy choices. An analysis of twenty-one policy evaluations will show how the deliberation process proceeds in practice.

5.2 THEORIES ON PRIORITIZING

In public administration science too, the phenomenon of setting priorities in a policy process is underexposed. It is surprising to see how little attention is paid to priority-setting, considering its relevance to all phases of the policy process. How much weight is attributed to the various policy issues? How important are the criteria included in a policy evaluation that determine the final judgement of that policy? Priorities affect the agenda, policy issues, and policy determination, implementation and evaluation. All the time the question turns up about the importance of a certain objective, the priority of a certain policy issue, the importance of policy instruments and their effects, and also how outcomes should be evaluated.

Establishing priorities is not as simple as determining how good or bad a policy alternative scores on a certain criterion. While the costs of highway construction can be established relatively easily, it is not that simple to establish whether these costs are of major or minor importance. As a rule, weights can only be determined subjectively. They often depend on individual preferences and may differ accordingly. To road users, the costs of highway construction may be a minor issue in relation to the advantages. To a government paying for the construction, costs may be a dominant aspect. Chadwick claims: 'A measure of the relative importance of objectives is difficult to arrive at ... but is important to evaluate proposed actions against all the objectives for the payoff mix ....' (Chadwick, 1971: 136).

Structural and cyclical approach

Setting priorities is concerned with the importance of problems, values, standards, objectives and policy instruments. Here the issue is restricted to prioritizing problems. Prioritizing concerns the precedence of issues, i.e. what should be done first or what is most important. In this description, priorities are equated with urgency; that is, the order in which problems should be dealt with. The importance attributed to problems or other matters can be structural, but it can also be cyclical. Values are generally assumed to have a structural priority. Equality, freedom, inner harmony or pleasure are more or less central to a person's conceptual framework, and their importance hardly changes during a lifetime (see Converse 1964, Barnes & Kaase 1979, Rokeach 1973). On a cyclical path, priority at time t also depends on the length of time the problem already exists, and on its priority at time t-1. The idea underlying the cyclical approach is that such problems as unemployment, inflation, crime and pollution do not change as such, but that their priority changes. Not a single problem is continuously attributed the highest priority. In the long term, cycli may be independent. In the short term, however, cycli may be influenced by fashion, disaster, extreme events or new information about a problem. Policy concerning shoplifting may get high priority when, at a certain moment, people get killed due to the occurrence of shoplifting. Vandalism may get high priority when things get out of hand, and racism may attract attention when the election results are dramatic or when a politician makes disputable remarks about the subject. At that time the priority increases, then reaches its peak and next makes a downswing in favour of another problem.

The objective approach

Regardless of whether or not priorities follow a cyclical path, the question remains how they are brought about. Is it possible to determine the importance of problems objectively, using a limited number of data? Is setting priorities a subjective affair that may differ from one individual to another, or is it the outcome of a collective and political process? In the past a number of suggestions have been made regarding how to determine the importance of problems objectively. Examples are Polsby's classification based on the magnitude of the policy domain, McFarland's classification based on the number of stakeholders, and Manis' classification based on the nature of the effects of problems. The terminology used here has been intentionally transformed to fit the conceptual framework frequently used in public administration science, without doing harm to their original intentions. A further discussion can be found in Van Schuur (1984); in part, his classification will be adhered to.

Polsby (1963) distinguishes four indicators used to determine the importance of problems. These are:

- the number of people affected by the outcome
- the types of community resources distributed by the outcome
- the quantity of resources distributed by the outcome
- the degree of disruption to present community resource distributions caused by the outcome.

Along with the fact that these criteria only partly indicate the importance of problems and that some of these criteria are rather vague, the validity of the indicators may also be questioned. The policy domains with which most of these means are concerned may not be the most important ones. The policy domain may also be one where structural items and items that are hard to alter (e.g. personnel costs) make up a relatively large part of the budget. Education, for example - which has the highest budget of all - is not a domain where everyone will claim the highest priority.

McFarland (1969) is mainly concerned with the actors involved. To him the indicators for the importance of problems are:

- the number of people actually engaged in activities concerning the issue
- the amount of money, time, and other resources invested
- measures of the intensity of conflict, particularly violence or near violence
- whether or not the issues involve possible changes in the procedural rules of the game.

Here too there are problems with operationalization. What is meant by the term 'engaged in'? The validity of indicators is also debatable. Rather than a function of the nature of the problem itself, the importance of problems seems to become a function of the extent to which some actors (for instance, the media) are able to create awareness of a certain issue.

Manis (1974) mainly considers the effects of problems. His criteria concerning the importance of problems are:

- primacy: what are the consequences of the problem, and how many consequences are there?
- magnitude: what are the dimensions of the consequences or effects of the problem?
- severity: how serious are the consequences of problems, in terms of damage?

Again, the criteria here are vague and hard to operationalize. All three classifications mentioned shift the issue of prioritizing problems to a second level. Instead of prioritizing political problems (first level), the question now raised is concerned with the relative weights (second level) of indicators for these problems. Polsby's classification, for example, disregards the question about the importance of the number of people affected by a problem in relation to the importance of the amount of government expenditure involved. This issue of the relative weighing of criteria can also be raised considering the classifications of McFarland and Manis.

The subjective approach

The subjective approach incorporates prioritizing in the definition of problems. A problem is defined as the difference between a personal standard and the perception of an existing or expected situation (Bressers and Hoogerwerf 1991: 21,22). The magnitude (importance) of a problem equals this difference. This implies that priority depends not only on the situation as it is perceived by an actor, but also on his subjectively defined standards. This approach may suggest that a scientific discussion about priorities is impossible. If taken to the extreme, this approach may lead to value relativism. In that case, both the personal standard and the perceived reality are determined subjectively, making a rational debate impossible. By definition, prioritizing then becomes irrational. This may well be why little attention has been paid to prioritizing in administrative science.

Priorities not determined independently of actual scores are another problem with this approach to attributing weights to criteria for impact assessment. After all, next to the personal standard the actual scores determine half the importance of a problem. When the costs of a policy alternative increase, the effect on the outcome of the analysis doubles. It will have a negative effect not only on the score on a criterion, but also on its weight because high costs are more important. In general, this approach results in criteria having various weights that are a positive function of the scores of alternatives on these criteria. To the extent that costs are higher, the weight attributed will also be higher. This is in contradiction to the recommendations found in literature concerning the weighing of criteria (Voogd, 1983).

According to the subjective approach, a person confronted with a choice will himself determine which weights to attribute to criteria according to his personal standards and his perception of these criteria. A very tall person buying a car will value the spatial aspect of different cars higher than will other car buyers. Nobody will contest his setting of priorities. The priorities attributed to criteria are often subjective and, in contrast to criterion scores, cannot be justified scientifically. There are many discussions in scientific literature about valuefree subjects and outcomes of research. No matter how much researchers disagree on those matters, they all seem to agree that the determination of weights is an issue that can be researched. The weights themselves, however, cannot be determined for others, not by any evaluator. This criticism also concerns consumer research. Different brands of a comparable product can be researched using a number of criteria. However, a price-quality ratio and buying suggestions will always depend on the weights attributed to quality and price criteria, which are not the same for individual consumers.

The political approach

According to the political approach to prioritizing, the attribution of relative weights to problems is not so much a subjective or objective matter depending on individual actors, but mainly a function of power relations, dependencies, conflicting interests and political culture. Power structures and structures of interest are the main political criteria for prioritizing problems. This is also the starting point for Kuypers, who claims 'Even when the 'principle of least damage to interests involved' is used with every deliberation, it is clear that the deliberation process is a struggle like all political processes.' (Kuypers, 1980:316) According to Kuypers, deliberation always takes place within a sphere of negotiation. Actions by negotiators tend to take all conceivable forms of political action, e.g. argumentation, persuasion, promises, seeking support, warning, manipulation, refusal to cooperate, threats and conflict (Kuypers, 1980: 316). According to Pröpper, it is not possible to simply dispose of political judgments by using decisionistic or technocratic models. Evaluation research can be carried out from different perspectives (using different criteria), exerting a different influence on the outcomes of such research. His claim is that: ' ... research conclusions cannot be adopted by policy people just like that. When research ... leads to the conclusion ... that policy is ineffective, this conclusion can only be adopted after checking whether the perspective from which the issue has been studied coincides with ones own perspective and the objectives of policy. This means scientific knowledge cannot be consumed by policy actors without any trouble, as is actually suggested by the decisionistic and technocratic model.' (Pröpper, 1989: 91)

The priorities that policy makers set for their problems involve not only the power structure but also political culture and political argumentation; that is, criteria determined politically. Whether the seriousness of, for example, problems with residential areas is primarily measured by crime rate, mobility or housing quality depends on political arguments with political consequences for the distribution of resources among different problem areas. Policy makers may incorporate in their deliberations the interest and priorities of different groups involved.

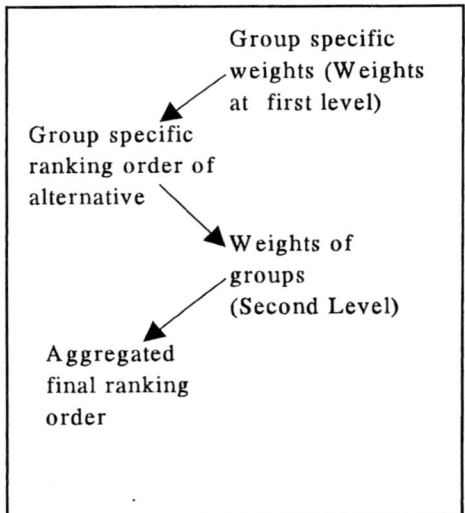

Figure 5.1 *Weighing at two levels*

Those directly involved are responsible for this prioritizing. As one of the founders of impact assessment stated 'These coefficients representing the respective weight of each criterion may result either from inquiry on the location factors in the branch, from the personal choice of the head of the firm, in terms of his cost factor, or again from a public decision.' (Guigou, 1971: 126) The importance attributed to these criteria also seems to be determined by the competence or legitimacy of the people choosing or evaluating. In a research about possible coastal extension between Hook of Holland and Scheveningen, it is stated that attribution of weights is the task of 'society through politicians, in dialogue with specific experts' (NEI, 1986: ii).

The consequences of such a position are, however, problematic. On the one hand, when politically sensitive issues are at stake, politically responsible people may be expected to take decisions concerning the inclusion or exclusion of criteria and their relative importance. Only policy actors (decision makers) seem to be able to decide whether, for example, housing stock, demographic aspects, social economic position or safety aspects should be the criteria used to determine priorities when the objective is to improve the social climate in residential areas. On the other hand, the question is how decision makers and politicians can be persuaded to make their priorities and consequently their criteria more explicit. The weights that policy actors (decision makers) attribute to various policy effects are often unknown. First, the people involved usually refuse to make such choices explicit. After all, it is important to politicians not to antagonize potential voters, which sometimes results in priorities being kept implicit. Secondly, weights may vary between different groups involved with a certain policy. Environ-mentalists set other priorities to the effects of environmental policy than do, for example, agricultural organizations. The deliberations about interests are different for these organizations. Both arrive at their own opinion about the policy to be preferred. This difference in attributing priorities also leads to different preferences regarding policy options. Hence, an impact assessment of possible locations for military exercise grounds based on 18 different sets of weights resulted in 18 different ranking orders. This way, the utility of such an assessment is very low. When aggregating such outcomes into one final ranking order, again the attribution of weights is very problematic.

Some people think an unprotested appeal to the authority of the decision maker can be made in order to solve the issue (NEI 1986: ii; this is called the instrumentalistic view). Others suggest a groupspecific approach; i.e. for each group a set of priorities is determined as is a separate ranking order of alternatives (Voogd, 1983: 64).
The weight of groups may also be determined in order to arrive at a general ranking order of alternatives, based, for example, on group power, group size or each group having the same weight. It should be noted that, again, the problem of attributing weights is displaced to the second level; in this case from criterion weights to group weights (Figure 5.1).

Displacement of the problem with regard to weighing criteria will also be an issue in the research discussed below. Different sets of weights, representing the opinion of different parties involved, are the weighing factors at first level. Usually groups are then combined, resulting in aggregate weighing in the final analysis. Aggregate weighing (implicitly) assumes the weighing of groups. Often the assumption is that each group has the same weighing factor (1.0); unweighed averages are then calculated on the basis of the priorities of each separate group. Nevertheless, this too is setting priorities and one of the determining factors of the outcomes of research.

5.3 METHODOLOGICAL ASPECTS OF WEIGHT DETERMINATION

This section will discuss the possibilities for investigating and measuring the priorities of policy actors. Although each technique has advantages and disadvantages, measuring priorities quantitatively will turn out to be possible.

Actual behaviour

Voogd (1980: 16) mentions three ways to investigate the weights of criteria that have been attributed by decision makers. The first is based on observed behaviour. The investigation focuses on finding out which criteria have been relevant in making the final policy choice and on making an estimation of their weights.

Wijbouw (1983) devised an inventive way to determine weights attributed by decision makers. His reasoning is as follows. If it is possible to calculate the utility of alternatives on the basis of criterion scores and weights, then it should also be possible to calculate weights when both utility of alternatives and criterion scores are known. If the utility of a business location is indicated by the number of companies that have been set up or expanded, and the characteristics of these locations are also known, then the weights that have been attributed to these characteristics by these companies can be calculated (see Table 5.1).

$$U_i = \sum_c (S_{ic})*G_c = S_{i1}*G_1 + S_{i2} + \ldots + S_{im}*G_m$$
$$U_j = \sum_c (S_{jc})*G_c = S_{j1}*G_1 + S_{j2} + \ldots + S_{jm}*G_m$$
$$\ldots\ldots$$
$$U_n = \sum_c (S_{nc})*G_c = S_{n1}*G_1 + S_{n2} + \ldots + S_{nm}*G_m$$

n = *number of alternatives (i,j)*
U_1 *and* S_{1c} *are given*
G_c *is to be calculated*

Table 5.1 *Inverse qualiflex method*

When the number of alternatives is equal to the number of criteria, it is possible to unambiguously determine weights ($G_1 \ldots G_m$). In that case there are just as many variables unknown (G_c) as there are equations, and the set of equations is solvable. As from the fourth version of SPSS PC, a module called ALSCAL is included that has been specially designed to determine afterwards what has been considered more or less important by a decision maker, given choices and criterion scores. If the number of alternatives is smaller than the number of criteria, the upper and lower limits of weights attributed by companies can be calculated. The equations do not have one unambiguous solution but can be partly solved by making a few assumptions. This method is called the inverse qualiflex procedure.

Scenarios

The second method for determining weights is to postulate alternative policy directions or scenarios. Different types of policy are represented by different sets of weights, specified by the investigator. The sources for such an approach are mainly written material. Policy memos, party programmes, government records and company reports can be analysed and evaluated to discover the relative importance of their objectives.

Preference analysis

The third method is based on preference analysis. Using questionnaires it can be investigated what level of importance respondents attribute to criteria when evaluating their policies. Actors are asked what they do or do not consider to be more or less important. Their answers can be used to indicate criterion weights. Such questions can be asked in various ways.

- Respondents may be asked to indicate one, two, three or more most important criteria from a list of criteria (select k out of n). All criteria can be listed pairwise and respondents can be asked to select the most important criterion from each pair of criteria. Using scale analysis techniques, criteria can be ordered according to their relative importance.
- Respondents may be asked to sort all criteria in order of importance. Here the Q sorting technique is relevant. Rietveld (1982) suggested analysing the outcomes of such sortings. Based on the assumption that the probability of each combination of weights is equal, given their ordinal ranking order, the expected

cardinal weights can be calculated. A debatable consequence of this approach is the fact that some criteria are attributed a relatively high weight while most are attributed a relatively low one. Jansen and Rietveld (1985) consider this to be in accordance with a number of a priori assumptions of evaluation research. However, they do not specify their argumentation for this remark, which makes the consequences of this approach no less debatable.

- The use of Likert scales is another possibility. According to its importance, each criterion is given a score on a scale ranging from 1-5 or 1-7. The final weight is determined by calculating the average score of all respondents. There are also more complicated preference analysis techniques, e.g. pairwise comparison where respondents are asked to compare each criterion with all other criteria and indicate for each pair which criterion is most important. Saaty (1977) suggests an approach where a Likert scale is combined with a pairwise comparison. The difference of importance between two criteria in a pair of criteria is valued on a nine-point scale, where 1 indicates equal importance and 9 indicates absolute dominance of one criterion over the other. The advantages of this technique are that the consistency of answering patterns can be traced and there is a possibility of calculating cardinal weights through transformation of scores.

- Next to these data collection techniques, the Delphi technique should also be mentioned. This technique can be particularly useful if the purpose of the investigation is to arrive at a set of weights acceptable to all people involved. This is because the Delphi technique aims at creating convergence of positions. This convergence is attained by respondents' anonymity, the argumentation of positions, and repetitive questioning in combination with the feedback of summarized, previous results in several rounds. Questions are asked not only about the relative importance of criteria but also about the supporting argumentation. Using anonymous interviews, a large number of arguments are gathered in order to arrive at a ranking order of criteria according to their weights.

- There are a large number of analytical techniques that produce a ranking order of criteria according to weights based on personal opinions. An example is straight counting, where criterion weights are determined by using the number of times (frequency) a criterion is considered to be most important.

Individual weight determination

Problems are smaller when a decision maker is able to determine criterion weights independently, as in a one-actor model. Whether costs are more or less important than benefits is determined by the decision maker himself. Nonetheless, some problems still remain. The extent to which individuals are capable of attributing weights to criteria depends on the number of criteria. Particularly when the number of criteria exceeds ten, reliability decreases considerably (Nijkamp, 1977: 54).

Secondly, the attribution of weights does not always comply with the transitivity requirement. One individual may consider industrial development to be more important than pollution, and pollution to be more important than employment, but still consider employment to be more important than industrial development. This raises the issue of circularity. Likewise, this problem becomes more serious with a large number of criteria.

Thirdly, with a ranking order based on weights that are determined subjectively, the relative importance of one criterion over another cannot be exactly indicated. Because most analyses require a quantitative set of weights, a distortion may occur as far as the actual set of weights of that individual is concerned.

Keep attribution of weight scores simple and transparent
Remove all irrelevant criteria
Start with the least important criterion
Determine weights independently of criterion scores

Table 5.2 *Recommendation concerning attribution of weights*

Pertaining to these problems, a number of recommendations can be made concerning the determination of weights.

- Keep the attribution of weight scores simple and transparent. The idea behind this recommendation is that outcomes of multi-criteria analysis are more valuable and more acceptable if it is made clear how the weights have been determined. Whether

results of research are used is a positive function of the extent to which its realization is understood.
- Remove all criteria with minimal relevance. The fewer criteria, the more reliable the weights attributed to them.
- Start with the least important criterion and deduce all other weights from the weight attributed to this criterion. As a rule, this criterion is valued 10. Another way is to distribute a predetermined number of points, say 100, over all criteria.
- Determine weights independently of criterion scores.

5.4 TRANSFORMATION OF WEIGHTS

Depending on the importance attached to weight attribution, weights can be transformed before being analysed. There are five techniques for doing this.

| Quantitative weights |
| Ranking order weights |
| Extreme weights |
| Random weights, controlled weight ranking order |
| Random weights, uncontrolled weight ranking order |

Table 5.3 *Five weight transformation techniques*

Quantitative weights is the most common way of treating weights. Criterion A, with a weight of 20, is twice as important as criterion B, which has a weight of 10.

With *ranking order weights* it is not exactly known how much more important criterion A is in relation to criterion B. Therefore, the original weights are transformed into a ranking order. Ranking order numbers are then treated as quantitative weights. In this case, it is irrelevant whether criterion A has a weight of 20 or 200, given criterion B has a weight of 10. By transformation, the ratio of analysed weights remains 2:1.

Extreme weights focuses on the extent to which a ranking order of alternatives changes while adding criteria to the analysis in decreasing order of importance. Here, alternatives are repetitively analysed. The first step is to base the analysis on only one - the most important - criterion (disjunctive analysis). The second step also includes the second most important criterion, which is attributed a weight equal to the most important criterion. The ranking order is recalculated and compared to the first ranking order to find out whether adding this criterion has altered the situation. This procedure continues until the least important criterion is included in the analysis. This transformation of weights provides a decision maker with the opportunity to investigate whether a change of the ranking order of alternatives, as a consequence of adding a possibly unimportant criterion, is justified. It could also be that the ranking order disregarding a certain criterion is better justified.

Random weights is another repetitive analysis. The assumption is that a decision maker has no idea about which criterion is more or less important than another. In such a case, random weights can be used. By repetitive calculation of a ranking order, using different and randomly chosen sets of weights, it can be analysed whether a preferred alternative exists regardless of the set of weights. The most dominant alternative will be the one that appears most frequently at the top of the list of alternatives.

Quantitative weights

Weights can be considered as quantitative weights if both criterion weights and the proportions of these weights are unambiguously meaningful, that is when criterion A having weight 20 and criterion B having weight 10 imply that A is twice as important as B. Then, both the score and the proportions of scores have meaning with regard to content, the variable 'weight' is at ratio level of measurement. In that case, following impact assessment techniques, weights G_c are transformed in such a way that the sum of all transformed weights G'_c, for all criteria, equals one. This implies that each criterion weight is divided by the sum of all criterion weights. The purpose of this transformation is to create comparability of impact assessments concerning different problems. By using this standard transformation, the unambiguity of calculated dominance scores is enhanced.

$$\sum_{c=1}^{m} G_c = 1$$

M is number of criteria

Formula 5.1 *Standardization of weights*

Ranking order weights

Usually, when the proportions of weights have no significance but their order does, the original weights are transformed into a ranking order. Table 5.4 shows the original weights Gc, and their transformation into a ranking order of weights Gc'. When transforming weights pertaining to n criteria, the lowest weight is valued 1 and the highest weight is valued n

Arguments

Original weights G_c	Ranking order G_c'	Quantitative weights G_c''
10	1	0.048
20	2	0.092
40	3.5	0.167
40	3.5	0.167
70	5	0.238
100	6	0.285

Table 5.4 *Ranking order weights*

The reason for this type of transformation is that the researcher assumes that the proportions of weights, in their ranking order, have a meaningful significance. Ranking order weights are standardized by the same transformation applied to quantitative weights. Each criterion weight is divided by the sum of all criterion weights. There are two objections to treating weights as ranking order weights, i.e.:

- With regard to content it can hardly be made plausible that ranking order weights are a better representation of proportions than the original weights.
- There are statistical drawbacks to calculating with ranking order numbers. In actual fact, variables expressed in ranking order are at ordinal level of measurement.

$$G'_c = \frac{G_c}{\sum_{c=1}^{m} G_c}$$

m = number of criteria

Formula 5.2 *Ranking order weights*

$$G_c = \frac{G_c}{\sum_{c=1}^{M} G_c} = \frac{G_c}{\tfrac{1}{2} n \ast (n-1)}$$

Formula 5.3 *Determination of standard weights from ranking order weights*

All the same, transforming weights into ranking order weights has become common practice. Reasons for this can mainly be found in the transparency and simplicity of such transformations. Also, the importance of common practice is the availability of a method for processing data independently of the researcher.

Extreme weights

Extreme weights is a third method for transforming weights whose proportions have no meaningful significance. Using this method, impact assessment is repeated as many times as there are criteria. Actually this method of transformation is a way to operationalize the effect of changing the decision rule from disjunctive to linear compensatory. The first evaluation maximizes the weight of the most important criterion and minimizes the weights of other criteria. The first impact assessment only considers the most important criterion. Then multi-criteria analysis is repeated, maximizing the two most important criteria and minimizing the rest of the criteria. This operation is repeated, adding the next most important criterion each round. With n criteria this results in n repetitions, where the last repetition uses weights $G_c = 1/n$ for all criteria.

$$G_{c_{max}} = 1$$
$$G_d = 0 \quad \text{for all other criteria}$$

Formula 5.4 *Maximization of the first criterion*

$$G_c = \tfrac{1}{2}$$
$$G_d = \tfrac{1}{2}$$
$$G_e = 0 \quad \text{for all other criteria}$$

Formula 5.5 *Maximization of the two most important criteria*

The significance of the extreme weights method is that it enables a researcher to examine whether adding a certain criterion will result in variation of dominance scores of alternatives. He can then decide to include or not include this criterion in the analysis. Application of this method enables the impact of each criterion to be analysed separately.

A second reason for using this method is that the researcher need not discriminate between weights of criteria included in the analysis. After all, each criterion included is weighed the same.

The disadvantages of this transformation are evident. The way of transformation is rather crude. One or more criteria with maximum weight are included, and the remaining criteria are completely left out of the analysis. The arguments with regard to the meaning of equalizing weights are just as weak as those for transforming them into ranking order weights. There is no reason, except tradition, to attribute equal weights to criteria.

Random + ranking order weights

A fourth method that has become popular lately is the transformation of weights into random weights. Here significance is attached only to the ranking order of criterion weights, not to the proportions or differences between these weights. The transformation procedure is as follows: based on the ranking order of criteria according to their weights, the most important criterion is attributed a weight of random value between 0 and 1000 (e.g. 274). The next most important criterion is now randomly valued between 0 and 274 (e.g. a weight of 160). The third most important criterion is randomly valued between 0 and 160 (e.g. a weight of 86). These random weights are then considered to be quantitative weights.

Transformations as they take place using quantitative weights are also applied to random weights. Finally, the dominance scores of alternatives are calculated. By repeating this procedure (say, 1000 times) each alternative can be examined to find out how many times it ends up in first, second or a subsequent position. The most dominant alternative is the one most frequently ending up in first position. Arguments for using the method of random weights are:

- Dominance scores are determined independently of the actual differences of weights between criteria.
- The extent to which dominance of an alternative depends on the weights attributed to criteria can be analysed. This dependency is high when the position of alternatives based on their dominance turns out to vary over 1000 repetitions.
- By using random weights, the determination of weights does not depend on the researcher or his interests.

Using random weights has the same disadvantages as using ranking order or extreme weights. A technical disadvantage, however, is its time consumption because of the many repetitions of the analysis that are needed. Doing the analysis by hand will lead to insurmountable problems. Time consumption using a computer depends on hardware capacity.

Random weights

This method, using completely random weights, operates in exactly the same way as the previous method, except that the ranking order of transformed weights does not necessarily correspond with the ranking order of the original set of weights. This method should be applied only when all information about weights is lacking. Another way to solve this problem is to make use of discordance evaluation in which all weights are considered equal. This method will be discussed in the next chapter. Transformation into completely random weights enables investigation of the extent to which a ranking order of alternatives depends on weights attributed. Usually this will be the case. Only when criterion scores themselves already indicate the dominance of one alternative, because its criterion scores are highest, will random weights produce an unambiguous result.

5.5 ATTRIBUTION OF WEIGHTS IN PRACTICE

Research design

In this section, twenty-one impact assessments will be investigated. The majority deal with town and country planning. The topics are: business location research, highway construction, location studies for (nuclear) power stations and wind turbines, the desirability of an industrial island, coastal extension, the quality of the housing stock in cities, a comparison of residential areas in two cities, a SWOT analysis of several cities and the conurbation in Western Holland, organization of two areas, drinking water supply, the consequences of land consolidation for landscape, mooring places for houseboats, scenario research for building in a large city, meal supply for the elderly, alternative expansion of civil aviation, and offshore industrial zones. Most research concerns ex ante evaluation commissioned by government authorities. The impact assessments studied have four characteristics in common.

They are all ex ante evaluation research. All investigations aim at assessing a number of alternatives a policy maker will have to choose from. The purpose of research is to be a tool in the policy preparation phase.

As a rule, the results of research have been used by policy makers. The outcomes of the investigation - a ranking order of alternatives - have become part of the policy deliberation process.

They are all impact assessment research. All alternatives are assessed using two or more criteria. Each criterion is attributed a weight expressing the importance attached to that criterion.

They are all contract research. External research bureaus have carried out investigations commissioned by local, province or national government.

In fifteen cases, research was carried out by a commercial bureau, and six cases were carried out by university institutions. Regarding government level, nine cases were commissioned by local government, five by county government, and seven by national government. From the time of publication of the reports it can be deduced that most studies are quite recent. The basic material consists of seven impact assessments carried out in 1990/1991, eleven in the 1980s, and three before 1980. The number of criteria used is on average ten.

Comparison of impact assessments

This section will present the results of the investigation of weight attribution. It is striking to note who has been setting priorities and who has attributed the actual quantitative weights to criteria. In the majority of cases, the researchers independently determine which criteria the decision maker should consider to be more or less important. Only three out of twenty-one reports show that consultation with people involved has taken place. In the majority of cases, the determination of weights occurs at the first level. This happens when the weights of criteria are directly determined by the researcher. In a few cases, weights are determined at second level. Different weight sets are aggregated into one overall set and the importance of different groups involved is set equal by the researcher. This outcome is all the more striking because, in as far as the reports mention the attribution of weights, it is continuously emphasized that the opinions of decision makers should be expressed in the attribution of weights. Only in one case it is explicitly indicated that the decision maker (in this case, a ministry) had determined the weights. However, the decision maker was presented with only a limited number of possibilities, actually giving the researchers a lot of influence on the final choice. In one case the commissioning authority explicitly indicated the preconditions within which weights could be varied by researchers. Another case used a questionnaire which allowed all parties involved to determine the weights.

The question now is which arguments are used to justify researchers taking over decision-making with regard to prioritizing, and whether these arguments are valid. Justification is lacking or inadequate in the majority of investigated evaluation reports. In five out of the twenty-one reports, justification is absent; in all others, justification is inadequate.

First, the length of argumentation is striking: in most cases it is very brief. Usually only one sentence is dedicated to the attribution of weights; there is hardly ever more than half a page of argumentation. This is surprising, considering the consequences of the attribution of weights. Weights are just as important as criterion scores in determining a ranking order. Nevertheless, the majority of reports show that much more attention is paid to establishing scores than to establishing weights.

Second, the content of argumentation is also striking. Usually only the method is discussed: 'Weights have been attributed in the following way ...' or 'Weights can be found in Table ...' Sometimes it is indicated that other weights are also possible but that no further research has been done due to all kinds of external factors. After that, the first set of weights is used to produce recommendations and a ranking order of alternatives.

Third, rationalizing and uncontrollable terms in the argumentation are also striking. Phrases used are e.g.: 'reasonable reflections of relative preferences', 'synthesis of facts', 'opinions and views', 'great accuracy', 'probability of weights', and 'pragmatic weight attribution'. This suggests that more importance should be attached to weight attribution than is actually possible.

Fourth, researchers - acknowledging the problems concerning weight attribution - try to ease their certainty about weight attribution by using adjectives. Yet, in the end this point is not referred to in the conclusion or the recommendations. Phrases used are e.g.: 'indicative weighing', 'indicative summary', 'relative weights', 'open to discussion', 'multi-stage approach', 'some inevitable subjectivity', and 'more or less qualitatively determined weights'. These terms do not clarify what is intended by the researcher. All that can be deduced is that researchers too have their doubts about the weights that have been attributed. In themselves these doubts are justified, but it hardly ever happens that researchers or policy makers draw conclusions accordingly. The ranking order of alternatives based on such dubious information is hardly questioned.

Fifth, despite recommendations in literature, researchers relate weight to the nature and quantity of data. Data that are less 'hard' will also be considered less important. A variable based on several indicators will be attributed a higher weight. Unreliable data are attributed a zero weight. Theoretically it seems hardly acceptable to suggest that a criterion such as criminality is not involved when assessing residential areas because data are lacking, just as mobility would be considered very important because of the abundance of data on this criterion. In evaluation research practice, however, this turns out to be the case. Some cases explicitly give argumentations for this point of view. According to these researchers, a criterion, quantitatively operationalized, is automatically more significant to the problem.

The sixth point concerns the reliability of weight attribution. In literature it is stated that prioritizing is a problem, particularly when the number of criteria exceeds ten. Weighing factors become less reliable when the number of criteria increases, because stability and reliability of prioritizing is reduced considerably. Intransitivity of weight attribution also becomes more probable when the number of criteria increases. Given these findings it might be expected that weight attribution will get more attention when more criteria are involved. The twenty-one cases investigated do not show any sign of this.

The seventh striking point is the diversity of ways in which to determine weights. There is not a single dominant technique used by the researchers. Saaty's method has been applied twice, as has the Likert technique. Distinguishing different scenarios occurs in one third of the investigations. Equalizing weights at first or second level occurs in one quarter of the investigations. Choices of treatment of weights are hardly argumented and turn out to be based on the personal preferences of researchers in the majority of cases.

By methodological and praxeological standards, the twenty-one reports analysed seem to be well organized. However, from the perspective of actors directly involved in policy, substantial criticism concerning the analysis is inevitable. The weighing of criteria is underexposed in the reports. It is merely indicated that weighing has taken place and that this is influential to the outcomes. However, the weighing scores are hardly ever substantiated. Policy actors do not sufficiently influence weighing. Although theory consistently emphasizes that weighing should reflect the opinion of the decision maker, in practice this turns out to be insufficiently the case.

This observation leads to the conclusion that the contribution of researchers is considerable. This is contrary to other research, which emphasizes only a small contribution of researchers with regard to evaluation research (Biegel & Smit, 1991). It is the researcher himself who determines weights without indicating or being able to indicate how he has arrived at his priorities. As we have seen, the assessment of policy measures to be taken is determined by the scores of alternatives on criteria and the weights of these criteria. The second element is also called the subjective element. As a rule, however, the analysed reports suggest that weight attribution is an 'objective' matter that can also be unambiguously done by researchers. This is contrary to the theoretical considerations and normative implications of prioritizing.

Possible explanations of findings

A remarkable conclusion from our analysis is that the assumption that a decision- or policy maker would determine the deliberation of criteria does not seem to correspond with the twenty-one impact assessments investigated here. A number of explanations can be put forward; however, their empirical correctness remains to be seen.

Decision makers consciously hand over weight attribution to researchers. Because weight attribution is a debatable activity, some decision makers consider it sensible to leave this to 'more objective' external research bureaus instead of entering the discussion themselves. Sometimes this is shown by the answer decision makers give when asked by people involved whether the weights mentioned in the report are really objective. This answer is: 'Do you know a more acceptable set of weights?'

Decision makers do not appreciate the importance of prioritizing. There is a subconscious acceptation of the fact that research bureaus attribute weights. To many, the impact assessment method is a kind of black box, input is 'objective data' and output is 'objective information'. This proposition is supported by the conclusion that argumentation of the set of weights used is minimal in many reports (usually not more than one sentence) and is mainly articulated in terms of operating procedures and not so much in terms of reasoning.

With regard to weight attribution, there is no difference between decision maker, stakeholders and the researcher. This statement is dubious. There is no reason to assume that policy priorities held by researchers are identical to those of policy makers.

Given the acceptable outcomes of research and the acceptable ranking order of alternatives, the determination of weights is also acceptable. This is also illustrated by apparent differences between (some) alternatives. If it is clear beforehand that alternatives are of very high or very low priority, then they are presented as such in the reports. Therefore, it is assumed that the ranks of other alternatives are also correct as are, consequently, the calculation of outcomes and the elements of that calculation.

Weight attribution is of less importance than assumed by the utility function. This could be demonstrated by sensibility analysis with a relatively stable ranking order, regardless of weights. However, as a rule this kind of analysis is lacking in the material analysed.

The weight of criteria

It has become clear that the attribution of weights to criteria is critical in impact assessment. Referring to Chapter 2 this can also be explained by the complex nature of prioritizing. Together the actor, choice and calculation systems influence the attribution of weights. It is clear the actor system affects prioritizing, considering that the attribution of weights is regarded as an objective, political or subjective matter. The choice system concerns the selection of alternatives and criteria. Adding or leaving out criteria is an implicit form of weight attribution and may also change the (relative) priority of all other criteria. The nature of alternatives can also alter prioritizing. In this respect, reference should be made to the section on bolstering. The calculation system plays a part because of the quantitative components of weights and the various ways to treat them. The next chapter will show that different analytical techniques of impact assessment can be distinguished by the way they take weights into account when determining the ranking order of alternatives.

5.6 CONCLUSION

This chapter discussed the problem of determining criterion weights. Some methods and recommendations were given regarding such determination. First, different theoretical approaches with respect to prioritizing were discussed. Then the methodological aspects were dealt with. Finally, twenty-one evaluation reports were analysed with regard to methods concerned with weight attribution to criteria.

This investigation shows that both policy makers commissioning impact assessment and external researchers evaluating policy do not pay sufficient attention to weight attribution. From a rational point of view, this is unsatisfactory because decision makers apparently take decisions based on priorities set by research bureaus and not by themselves. From a democratic point of view, this is particularly unsatisfactory because people elected to make political deliberations and to allocate scarce resources turn out not to make these decisions themselves but leave this power to (uncontrolled) research bureaus.

6 Compilation into a ranking order

> This chapter focuses on the compilation methods of seven analytical techniques. By using the same example for each technique, it will become clear how ranking orders are brought about. After clarifying a compilation method, the rationale behind the technique will be discussed.

Tasks
|
Alternatives
|
Criteria
|
Test scores
|
Importance of criteria
|
Compilation of data
|
Analysis of ranking order
|
Leave decisions to the decision maker

INTRODUCTION

After all data regarding the calculation of scores of alternatives on criteria and criterion weights have been collected, they need to be made comparable and subsequently compiled, by reckoning their weights, into a utility score for each alternative. Philosophically, choosing from alternatives on the basis of utility optimalization is a familiar phenomenon. By way of introduction to the seven statistical techniques, this utilitarian philosophy will be briefly discussed. Then a series of decision rules and their significance will be dealt with.

Finally, seven more recent variants of the linear compensatory decision rule will be discussed. Using the same example for each analytical technique, their operations will be explained.

6.1 UTILITY OF ALTERNATIVES

The objective of all policy evaluation is to indicate the utility of policy. One of the characteristics common to both ex ante and ex post evaluation is the objective to determine the value or utility of alternatives on the basis of explicit criteria. This concerns alternatives with regard to the continuation, modification or termination of policy, or alternatives with regard to choosing from various policy instruments. Criteria are either deduced from policy objectives or are indicative of policy effects (intended and unintended). The idea that the value of each action can be determined, being the purpose of evaluation, originates in utilitarian philosophy. This section will deal with the characteristics of this philosophy and its two main protagonists, Jeremy Bentham and John Stuart Mill. Some people consider the determination of utility, usually expressed in terms of recommendations, to be outside the realm of science. Others consider it to be the true purpose of evaluation research (Scriven, 1972; Cronbach, 1982; Stufflebaum & Webster 1980). Stufflebaum & Webster classify this type of evaluation as 'true evaluations', in contrast to summative evaluations, which they classify as 'quasi-evaluations', and legitimizing evaluations, which they classify as 'pseudo-evaluations'. Thinking of the term 'utility', leaving out emotionally charged connotations such as egoistic behaviour, other terms come to mind, such as attractiveness, success, more or less frustrating, advantage, deliberation of costs and benefits and, more generally, the value of policy.

Because the term 'evaluation' means nothing more than assessing value, and because value is synonymous with utility, the discussion below will focus on this term as being central to any form of evaluation. Utility theory will be discussed as it was originally formulated by Jeremy Bentham and later supplemented by John Stuart Mill.

Regarding utility theory, the same debate as the one among evaluation researchers has taken place. This is the second reason to discuss utility theory. A typical difference between the conceptions of Bentham and Mill is that Bentham only takes into consideration the utility of behaviour by the actor himself, whereas Mill uses a broader definition of utility distinguishing between higher (altruistic) and lower (egoistic) levels of utility optimalization.

6.1.1 Bentham

The eighteenth-century philosopher Jeremy Bentham founded utilitarianism as we know it today. The phrase most quoted from his The Principles of Morals and Legislation (1780) indicates what determines and explains human behaviour and how it can be regulated and controlled.

> 'Nature has placed mankind under the governance of two sovereign masters, pain and pleasure. It is for them alone to point out what we ought to do, as well as to determine what we shall do. On the one hand the standard of right and wrong, on the other the chain of causes and effects, are fastened to their throne. They govern us in all we do, in all we say, in all we think: every effort we can make to throw off our subjection will serve but to demonstrate and confirm it.'
> (Bentham, 1780, Ch. 1, Section 1)

This hedonistic principle was elaborated by Bentham, whose aim was to arrive at an argumentation on which the conclusion could be based that costs and benefit are interchangeable. A quantity of something offsets a quantity of something else. Obviously this involves weighing, for which Bentham suggested seven criteria: intensity, durability, (in)security, commitment at a distance, chance of repetition, purity, and the number of people affected.

Intensity
Durability
(In)security
Commitment at a distance
Chance of repetition
Purity
The number of people affected

Table 6.1 *Bentham's criteria*

According to Bentham, his principle of utility can be generally applied, for example, to compare matters that are completely different. Somewhat provokingly, he claimed that a game for children could be equivalent or even of higher utility than reading poetry. This kind of comparison, which was completely contradictory to the conceptions that had been held since the days of early Greek civilization, made his theory highly debatable. They are, however, a direct consequence of his theory. A second debatable issue which brought Bentham's utilitarianism into discussion is his conception of atomized individualism. The assumption here is that only individuals can determine what gives them 'pleasure'. Third parties are unable to do so. The consequence of this position is that government cannot and should not focus its attention on stimulating good fortune; instead, it should concentrate on avoiding bad fortune. This standpoint led to aversion particularly at the rise of the welfare state. In the welfare state, the purpose of government is more than to merely regulate a competitive and individualistic society.

6.1.2 John Stuart Mill

John Stuart Mill was one of the first people to criticize Bentham's ideas. His first claim was that society is not just an amalgamate of individuals, but also consists of social structures. To understand changes taking place in society, it is important to pay attention to these structures and the developments within them. Secondly, Mill uses a much broader definition of utility:

> 'I regard utility as the ultimate appeal on all ethical questions; but it must be utility in the largest sense, grounded on the permanent interests of man as a progressive being.

By formulating utility in this way, Mill is also able to distinguish between higher and lower 'pleasures'. About Bentham he mockingly remarked it would be better to be a dissatisfied Socrates than a satisfied pig (Wolfe and McCoy, 1972: 171). Mill's explanation is based on distinguishing two forms of good fortune: egoism, which is good fortune strived for by individuals, and altruism, which is good fortune strived for by individuals, because it makes other people happy. Pleasures of the second type are at a higher level than pleasures of the first type. First of all because they eventually lead to the principle which says 'The greatest happiness for the largest number of men', and secondly because people familiar with and appreciating both types eventually choose the second.

Utility of freedom serves as an example. According to Mill, the utility of freedom lies in the increasing individuality necessary to enable moral progress. The difference between him and Bentham appears not to be a fundamental one. Mill considers himself to be making 'amendments'. In the end the difference revolves around the weighing of various criteria for 'pleasure', seven of them already given by Bentham. Whereas Bentham underrates the criterion that concerns the number of people affected by a choice, this criterion is highly appreciated by Mill.

6.1.3 The utility formula

The utility of actions is not an abstraction but can be represented by a formula. This formula implicates that choices depend only on the value of the outcomes or effects S_{ic}, as determined by a decision maker, and the probability $P[S_{ic}]$ of the occurrence of these effects. As can be seen in Formula 6.1, the outcome of each effect is (artificially) multiplied by 1 (Buchanan, 1969; Page 1960).

$$U_i = \sum S_{ic} * P[S_{ic}] * 1$$

U_i = Utility of alternative i
S_{ic} = effect c caused by option i
$P[S_{ic}]$ = probability of effect Sic

Formula 6.1 *Expected utility*

This reflects the assumption that in a utility function all effects are equally important. This way the formula appears to be objective and valuefree. However, implicitly a choice has been made by considering each effect to be equally important. This is only possible when the same unit of measurement (e.g. money) is used for each effect. If the unit of measurement of effects differs, equalization of weights is actually value bound. Formula 6.2 explicitly presents the priority of each effect, i.e. its weight (G_c).

Obviously, weights are a crucial factor. Their determination cannot be done by evaluators, as was demonstrated in the previous chapter. After all, evaluators do not have the authority to determine which effects are or are not important.

Compilation into a ranking order 153

$$U_i = \sum S_{ic} * P[S_{ic}] * G_c$$

U_i = Utility of alternative i
S_{ic} = effect c caused by option i
$P[S_{ic}]$ = probability of effect Sic
G_c = Importance of effect c

Formula 6.2 *Extended formula for expected utility*

By taking into account the effects themselves, the probability of their occurrence and the importance attached to them, the utility function can be generally applied to the utility determination of alternatives, regardless of whether criteria have been measured at the same level of measurement. Conjointly all weights of criteria (e.g. pollution measured in CO_2 quantities, noise nuisance measured in dB and costs measured in money terms) determine the utility of alternatives. In this chapter, the general formula is simplified by keeping the probability of all criterion scores at 100% (=1).

6.2 DECISION RULES

Determining the ranking order of alternatives is the last step of the multi-criteria model. A decision rule has to be chosen to determine the best alternative. There are many possible ways to do this. Making decision rules explicit is an advantage of the model. A scorecard without decision rule results, as research shows, in intuitively determined choices. In that case options are presented simultaneously, the multitude of criteria being too complex to comprehend. This intuitive decision rule, earlier called 'affect referral', is excluded from impact assessment precisely because its objective is to avoid this kind of decision rule. It is not the prejudices with regard to alternatives that are central, but the scorecard. It is no longer possible to determine which alternative should be preferred on the basis of emotion, 'a primary affective reaction'. Impact assessment also has the advantage that a subconscious transition from one decision rule to another becomes highly unlikely.

Even then there are many ways to arrive at a ranking order. Impact assessment uses the most simple solution, i.e. the linear compensatory decision rule. Each criterion score is weighed according to its importance and the sum of weighed scores determines the value of each alternative.

Other decision rules are also possible. Nonlinear compensatory decision rules do not calculate a sum of weighed scores, but use multiplication or a polynomic function. Multiplication and particularly polynomic functions distinguish themselves from linear decision rules because their outcomes are mainly determined by the extreme values of criterion scores and weights. This can be seen in the following example.

	alternative		weight
	I	J	
criteria			
c1	3	1	1
c2	3	3	1
c3	3	5	1

linear compensatory decision rule
$U_i = 3 + 3 + 3 = 9$
$U_j = 1 + 3 + 5 = 9$

cumulative decision rule
$U_i = 3*3*3 = 27*$
$U_j = 1*3*5 = 15$

polynomic decision rule
$U_i = 2^3+2^3+2^3 = 24$
$U_i = 2^1+2^3+2^5 = 42*$

* preferred alternative

Table 6.2 *Elaboration of decision rules*

Suppose alternative A scores 3 on three criteria and alternative B scores 1, 3 and 5, respectively. Using the linear compensatory decision rule, the alternatives are equivalent (3+3+3=1+3+5). Using the cumulative decision rule, alternative A is preferred (3*3*3>1*3*5). Alternatives scoring average on all criteria will have the highest value.

If a polynomic decision rule is applied, alternative B will be preferred ($2^3+2^3+2^3<2^1+2^3+2^5$). With polynomic decision rules, the value of alternatives with more extreme criterion scores is higher than the value of alternatives with values closer to average. This is even more so as the base (in this case, 2) increases. Of course, which type of decision rule should be used also depends on the policy maker's preference.

Alternatives can also be put into ranking order by using lexicographic decision rules. Criteria are considered stepwise in order of importance, and alternatives are removed from the analysis if they do not have a maximum score on the criterion under consideration.

Additive difference is the last decision rule to be mentioned here. In this, alternatives are compared pairwise. Chapter 8 will show this decision rule to be the only one complying with the requirements of logic. Using the linear compensatory decision rule in our model has the advantage that it corresponds with the way many actors generally make choices; Timmermans mentions a percentage of 79 (Timmermans, 1991: 86). This correspondence mainly occurs when options are not presented simultaneously but consecutively (Plott and Levine, 1978; Tversky and Satteh, 1979; Cooper, 1980).

Compared to polynomic and cumulative decision rules, the linear compensatory decision rule tends towards a combination of conjunctive and disjunctive decision rules. Conjunctive decision rules are rules that reject alternatives on the basis of the worst score on a criterion, or on the basis of alternatives having to satisfy minimum requirements. This is comparable to what were earlier called veto criteria. Disjunctive decision rules are rules that consider extreme positive scores on a certain criterion. Whether an alternative has the most optimal score on all criteria is not crucial; what is important is whether an alternative sticks out on one criterion. In soccer, one might think of an excellent attacker being preferred because he scores many goals, regardless of whether he has any other stories to tell. If business location is an issue, one might think of a location with optimal accessibility but without any other advantages. When selecting personnel, an applicant can be selected on the basis of his knowledge in a specific area, while he scores badly on a large number of other characteristics.

The following is mainly concerned with the determination of the utility of alternatives according to seven versions of the linear compensatory decision rule.

6.3 THE EXAMPLE

Consider the following problem of choice. There are three alternatives and four criteria, and the criterion scores and weights are known. This is enough information to create a ranking order of alternatives according to preference. The information is given in Table 6.3, a completely filled-in scorecard.

	Alternatives			
Criteria	*I*	*J*	*K*	*G*
$c1$	1	2	5	30
$c2$	1000	1000	500	-50
$c3$	4	4	10	10
$c4$	50	75	25	10

Table 6.3 *The input data*

Deliberately, the scores on I and J on the second and third criterion are equal. The weights on the second and third criterion are also equal. The second criterion is to be minimized, which can be seen by the negative sign of its weight. This criterion could be interpreted as a cost criterion. The other criteria are to be optimized. Criterion 2 is most important: the absolute value of its weight is 50.

6.4 VARIOUS ANALYTICAL TECHNIQUES

The methods already mentioned all assume the following principles:

- There are at least two choice possibilities (alternatives).
- There are at least two criteria on which to compare the alternatives.
- Criteria are attributed weights according to their relative importance.
- Alternatives can be put into ranking order on the basis of their scores on various criteria, taking into account the weights of these criteria.
- The most dominant alternative (i.e. the one with the highest utility) is the preferred one.

Compilation into a ranking order

Differences between the analytical techniques are concerned with the possibilities of incorporating quantitative and qualitative criteria, the way differences in level of measurement of criteria are dealt with, and the way total (dominance) scores for alternatives are calculated. Usually evaluation methods are distinguished by the level of measurement of criterion scores and their weights.

	quantitative weights	qualitative weights
quantitative scores	expected value evamix con-discordance	
qualitative scores	permutation regime evamix concordance	permutation regime

Table 6.4 *Differences between methods*

It is striking to note that no specific methods have been developed for the assessment of alternatives having quantitative criterion scores, while the criteria themselves have been put into ranking order of importance qualitatively. It is relatively simple to make such techniques as concordance, expected value or evamix applicable to the analysis of problems with qualitative criterion weights. The Salomo computer program enables experiments with the treatment of weights. With Salomo, problems can be analysed with quantitative scores and qualitative weights, and the latter can be transformed into quantitative weights using ranking order or random weight treatment (see Chapter 5).

All analytical techniques follow this stepwise procedure:
- Standardization of weights G_c for all c criteria. This enables the comparison of different evaluations.
- Standardization of scores S_{ic} of all i alternatives on all c criteria. This enables the comparison of scores. Scores measured in

158 *Compilation into a ranking order*

money terms are made comparable to characteristics measured in square metres.
- The utility of each alternatives is calculated by:
  - Multiplication of S_{ic} and G_c for each criterion
  - Addition of the outcomes of these multiplications, which results in a utility score for each alternative.
  - Alternatives are put into ranking order based on utility scores.

Step 1. Standardization of weights and criterion scores

Standardizing weights and criterion scores is the first operation in all methods to be discussed. The scorecard becomes easier to interpret this way. All analytical methods standardize weights by dividing each weight by the sum of all absolute weights. In our example, the sum of weights of all criteria equals one hundred (30+50+10=100). It is also possible, before standardizing weights, to transform them into ranking order weights or into random weights based on the original ranking order.

Except for evamix, all analytical methods standardize criterion scores by dividing scores on a criterion by the maximum score for that criterion. In our example, the maximum score of criterion 1 equals 5, and the maximum score of criterion 2 equals 1000. Table 6.5 is a standardized scorecard showing which alternative scores best, or worst, on which criterion (those valued 1.0). Standardized scores are comparable. Whereas Table 6.1 is about scores that are measured at different levels, in Table 6.5 all scores are expressed in one standardized unit of measurement. In everyday language: apples and pears are seen as fruits

$$G'_c = \frac{G_c}{\sum_{c=1}^{M} |G_c|}$$

G'_c is the transformed weight

G_c is the original weight

$\sum_{c=1}^{M} |G_c|$ is the sum of all absolute weights

Formula 6.3   *Standardization of weights*

Compilation into a ranking order

	Alternatives			Weight
Criterion	*I*	*J*	*K*	*G*
c1	0.2	0.4	1.0	0.3
c2	1.0	1.0	0.5	-0.5
c3	0.4	0.4	1.0	0.1
c4	0.66	1.0	0.33	0.1

Table 6.5 *The standardized scorecard*

It is possible to standardize weights and criterion scores in exactly the same way. This can be done by using either Formula 6.3, 6.4 or 6.5 for both criterion scores and weights. Calculating z scores (statistical standard scores) is also a possibility. Normally, the evamix method uses Formula 6.5 to standardize criterion scores. Regardless of which method has been used, after standardization the highest value scored on a criterion is transformed into a standard score equal to 1.0.

$$S'_{ic} = \frac{S_{ic}}{\max S_c}$$

S'_{ic} is the standardized score
S_{ic} is the original score
$\max S_c$ is the maximum score on a criterion

Formula 6.4 *Standardization of scores*

$$S'_{ic} = \frac{S_{ic} - \min S_c}{\max S_c - \min S_c}$$

$\min S_c$ is the minimum score on c
$\max S_c$ is the maximum score on c

Formula 6.5 *Standardization of scores according to evamix*

Additionally, using Formula 6.5, the minimum score of a criterion or weight is transformed into 0.0. In the case of weight standardization, this is problematic because the criterion having the lowest weight, ergo a standard weight of 0.0, will then be disregarded.

Step 2 Utility Compilation

$$U_i = \sum_{c=1}^{n} S''_{ic} * G'_c$$

Formula 6.6 *Utility function*

Although all methods assume the linear compensatory decision rule given in Formula 6.6, they differ in the way standard scores S''_{ic} are entered into the formula. The value of S''_{ic} can be equal to the standardized score of an alternative on a criterion (expected value method, $S''_{ic}=S'_{ic}$), the difference between standard scores of alternatives ($S''_{ic}=S'_{ic}-S'_{jc}$, evamix, con-discordance), or the sign of the difference between standard scores of alternatives ($S''_{ic}=1$ when $S'_{ic}>S'_{jc}$ and $S''_{ic}=-1$ when $S'_{ic}<S'_{jc}$). The latter transformation is useful when criterion scores are at ordinal level of measurement.

The expected value method

The expected value method to determine the total value of an alternative is most common when all criteria and weights have been expressed in quantitative terms. In that case, criteria are measured at interval or ratio level in terms of e.g. money, square metres or decibels. The example in the first section shows the precise operation of this method.

Simplicity, transparency and logic are the strong points of the expected value method. If the values of criteria on all alternatives are known, as well as the importance of criteria, the expected value method produces an unambiguous ranking order of alternatives. For each alternative, each criterion score is multiplied by its related criterion weight. For each alternative, these multiplications are added up to produce a dominance score indicating its utility. Table 6.6 shows alternative K to have the highest utility score (dominance). Given criteria and weights, alternative K is to be preferred over alternative J and the worst alternative I.

	Alternative		
	I	j	k
Criterion			
c1	0.06	0.12	0.30
c2	-0.50	-0.50	-0.25
c3	0.04	0.04	0.10
c4	0.067	0.10	0.033
Utility	-0.33**	-0.24	0.183

*   0.06 is the standardized criterion score (0.2) multiplied by the standardized criterion weight (0.3) See Table 6.5.
** -0.333 (=0.06+-0.5+0.04+0.067) is the final utility score of alternative I

Table 6.6   *Ranking order of alternatives using the expected value method*

The concordance method

To the concordance method only criterion weights are important. Criterion scores are irrelevant and analysed at ordinal level of measurement, that is they will only be interpreted in terms of 'higher' and 'lower'. If on a criterion the score for alternative I is higher than the score for alternative J, the related criterion weight is added to the utility score of alternative I and subtracted from the utility score of alternative J. If the scores are equal, dominance scores remain unchanged. This is repeated for all criteria. To control the calculation, the sum of dominance scores of all alternatives should equal 0.0. Dominance scores (U=utility) of alternatives I, J and K are given in Table 6.7.

Again, following the concordance method, alternative K is preferred over alternatives I and J. Again alternative I is the least preferred. Using the concordance method involves two questions. First, does alternative I score better or worse on a certain criterion, and secondly, what is the weight of that criterion? If I scores better on C1 than J, the absolute weight of C1 is assigned to I, if not to J, regardless of the magnitude of the difference between I and J. According to this principle, all alternatives are compared for all criteria. This results in a ranking order of dominance independent of the magnitude of differences and therefore independent of standardization of the original scores. After all, standardization does not change the ranking order of scores on a criterion.

	Alternative			Weight
	I	J	K	
Criterion				
C1	+	++	+++	0.3
C2	++	++	+	-0.5
C3	+	+	++	0.1
C4	++	+++	+	0.1

+ indicates a relatively positive valuation

sum of dominance scores
U_i = -0.3^a - 0.3 (+ 0.0) -0.5 (+0.0) - 0.1 - 0.1 + 0.1 = - 1.2
U_j = $+0.3^b$ - 0.3 (+ 0.0) -0.5 (+0.0) - 0.1 + 0.1 + 0.1 = - 0.4
U_k = +0.3 +0.3 + 0.5 +0.5 +0.1 + 0.1 - 0.1 - 0.1 =+1.6*

*preferred alternative

a   This is -0.3 because alternative I scores worse on criterion C1 than alternative J. The weight of criterion C1 (0.3) is subtracted from the dominance score of I.
b   This is 0.3 because alternative J scores better on criterion C1 than alternative I. The weight of criterion C1 (0.3) is added to the dominance score of J.

Table 6.7 *Ranking order of alternatives using the concordance method*

The discordance method

To the discordance method the values of weights are irrelevant. Only the sign of weights, whether they are costs or benefits, is taken into consideration. Alternatives are compared using the differences between standardized criterion scores. If alternative I scores worse on a criterion than alternative J, taking the sign of the criterion weight into consideration, the absolute difference between the scores on I and J is added to the dominance score of I and subtracted from the dominance score of J. The dominance scores (U=utility) of alternatives I, J and K are given in Table 6.8. In this case, the alternative having the lowest dominance score is to be preferred. Again, K is most preferred and I is the worst option.

	Alternative			Weight
Criterion	I	J	K	
C1	0.2	0.4	1.0	1*
C2	1.0	1.0	0.5	-1
C3	0.4	0.4	1.0	1
C4	0.67	1.0	0.33	1

U_i = 0.2 + 0.8 + 0.0 + 0.5 + 0.0 + 0.6 + 0.33 - 0.33 = 2.1
U_j = -0.2 + 0.6 + 0.0 + 0.5 + 0.0 + 0.6 - 0.33 - 0.67 = 0.5
U_k = -0.8 - 0.6 - 0.5 - 0.5 - 0.6 - 0.6 + 0.33 + 0.67 = -2.6**

sum of dominance scores   0.0

* only the sign of weights is relevant
** preferred alternative

Table 6.8 *Ranking order of alternatives using the discordance method*

The discordance method takes into account only the magnitude of differences of standard scores on criteria and not their weights. If I scores better on C1 than J, the absolute difference of scores is assigned to J, that is it will be subtracted from the dominance score of J. The alternative having the lowest negative total utility score is the dominant alternative. Here, standardization is of great influence to the final dominance of I over J. Only the signs of criterion weights are relevant. Whether a criterion has a weight of 1 or 100 is irrelevant to the outcomes of the discordance method.

The con-discordance method

The con-discordance method is a combination of concordance and discordance methods. The outcome of this method equals the outcome of the concordance method minus the outcome of the discordance method. This results in the dominance scores given in Table 6.9.

	Concordance -	Discordance	= Con-discordance
$U_I =$	(− 1.20) −	(+2.10) =	− 3.30
$U_J =$	(− 0.40) −	(+0.50) =	− 0.90
$U_K =$	(+ 1.60) −	(− 2.60) =	+ 4.20
	Sum of dominance scores	=	0.00

Table 6.9 *Ranking order of alternatives using the con-discordance method*

As its name suggests, the con-discordance method is derived from the concordance method and the discordance method. Both take into account only one aspect of multi-criteria analysis, i.e. either scores or weights. The con-discordance method calculates the dominance score of alternative I by subtracting the dominance score of I according to discordance from the dominance score of I according to concordance.

Fictitious example

	I	J	weight
C1	0.5	1.0	4
C2	1.0	0.25	2

Outcome according to concordance
$U_I = -0.66 + 0.33 = -0.33$
$U_J = 0.66 - 0.33 = +0.33*$

Outcome according to discordance
$U_I = 0.5 - 0.75 = -0.25*$
$U_J = -0.5 + 0.75 = 0.25$

Outcome according to con-discordance
$U_I = -0.33 - -0.25 = -0.08$
$U_J = 0.33 - 0.25 = 0.08*$

*gives preferred alternative

Table 6.10 *Consequences of different standardization techniques for con-discordance*

The outcome of this method is a combination of differences between alternatives on criteria and the importance of these criteria.

Here we are faced with the consequences of standardizing weights differently from standardizing scores. Where two alternatives are considered equal by other analytical methods, this method enables preference to be given to an alternative because of the standardization technique. For example, the score on criterion C1 for alternative I is twice the score for alternative J. Alternative J scores four times as high as alternative I on criterion C2. The weight of C1 is twice the weight of criterion C2. Normally there would be no dominance of one alternative over the other. However, Table 6.10 shows that the con-discordance method does give preference to one or the other.

The regime method

The regime method operates exactly like the concordance method. Here too only the actual weights and the ranking order of criterion scores are taken into account. The difference from the concordance method is that alternatives are compared pairwise for all criteria. If alternative I scores better on a criterion than another alternative, the weight of that criterion is added to the dominance score of I. Otherwise the weight of that criterion is subtracted from the dominance score of I. This results in the pairwise dominance scores given in Table 6.11.

$U_{I,J}$ = -0.3 +0.0 +0.0 -0.1 = -0.4 => I<J
$U_{I,K}$ = -0.3 -0.5 -0.1 +0.1 = -0.8 => I<K
U_I = -1.2

$U_{J,I}$ = +0.3 +0.0 +0.0 +0.1 = +0.4 => J>I
$U_{J,K}$ = -0.3 -0.5 -0.1 +0.1 = -0.8 => J<K
U_J = -0.4

$U_{K,I}$ = 0.3 +0.5 +0.1 -0.1 = +0.8 => K>I
$U_{K,J}$ = 0.3 +0.5 +0.1 -0.1 = +0.8 => K>J
U_K = +1.6

Table 6.11 *Ranking order of alternatives using the regime method*

Although addition is different, the outcomes of the regime method are identical to the outcomes of the concordance method. Again alternative K is preferred, then J and finally I. Dominance scores are identical to those of the concordance method.

The regime method differs from previous methods because it can also be applied when only qualitative criterion scores are available. Although alternatives can be distinguished by their scores on criteria, this is only done on the basis of i being better or worse than j. Scores are measured at ordinal level which makes it impossible to calculate sum totals or averages. The multiplication of scores with quantitative or qualitative weights is also meaningless.

Basic to the method is the pairwise comparison for each criterion. The sign of the difference of criterion scores (plus or minus) between pairs of alternatives is multiplied by their related criterion weights. The sum total of scores over all criteria indicates whether I is better or worse than J.

The evamix method

The evamix method assumes two kinds of criteria, i.e. qualitative and quantitative criteria. Quantitative scores are standardized according to Formula 6.7.

$$S'_{ic} = \frac{S_{ic} - \min S_c}{\max S_c - \min S_c}$$

$\min S_c$ is the minimum score on c
$\max S_c$ is the maximum score on c

Formula 6.7 *Standardization of scores according to evamix*

Step one: the original scorecard is divided into two, because quantitative criteria allow for more analytical possibilities than do qualitative criteria, and because the objective of this method is to actually use all information contained in the data when calculating total scores. One scorecard lists qualitative criteria, the other lists quantitative criteria.

Step two: alternatives are compared on the basis of qualitative criteria. If I scores better than J on a criterion, the first alternative dominates the second, and a value equal to the weight of the criterion is attributed to I. If I scores worse than J, this results in a negative dominance.

Step three: the total dominance of one alternative over another is calculated by repeating the second step for all criteria and adding up the resulting dominance scores. This way a dominance matrix results that contains the total dominance of each alternative over any other alternative, with regard to qualitative criteria.

Step four: the values of all quantitative criteria are standardized. This can be done by, for example, dividing each value by the maximum value scored on the criterion concerned. The weight of a quantitative criterion is multiplied by the value difference of two alternatives regarding the criterion concerned. The outcome determines the extent to which one alternative dominates the other, or the other way around. This produces a dominance matrix that contains the total dominance of each alternative over any other alternative, with regard to quantitative criteria.

Step five: evamix makes a comparison of both dominance matrices. To do this, the standardization of both matrices is necessary. All values in the qualitative dominance matrix are added up and all values in the matrix are divided by this sum.

Step six: the total weight of the qualitative dominance matrix is determined by adding up the weights of all qualitative criteria. The same procedure is followed with regard to the weight of the quantitative dominance matrix.

Step seven: the extent to which one alternative dominates another is calculated as follows. Each value in the standardized qualitative matrix is multiplied by the total weight of all qualitative criteria, and each value in the standardized quantitative matrix is multiplied by the total weight of all quantitative criteria.

Step eight: qualitative and quantitative matrices can now be combined. The total dominance of alternative I is calculated by adding up the dominance scores of alternative I over all other alternatives (the values in the final dominance matrix are added up horizontally). It can be seen that the value of any alternative is influenced by the values of other alternatives in a number of steps, because of standardization.

Step nine: the ranking order of alternatives is determined in such a way that the worst alternative influences the ranking order of better alternatives equally as much as the differences between the better alternatives mutually.

The standardized scorecard is divided into a quantitative and a qualitative scorecard. Suppose in this example C1 and C3 are qualitative criteria and C2 and C4 are quantitative criteria. The resulting two scorecards are presented in Table 6.12 and Table 6.13.

	Alternatives			G
Criteria	I	J	K	
C2	1.0	1.0	0.0	-0.5
C4	0.5	1.0	0.0	0.1

The sum of the absolute weights is 0.6

Table 6.12 *Quantitative standardized scorecard*

	Alternatives			G
criteria	I	J	K	
C1	+	++	+++	0.3
C3	+	+	++	0.1

The sum of the absolute weights is 0.4

Table 6.13 *Qualitative standardized scorecard*

The qualitative scorecard is analysed in the same way as is done by the regime method. Only criterion weights are taken into consideration. The analysis of quantitative scores uses the differences between criterion scores of pairs of alternatives. This is multiplied by criterion weights and results in dominance scores of one alternative over another according to Formula 6.8.

$$D_{ij} = \sum_{c=1}^{k} (S_{ic} - S_{jc}) * G_c$$

S_{ic} and S_{jc} are the scores of alternatives i and j on criterion c

Formula 6.8 *Regime method*

This results in two dominance matrices (Table 6.14 and 6.15)

	I	J	K
I	---	-0.05	-0.45
J	0.05	----	-0.40
K	0.45	0.40	----

The sum of the absolute scores is 1.8

Table 6.14 *Dominance-matrix quantitative*

	I	J	K
I	---	-0.3	-0.4
J	0.3	----	-0.4
K	0.4	0.4	----

The sum of the absolute scores is 2.2

Table 6.15 *Dominance-matrix qualitative*

Then the dominance relations between alternatives over quantitative and qualitative criteria are combined into one score.

The pairwise dominance of qualitative and quantitative criteria are added up, taking into account the total weight of quantitative and of qualitative criteria and also the sum of all absolute dominance scores in both matrices. This results in the rather complicated Formula 6.9.

$$U_i = \sum_{j=1}^{n} \left[\frac{D_{quan}(i,j)}{\sum_{i=1}^{n}\sum_{j=1}^{n}|D_{quan}(ij)|} * \sum_{c=1}^{K}|G_{cquan}| + \frac{D_{qual}(i,j)}{\sum_{i=1}^{n}\sum_{j=1}^{n}|D_{qual}(ij)|} * \sum_{c=1}^{L}|G_{cqual}| \right]$$

$D_{quan}(i,j)$ is dominance of alternative i over alternative j based on the quantitative criteria (see Table 6)

$D_{qual}(i,j)$ is dominance of alternative i over alternative j based on the qualitative criteria (see Table 7)

$\sum_{c=1}^{K}|G_{cquan}|$ and $\sum_{c=1}^{K}|G_{cqual}|$ are weight summations of respectively K absolute quantitative and L absolute qualitative criteria

Formula 6.9 *Utility in Evamix-method*

All this leads to the dominance scores given in Formula 6.10. According to Tables 6.14 and 6.15, the sum of all quantitative criterion weights equals 0.6 and the sum of all qualitative criterion weights equals 0.4. Here too alternative K is the preferred alternative, and I is the worst alternative.

$$U_I = \frac{-0.05}{1.8}*0.6 + \frac{0.45}{1.8}*0.6 + \frac{-0.3}{2.2}*0.4 + \frac{-0.4}{2.2}*0.4 = -0.294$$

$$U_J = \frac{0.05}{1.8}*0.6 + \frac{-0.4}{1.8}*0.6 + \frac{0.3}{2.2}*0.4 + \frac{-0.4}{2.2}*0.4 = -0.135$$

$$U_K = \frac{0.45}{1.8}*0.6 + \frac{0.4}{1.8}*0.6 + \frac{0.4}{2.2}*0.4 + \frac{0.4}{2.2}*0.4 = 0.429$$

Formula 6.10 *Result of Evamix method*

The Evamix method operates in a way similar to that of the expected value method. The main difference is that Evamix allows for both

170 Compilation into a ranking order

quantitative and qualitative criteria - qualitative in the sense that it is known that alternative I scores better than alternative J on a criterion, but how much better is unknown. Again, the objective is to calculate total scores for alternatives on the basis of standardized criterion scores and the standardized weights of criteria. This results in a ranking order of alternatives based on dominance as given in Formula 6.10.

The permutation method

The objective of the permutation method is to find not the best alternative but the best ranking order of alternatives. Here too criterion scores are taken to be qualitative. Only criterion weights and the sign of the difference between scores are taken into consideration. In our example, six ranking orders are possible.

I J K
I K J
J I K
J K I
K I J
K J I

Table 6.16 *All possible permutations given three alternatives*

Suppose the first ranking order is correct. This implies I being better than J, J being better than K, and I being better than K. The permutation method compares this with the actual ranking order according to each criterion. If both ranking orders match, the value of this ranking order is augmented by the value of the weight of the criterion. In the reverse case, the value of this ranking order is reduced by the value of the weight of the criterion.

Each of the six ranking orders corresponds to a greater or lesser extent to the actual ranking order of alternatives on criteria. The objective is to find the ranking order that corresponds best to the criterion scores and weights. The first ranking order is completely contrary to the ranking order according to the first criterion C1. Both ranking orders are exactly opposite for all pairs of alternatives (I,J), (I,K) and (J,K). Therefore, the value of this ranking order is subtracted by three times the weight of the C1. For both the second and the third criterion (C2 and C3), the ranking orders are opposite twice and do not correspond once. This results in another negative score for this ranking order equal to 2*0.5+2*0.1. Regarding the fourth criterion, the ranking orders correspond twice and are opposite once, which results in a positive score of (2-1) times the weight of C4. The score for ranking order IJK now becomes: -3*0.3+-2*0.5+-2*0.1+1.0.1=-2.0. Of all permutations the ranking order KJI scores highest: its value equals 2.0. So K is the best alternative, followed by J and finally I.

The permutation or qualiflex method focuses not on the scores of alternatives, but on the best ranking order of alternatives. Starting off with qualitative scores, a dominance score is calculated for each possible ranking order. A ranking order may completely correspond to the scores of alternatives on a criterion. In that case, the dominance of this ranking order is augmented by the weight of that criterion multiplied by the number of times this ranking order corresponds with the ranking order of scores of alternatives on that criterion. Having two alternatives and a weight equal to 0.66, this complete correspondence results in a dominance equal to 2*0.66. The maximum dominance score of a ranking order of alternatives now equals the number of alternatives (the sum of weights being equal to 1.0). The criterion scores of the alternatives themselves are of little importance. Mainly the criterion weights are significant in determining the best ranking order of alternatives.

6.5 INTERPRETATION OF RANKING ORDER

6.5.1 Variation of outcomes with identical scores

It is of course possible that different analytical techniques using the same set of criterion scores and weights will produce different ranking orders of alternatives. First of all, this may indicate that differences between alternatives are small. Therefore, it is recommended not to study just the ranking order but also the dominance scores, which may indicate an almost equivalent position of the alternatives. If dominance scores turn out to be relatively wide apart, the individual preference of a decision maker for one or the other analytical technique becomes important. Recently, the practice of multi-criteria evaluations seems to have developed a preference for the permutation method. The next chapter will show how unfortunate this preference is. It can be very useful to separately analyse two alternatives whose place in the ranking order is uncertain, because their relative positions may be determined by the positions of other alternatives.

6.5.2 Input of scores in a new analysis

A second issue is the stepwise approach as suggested in Chapter 3. If the number of criteria exceeds six to eight, it is recommendable to divide the analysis into two or more analyses. Utility can then be first calculated on the basis of, for example, financial criteria, then feasibility criteria and finally criteria with regard to content. These three analyses will produce three ranking orders and three series of dominance scores. Dominance scores or ranking orders can be used as input for an overall analyses, provided weights are attributed to the main criteria. Criterion scores in the overall analysis are qualitative when ranking orders are used. Formally, criterion scores in the overall analysis are also qualitative when they are based on dominance scores resulting from an analysis of qualitative criterion scores. However, it can be useful to consider these dominance scores as quantitative, at interval level of measurement. Some people hold the opinion that dominance scores contain more information, reflecting the proportionate relations between alternatives better than a ranking order. Others claim that, formally, dominance scores do not contain enough information to attribute any meaning to these proportionate relations between alternatives.

6.6 CONCLUSION

Seven analytical techniques for impact assessment were discussed in this chapter. The arithmetic operations and the rationale of each technique was elaborated. It was then discussed how to interpret a ranking order of alternatives on the basis of their utility, and how the output of impact assessment may serve as input for a new evaluation. Here a warning should be given. Impact assessment suggests an unambiguous ranking order; however, the next chapter will show this suggestion to be incorrect. Also, a critical reader might wonder whether such algorithms can replace the choice process of a decision maker. In this respect, a remark by McNamara is interesting:

> 'It is true enough that not every human situation can be fully reduced to lines on a graph or to percentage points on a chart. But all reality can be reasoned about, and not to quantify what can be quantified is only to be content with something less than the full range of reason.' (McNamara, 1968)

7 Analysing the outcomes

> This chapter focuses on the analysis of outcomes, possibilities and limitations. There are two basic conditions multi-criteria evaluation methods should satisfy in order to be meaningful. The influence of adding criteria and/or alternatives with regard to outcomes will be discussed. Outcomes will turn out to vary by adding alternatives and/or criteria. Finally, recommendations will be made concerning the use of the analytical methods.

Tasks
|
Alternatives
|
Criteria
|
Test scores
|
Importance of criteria
|
Compilation of data
|
Analysis of ranking order
|
Leave decisions to the decision maker

INTRODUCTION

In the Middle Ages, the philosopher Buridan was attacked by his critics for his theory on psychological determinism, which suggested that people cannot but make the most preferable choice. His critics invented the well-known ass (later known as Buridan's Ass) who had to choose between two identical stacks of hay, but could not. According to Buridan, the ass could not but make the best choice. According to the critics, the ass - being offered identical stacks - could not choose and thus had to starve amidst plenty.

Scientists using multi-criteria evaluation may well claim to have solved this problem. Their answer is: 'Increase the number of criteria by which the alternatives are compared, and a dominant alternative will appear.' They claim to be able to compare even more than two

174 *Analysing the outcomes*

alternatives on the basis of many criteria, where each criterion has its own weight. Furthermore, they provide algorithms, making such an evaluation more 'objective'.

Multi-criteria evaluation methods are comparable to cost-benefit analysis. However, the advantage of multi-criteria evaluation methods is that they enable criteria measured in units other than price to be considered. In this chapter, it will be shown that these techniques have some serious shortcomings.

7.1 DECISION REQUIREMENTS

The outcomes of impact assessments suggest an unambiguous ranking order. This suggestion is founded on two basic conditions. Firstly, further alternatives should not influence the utility of other alternatives. Secondly, criteria that do not discriminate between alternatives should not influence the utility of alternatives.

These two requirements are part of a list of requirements that rational decisions have to meet. In 1954 Milnor formulated ten criteria that decisions should satisfy (J. Milnor, in: R.M. Thrall et al., 1954; see also Arrow, 1951). He used these criteria to study the Laplace principle (maximization of average output), the Wald principle (minimax), the Hurwicz principle (optimism) and the Savage principle (minimax regret). Milnor's ten axioms are the following:

Transitivity	Transitivity is when $r_i > r_j$ OR $r_j > r_i$, but not $r_i > r_j$ AND $r_j > r_i$ (r is priority or dominance and i,j are options). The latter case would be circularity.
Symmetry	Priority ranking is independent of the order of presentation of alternatives and criteria in all choice situations. This means that the preference for options depends only on their relevant characteristics and not on the way they are presented.
Strong dominance	If the score of r_i on each criterion is better than the score of r_j, then $r_i > r_j$.
Continuity	If in the case of k multiple choices between the same alternatives, criteria and effect scores, rk>rk', then r>r' applies to the limit row. If the content of the choice situation does

	not alter, neither may the ranking of the options.
Linearity	Ranking does not change when all criterion scores of all alternatives are transformed in the same way: $a'_{ij}=\lambda a_{ij}+\mu$, $\lambda>0$. The unit by which the criteria are measured (e.g. pounds, dollars or marks) may not have any impact on the priority ranking of options.
Row adjunction	Ranking of alternatives does not change when new alternatives are added. The principle of row duplication was formulated later; it states that the ranking of options is invariant to uniform extension of the set of choices (Yellot, 1977).
Column adjunction	Ranking of alternatives does not change when criteria are added, provided these criteria are constants. When all options have the same score on a particular criterion, the ranking of alternatives should be identical before and after addition of that criterion.
Column duplication	Ranking of alternatives does not change when criteria are added that are identical to the original criteria.
Convexity	If the scores of a fictitious alternative A are equal to the average of two other equivalent alternatives B and C, the preference for A will be greater than for B (no bias against randomizing). If two alternatives are equivalent, there is no objection to selection by the toss of a coin.
Special row adjunction	Ranking of alternatives does not change when new alternatives are added that score lower on all criteria than the original alternatives. This axiom was elaborated by Luce, and is now known as Luce's first axiom.

From these axioms it can be concluded that two alternatives are equivalent when the only difference between them is the order of presentation of effect scores. It can also be concluded that the choice between alternatives should not change when new alternatives are added that are dominated by at least one original alternative.

The axioms are particularly concerned with the framing problem. That is, choices should not change just because the presentation of the problem changes while its content remains the same. The axioms are concerned with the inherent logic underlying decision-making. The better the decision process satisfies the axioms, the better (more rational) the decision. In this respect, the axioms of Luce and Yellot (row adjunction and special row adjunction) are crucial. When these two conditions are not met, the conditions of transitivity, strong dominance, continuity, linearity and convexity will not be completely met. The extent to which these basic conditions are violated by each analytical technique determines the incorrectness of resulting policy choices and the extent to which they may be subjected to criticism.

Here, the intention is not to discuss the external problems of evaluation methods, such as the question how weights and criterion scores can be determined; the issue is the sensitivity of evaluation methods to the adding or leaving out of criteria and alternatives, as a consequence of the algorithm chosen to calculate dominance scores for alternatives. The three major problems with regard to the outcomes of impact assessment are:

- The outcomes are sensitive to the adding of alternatives that are a priori insignificant because of a relatively low score on all or most relevant criteria.
- The outcomes are sensitive to the adding of criteria that do not discriminate between alternatives because criterion scores on all alternatives are equal.
- The final ranking order does not always satisfy the transitivity requirement. This means that the utility of I does not have to be greater than the utility of K, although the utility of I is greater than the utility of J and the utility of J is greater than the utility of K.

The first problem occurs when a choice between two alternatives is framed in a choice problem that considers three alternatives. Framing may not influence the relative ranking order of the first two alternatives. In that case, the method drops into the pitfall of irrationality it was designed to avoid. You do not think Oprah Winfrey is more amusing than Jerry Springer because Jenny Jones is so boring. A similar problem occurs when adding criteria. Suppose a third criterion (for instance, political feasibility) with equal scores on all alternatives. Such a criterion is not allowed to influence the outcomes of a multi-criteria analysis. The question is, does it influence outcomes? This chapter deals with the question whether impact assessment methods satisfy the following two basic requirements.

Condition 1
Evaluation methods are expected to produce a ranking order of alternatives according to a preference that does not change when adding a third alternative that is worse than the first two.

It will be demonstrated that none of the evaluation methods discussed fully satisfies this condition. The question will be asked whether methods can be put into a ranking order of sensitivity and whether recommendations can be made to minimize the consequences of this problem.

Condition 2
Evaluation methods are expected to produce a ranking order of alternatives according to a preference that does not change when adding criteria that score equally on all alternatives.

We will see, however, that evaluation methods are different regarding sensitivity. There are other conceivable conditions in addition to the two given above; however, they will be only briefly mentioned here. First, preference analysis in psychometrics uses requirements regarding strong, limited or weak transitivity. This condition is concerned with the extent to which alternative I is preferred over alternative K, given that I is preferred over J and J is preferred over K (Coombs, 1983; Luce 1959, 1977; Tversky 1969). Second, Luce's choice axioms may be mentioned (e.g. the axiom stating that a choice is independent of the order in which criteria are taken into consideration). The third is Yellot's axiom (1977), which states that the probability of choices should not change when the number of alternatives is uniformly extended. When a cup of coffee is preferred over a cup of tea or a glass of milk, this should also be the case when the number of alternatives is extended to, for example, 100 cups or glasses of each. Here, the main issue is individual choice behaviour, but the axioms are also applicable to comparisons of the characteristics of 'objective' choice algorithms, i.e. evaluations.

7.2 A SIMPLIFIED EXAMPLE

To clarify the first problem, an example using the expected value method will be presented. The other two problems will be dealt with later in this chapter. Suppose a policy maker is dealing with a problem concerning the increasing traffic in inner cities. Fictitiously he might have a choice of two alternatives:

I   Extension of parking facilities in the centre.
J   Extension of parking facilities in the suburbs and improvement of public transport into the centre.

The two criteria that will be used to make a decision are:

C1   Costs in millions of dollars.
C2   Percentage increase of the number of visitors.

The importance of both criteria should be determined. However, stakeholders cannot decide which criterion is more important than the other. Both criteria are attributed equal weights, for example, 1. Because costs are negative and the increase of visitors is positive, the resulting weights are:

G_1 -1.
G_2 1.

Using fictitious scores Table 7.1, a so-called scorecard presents the alternatives and criteria. This example shows that alternative I is more expensive than alternative J, but also that the percentage increase of visitors is higher with alternative I than with J.

Example	*Alternative*		*Weight*
	I	J	
Criterion			
Costs	$ 20 million	$ 10 million	- 1
increase	16%	8%	+1

Table 7.1   *An example where both alternatives have equal dominance*

Analysing the outcomes

This results in the two alternatives being equally preferred. The expected value method produces the dominance scores presented in Formula 7.1.

$$U_I = [\frac{20}{20} * -\frac{1}{2}] + [\frac{16}{16} * \frac{1}{2}] = 0.0$$

$$U_J = [\frac{10}{20} * -\frac{1}{2}] + [\frac{8}{16} * \frac{1}{2}] = 0.0$$

Formula 7.1 *Calculation of dominance scores*

The outcomes indicate that both alternatives have equal utility. This approach to problems of choice has, as stated earlier, its own inherent logic. The pros and cons of alternatives considering several criteria are taken into account. The criteria have been made comparable and the importance of criteria is also accounted for. It is this logic that has led to the increased use of impact assessment by policy makers.

Nevertheless, such an evaluation method can produce peculiar results. Suppose there is a third alternative, namely a traffic circulation plan. Its costs are 40 million and an increase of the number of visitors is not expected. In other words, this is a bad alternative. When dominance scores are calculated taking into account also this alternative, the outcomes will be as given in Formula 7.2.

$$U_I = [\frac{20}{40} * -\frac{1}{2}] + [\frac{16}{16} * \frac{1}{2}] = 0.250$$

$$U_J = [\frac{10}{40} * -\frac{1}{2}] + [\frac{8}{16} * \frac{1}{2}] = 0.125$$

$$U_K = [\frac{40}{40} * -\frac{1}{2}] + [\frac{0}{16} * \frac{1}{2}] = -0.500$$

Formula 7.2 *Calculation of dominance scores using a third alternative*

It is now suggested that alternative I (extension of parking facilities in the centre) is better than alternative J. Obviously this outcome is artificial. The proportions between alternatives have not changed at all. The result is a consequence of the method used and of adding a third alternative. It turns out that the expected value method is sensitive to the adding of alternatives. The question now is whether other methods of impact assessment also show this sensitivity.

7.3 THE ANALYSIS

7.3.1 Adding bad alternatives

Consider the 'city marketing' problem with three alternatives and two criteria. Alternative I is to extend of parking facilities in the centre, alternative J is to extend parking facilities in the suburbs and improve public transport, and alternative K is a traffic circulation plan. Alternatives I and J are equally dominant, though alternative I is twice as expensive as alternative J, but also twice as effective. To analyse the influence of bad alternative K on the other two alternatives, the data in Table 7.2 will be used.

	Alternatives			Weight
	I (PFC)	J (PFS)	K (TCP)	
criteria				G
Costs	100	50	variable	-1
effectivity	10	5	2.5	+1

Table 7.2 *Scorecard*

The only unknown (variable) is the value of alternative K regarding costs. This value should be 25 or higher because we want alternative K to be irrelevant. In that case the total dominance score of alternative K should be lower than the total dominance scores of either I or J. We must remember here that the weight of costs is negative. The effectiveness of alternative K has been fixed at half the effectiveness of alternative J, scoring lower than I on that criterion.

Sensitivity of the expected value method

Figures 7.1 and 7.2 illustrate the variation of dominance of I and J as a function of costs, using two evaluation methods. For both analytical techniques, the dominance of extending parking facilities in the centre (I) and the dominance of extending parking facilities in the suburbs and improving public transport (J) are represented on the y axis. The x axis represents the costs of a traffic circulation plan (C_K).

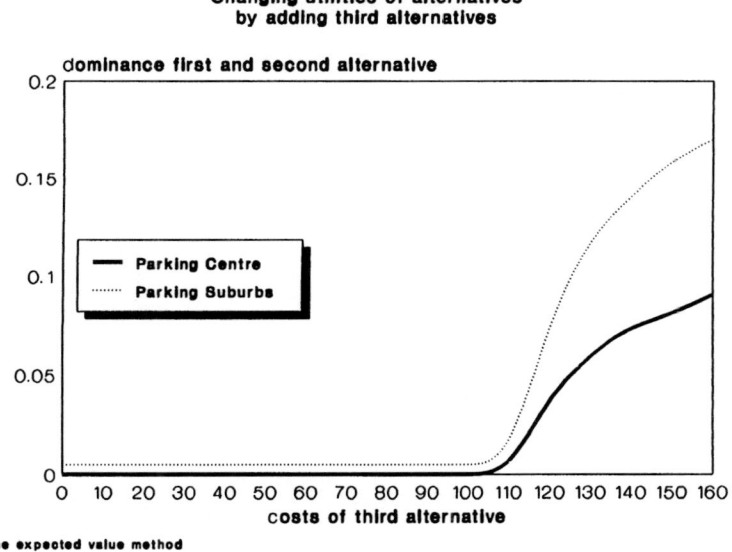

Figure 7.1   *Sensitivity of the expected value method*

Two limitation values are important to the interpretation of the figures. The first limitation value is when the costs of K equal 50, making the costs of K higher than costs of J. This changes the position of J in the ranking order of costs from 2 to 1. The second limitation value is when the costs of K equal 100. This makes the costs of K higher than the costs of I (so far the maximum score). In that case, alternative K (the traffic circulation plan) scores worst on both criteria. At the two limitation values, all figures clearly show a change of behaviour of the two best alternatives I and J.

Figure 7.1, the expected value method, shows that the costs of a traffic circulation plan (C_K) do not affect the ranking order of the two best alternatives as long as these costs do not exceed the maximum score of 100. When the costs of a traffic circulation plan do exceed 100, making it a really bad alternative, alternative I starts to dominate alternative J. The difference between I and J increases when costs of K increase.

Sensitivity of the permutation method

The results of analysing the permutation method are similar to those of the concordance method. Figure 7.2 shows that as long as the costs of a traffic circulation plan (C_K) are between 50 and 100, alternative I dominates alternative J. If the costs of alternative K (C_K) exceed 100, however, the dominance scores of alternative I and alternative J again

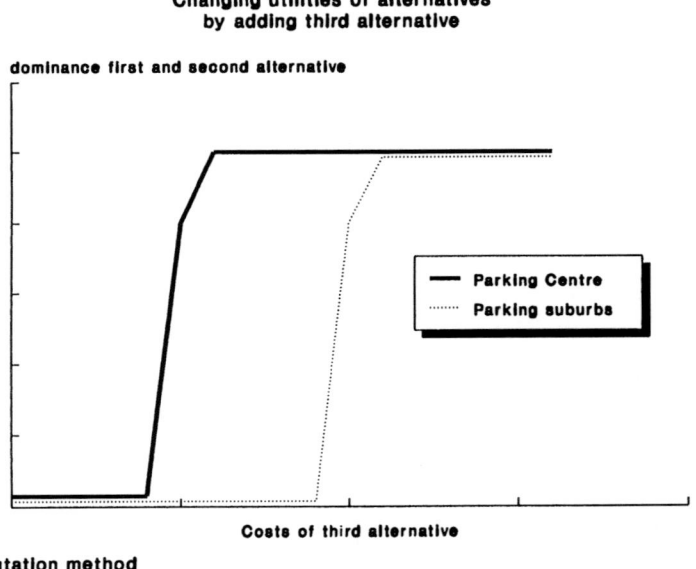

Figure 7.2 *Dominance of alternatives I and J affected by an alternative K*

become equal, at a higher level. Here too the conclusion may be that the permutation method is sensitive to the adding of bad alternatives if the scores of those bad alternatives disturb the ranking order of scores on criteria of the original alternatives.

7.3.2 Adding criteria

This section will present an analysis similar to the previous one. The sensitivity of evaluation methods to the adding of non-discriminatory criteria will be investigated. Non-discriminatory criteria are criteria for which all alternatives have the same score. It may be expected that evaluation methods are insensitive to the adding of such a criterion.

The same city-marketing policy problem used in the previous analyses will be used here. Alternative I is to extend parking facilities in the centre, alternative J is to extend parking facilities in the suburbs and improve public transport, and alternative K is a traffic circulation plan. The scores (which have been somewhat altered in order to help clarify the problem) are presented in Table 7.3.

Criteria	Alternatives			Weight
	I	J	K	
Costs	50	150	200	-2
Effectiveness	5	10	2.5	4
Political feasibility	8	8	8	variable

Table 7.3 *Analysis of condition 2*

The difference between the costs of I and the costs of J is half the difference between the effectiveness of I and the effectiveness of J. Because effectiveness weighs twice as much as costs, the outcome of the evaluation is that these two alternatives are equivalent. Alternative K is added with costs higher and effectiveness lower than the other alternatives I and J.

This analysis is about adding a third criterion (e.g. political feasibility) on which all three alternatives score equally. The weight of this criterion is variable. Dominance scores, as a function of a non-discriminatory criterion, indicate the sensitivity of evaluation methods to the adding of criteria. Figure 7.3 shows the outcomes of the analysis using the expected value method.

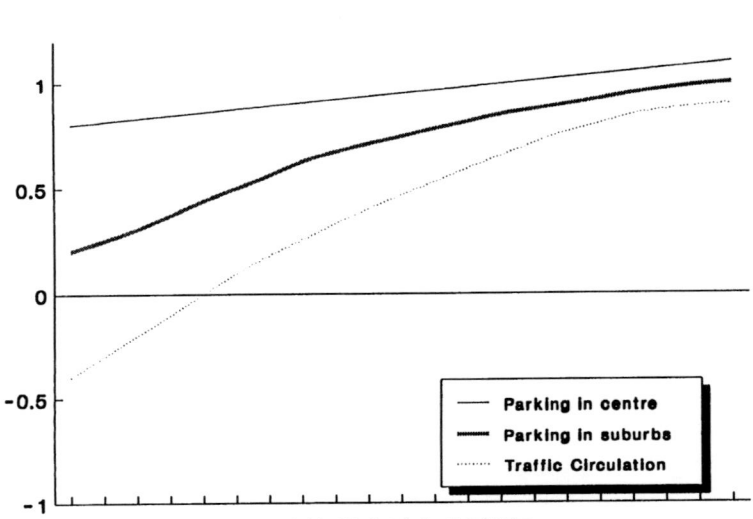

Figure 7.3 *The influence of adding irrelevant criteria*

First of all, the ranking order of dominance of the alternatives does not change. The discordance method even turns out to be completely insensitive to the adding of criteria. However, a drawback to this method is that the best two alternatives are not considered to be equivalent, even without the third criterion. This is a consequence of the discrepancy in the way weights and scores are standardized, and applies to all methods using qualitative scores.

The expected value method does not show a noticeable change between the two best alternatives. However, when criterion scores of the added criterion are slightly different from each other, this may change dramatically. In that case, the ranking order of alternatives changes directly. Secondly, it turns out that the difference between alternatives becomes smaller when the weight of the non-discriminatory criterion increases. The latter phenomenon can be seen when using the expected value, evamix, regime, concordance or con-discordance method.

With the permutation method, the ranking order of dominance is insensitive to the adding of new criteria. Analysis shows that differences between alternatives are smaller when the weight of the added criterion is extremely high. These changes, however, remain minimal.

7.4 STEPWISE AND PAIRWISE ANALYSIS

Does this analysis of the adding of bad alternatives and non-discriminatory criteria lead to the conclusion that multi-criteria analysis has become useless? The presented results provide arguments to support this. However, there are four reasons why this would be an unsatisfactory conclusion.

Firstly, there is a need for techniques that 'objectify' decision processes. Presenting the dominance of alternatives in relation to each other in one single figure can be a powerful argument in the final decision-making process.

Secondly, deliberations in a decision-making process become clear and verifiable by using multi-criteria analysis. As was stated in Chapter 1, multi-criteria analysis has an intrinsic value that is not completely cancelled out by its shortcomings.

Thirdly, the algorithms on which multi-criteria analysis is based are open to improvements. New standardization methods or new methods of standardizing weights and criterion scores identically could be developed.

Fourthly, it is not necessary to reject the good with the bad. Despite its shortcomings, and provided it is applied carefully, multi-criteria analysis can enhance the rationality of policy choices. Multi-criteria analysis is the optimalization of utility functions. However, in general choices primarily involve the most dominant alternative and to a much lesser extent the alternatives that are in third or fourth place. Despite the shortcomings of the method, this most dominant alternative can be found in a reliable way. In order to arrive at reliable outcomes, the following procedure is recommended.

First of all, all irrelevant criteria need to be removed, i.e. the ones that hardly play a part in the decision process because they do not discriminate between alternatives. Criteria that do not discriminate alternatives at all need to be kept outside the analysis, regardless of their importance. If they were included in the analysis, the results might become distorted because differences between alternatives would be underestimated. Indicating a factor of discrimination for each criterion when presenting a multi-criteria analysis is recommended in order to improve verifiability of the results. For each criterion, such a factor of discrimination can be calculated by using e.g. Formula 7.3. When all discrimination factors are equal, or have a value of at least 1.0, the results of multi-criteria analysis seem to be more reliable. Reliability is less when the discrimination factor of one or more criteria is close to zero. The Salomo software program automatically gives the discrimination factor for each criterion.

$$\frac{Max\ S_c - Min\ S_c}{\overline{S_c}}$$

Formula 7.3 *Discrimination factors*

Two procedures can be used in multi-criteria analysis to reduce the effect of third alternatives on a ranking order of dominance.

The first is called *pairwise evaluation*. Each pair of alternatives is evaluated separately. The alternative that scores better than all other alternatives, pairwise, is the dominant one. A disadvantage of this approach is its labour intensity. With n alternatives, $½*n*(n-1)$ evaluations are required.

The second procedure is called *stepwise evaluation* and is less laborious. First, the analysis is done over (n) alternatives. This results in a ranking order of dominance. Then, the least dominant alternative is left out and the analysis is repeated using n-1 alternatives. This goes on until two alternatives remain; thus n-1 evaluations are necessary. With six alternatives, a pairwise evaluation implies 15 repetitions, and a stepwise evaluation implies 5 repetitions. With stepwise evaluation, the utility of the most dominant alternative is finally determined by the outcome of multi-criteria analysis over the two most dominant alternatives. The disadvantages of this approach are its lower accuracy and the need to satisfy the requirement of transitivity, e.g. if alternative A is worse than B and B is worse than C, then A should also be worse than C. The validity of stepwise evaluation depends on whether the transitivity of the outcomes can be assumed. The problem with leaving out worst alternatives is that, just like the best alternative, the worst alternative can also be an artefact of the number of alternatives.

In psychometry, extensive research has been done about transitivity and intransitivity when determining subjective preferences. Strong transitivity of outcomes X, Y, and Z exists when the following two conditions have been satisfied.

$$X>Y \text{ and } Y>Z \Rightarrow X>Z$$
$$X=Y \text{ and } Y=Z \Rightarrow X=Z$$

With impact assessments, an alternative can only be the worst alternative if it is dominated by all other alternatives. To investigate whether transitivity is always the case with impact assessments, the alternatives are evaluated pairwise in two cases. Only in one case can the outcome be interpreted unambiguously; namely, when the results are as presented in Table 7.4.

Taken together	is pairwise dominant over
Alternative A	4 alternatives
Alternative B	3 " "
Alternative C	2
Alternative D	1
Alternative E	0

Table 7.4 *Order of dominance*

The evaluation of all alternatives together results in alternative A being the most dominant, followed by alternatives B, C, D and E. Pairwise evaluation also shows A to be the best alternative. Alternative A dominates the other four alternatives. Alternative B is second and dominates the remaining three alternatives. This goes on up to alternative E not dominating any other alternative. Alternative E is dominated by all other alternatives. Another possible outcome is given in Table 7.5.

Here there can be no transitivity. Pairwise, alternative D and E both are dominant over one of the other alternatives. In at least one case this has to be a dominance over alternative A, B or C. By leaving out alternatives D and E stepwise, an alternative that is better than one of the remaining alternatives is removed from the analysis. In the case of such a

188 *Analysing the outcomes*

result, a stepwise procedure is impossible and pairwise evaluation should be used. Whether this kind of problem does occur in reality will be discussed in the following section.

Taken together	is pairwise dominant over
Alternative A	3 alternatives
Alternative B	3 " "
Alternative C	2 " "
Alternative D	1 alternative
Alternative E	1 " "

Table 7.5 *Order of dominance*

7.5 THE 'LOCATIONS FOR A NUCLEAR POWER STATION' CASE

In 1985, an impact assessment commissioned by the Dutch Ministry of VROM was made about possible locations for a new nuclear power station. Nine locations were considered and their appropriateness was evaluated using fifteen criteria.

Table 7.6 presents the scores of the fifteen criteria on the nine locations. A low score on a criterion is better than a high score. All criterion scores are ordinal. The only observation that can be made is whether one alternative is better or worse than another alternative. How much better or worse cannot be deduced from the criterion scores. Weights, as they have been used in the analysis, are also shown in Table 7.6. A low weight indicates a criterion of higher importance. Originally four sets of weights were distinguished. The analysis here only considers the economic weight set that was used.

Given the nature of criterion scores and weights, only some evaluation methods can be used. Originally the analysis was made on the basis of the permutation or qualiflex method. The alternatives in ranking order of dominance are presented in Table 7.7.

There is no doubt that economically the Maasvlakte turns out to be the best location for a new nuclear power station, given the criteria and weights attributed to them. In the original analysis this alternative was qualified as 'very good'. Flevo-Noord, Ketelmeer and Noordoostpolder were qualified as 'good', Eemshaven as 'moderate', Borssele and Wieringermeer as 'bad', and Bath and Moerdijk as 'very bad'.

location criteria	1	2	3	4	5	6	7	8	9	weights
1	3*	3	1	2	2	3	4	1	1	1**
2	1	2	1	1	1	2	1	1	1	5
3	2	2	2	2	2	1	3	2	2	2
4	1	4	3	2	1	5	3	1	1	2
5	1	1	1	2	2	1	2	2	2	3
6	2	1	1	1	1	1	3	1	1	2
7	2	1	2	3	3	1	2	3	3	4
8	2	2	2	2	2	1	2	2	2	2
9	3	2	2	2	3	1	2	3	3	2
10	2	3	3	2	1	2	4	1	1	5
11	3	1	1	1	3	1	2	3	3	6
12	3	1	3	1	2	1	1	1	1	5
13	2	2	3	1	1	2	2	2	3	2
14	2	1	1	2	2	1	1	2	2	2
15	2	3	3	2	2	4	3	1	1	2

*lower scores are better scores
**lower scores are more important

Locations: 1. Bath 2. Borssele 3. Eems 4. Flevo 5.Ketelmeer 6.Maasvlakte 7.Moerdijk 8.Noordoostpolder 9.Wieringermeer

Criteria: 1 population density 2 evacuation possibility 3 pollution of agricultural land 4 danger to industrial areas nearby 5 polluted surface water 6 cooling water (quantitative) 7 cooling water (qualitative) 8 decrease air pollution 9 utility of residual heat 10 indirect space occupation 11 landscape effects 12 natural environment effects 13 connection to net structure 14 connection to infrastructure 15 appropriateness for using coal

Table 7.6 *Evaluation matrix of locations for a nuclear power station*

The second column in Table 7.7 presents the outcomes of a pairwise impact assessment. The table shows for each alternative how many other alternatives are dominated when compared pairwise. Criteria on which both alternatives in a pair have identical scores are removed from the analysis.

Permutation method ranking score=5.67	pairwise dominant over
Maasvlakte	8
Flevo Noord	5
Noord Oost Polder	7
Ketelmeer	3
Eems	5
Wieringermeer	4
Borssele	3
Bath	1
Moerdijk	0

Table 7.7   *Alternatives in ranking order of dominance*

Undoubtedly the Maasvlakte is again the best alternative and turns out to dominate all eight other alternatives. The position of Moerdijk is also evident. The alternative is dominated by all other alternatives (score 0).

Undisputed also is the position of Bath/Hoedekenskerke. This alternative is dominant over Moerdijk only, and is dominated by all other alternatives. The ranking order of dominance of the remaining six alternatives is striking. While the original analysis showed Flevo-Noord as the second location to be preferred, a pairwise analysis indicates that this alternative dominates only five rather than seven other alternatives. The outcome of pairwise analysis is that Noordoostpolder is dominant over Flevo-Noord. Noordoostpolder is worse than Maasvlakte, but it dominates all other alternatives (score 7). The position of this alternative is also unambiguously determined. So, four out of nine alternatives are clearly positioned by pairwise analysis. Maasvlakte dominates the other eight alternatives and Noordoostpolder dominates the remaining seven alternatives. Moerdijk is worse than the other eight alternatives and Bath/Hoedekenskerke dominates only Moerdijk and is dominated by the other seven alternatives.

The dominance scores of the remaining five alternatives cannot be interpreted unambiguously. Flevo-Noord and Eemshaven are dominant over five alternatives, Ketelmeer and Borssele are dominant over three alternatives, and Wieringermeer dominates four alternatives.

When these alternatives are evaluated simultaneously using the permutation method, two ranking orders turn out to be equally good. In other words, when analysing the five alternatives, Flevo-Noord and Wieringermeer seem to score equally well. A pairwise analysis of the ranking order of dominance of these five alternatives is even more interesting. The outcomes are presented in Table 7.8.

Again it can be seen that pairwise comparisons cannot be interpreted unambiguously. Flevo-Noord dominates only three of the four remaining alternatives.

Wieringermeer dominates only two alternatives, and the previously considered worst alternat-ive, Borssele, now turns out to be pairwise dominant over one other alternative.

Under the assumption of transitivity, it is expected that Flevo-Noord is a better location than Wieringermeer, provided that Flevo-Noord is better than Eemshaven and Eemshaven is better than Wieringermeer. This conclusion turns out to be incorrect. Compared pairwise, Wieringermeer is a better location than Flevo-Noord. Thus transitivity is out of the question.

alternative			pairwise dominant over
Flevo-Noord	3	viz	Eems, Borssele and Ketelmeer
Eemshaven	3	viz	Wieringermeer, Borssele and Ketelmeer
Wieringermeer	2	viz	Flevo-Noord and Ketelmeer
Ketelmeer	1	viz	Borssele
Borssele	1	viz	Wieringermeer

Table 7.8 *Pairwise analysis of five locations for a nuclear power station*

Another case is when the three alternatives Flevo-Noord, Wieringermeer and Borssele are analysed. In the original analysis, Borssele was the worst alternative, Flevo-Noord was a good alternative and Wieringermeer a reasonable alternative. Table 7.9 shows the new ranking order of locations using a pairwise analysis based on the economic weight set. Again there is no transitivity because Wieringermeer is better than Flevo-Noord, Flevo-Noord is better than Borssele, and Borssele turns out to be better than Flevo-Noord. The only conclusion is that all three alternatives should be considered equivalent.

When compared with the ranking order of alternatives in the original analysis, these results indicate both similarities and differences.

Similarities can be found in the positioning of the Maasvlakte as being a very good alternative and in the positioning of Bath/Hoedekenskerke and Moer-dijk as being very bad alternatives. Differences can be found in the positioning of the remaining locations for a nuclear power station. Particularly the change in position of Borssele, Wieringermeer and Flevo-Noord is remarkable. The original analysis concluded that Borssele and Wieringermeer were bad alternatives, Flevo-Noord, Ketelmeer and Noordoostpolder were good alternatives, and Eemshaven was a moderate alternative. Given the intransitivity of these alternatives, the conclusion of our analysis is that they are all equivalent alternatives that cannot be unambiguously put into ranking order of dominance for reasons of circularity.

7.6 CONCLUSION

This chapter focused on the sensitivity of various techniques of multi-criteria analysis to the adding of alternatives that score relatively badly on criteria. As well as this, the sensitivity of these techniques was investigated with regard to the adding of criteria that do not discriminate between alternatives.

All seven evaluation methods are sensitive to the adding of relatively bad alternatives and non-discriminatory criteria. This concerns not only alternatives that score badly on all criteria (whose removal from the analysis is recommended in the literature), but also alternatives that are bad considering all criteria together, but that score not so badly, or even relatively well, on some of the criteria. Particularly evamix, con-discordance, permutation and concordance are sensitive to the adding of alternatives. As to adding non-discriminatory criteria, permutation and discordance in particular are robust (insensitive) methods. Characteristic of the other evaluation methods is the decrease in differences between dominance scores as the weight of the added criterion increases. The main reason for this variation of robustness seems to be the standardization of criterion scores and weights, and also the limited number of alternatives and criteria typical of most multi-criteria analyses. Nevertheless, standardization is a necessary condition in multi-criteria analysis. These evaluations can only be done if scores and weights are standardized. At the same time, this is one of the causes of their sensitivity to violation of the two basic conditions mentioned before.

Using a case study, the possibilities of stepwise impact assessment were investigated as was whether a more laborious pairwise evaluation should be preferred. It was argued that this depends on the question whether transitivity of outcomes will always exist. Impact assessment practice shows that intransitivity may occur.

The conclusion of these analyses is that impact assessment methods, while suggesting that the resulting ranking order is 'objective', can also produce an intransitive ranking order of alternatives. Transitivity is not always the case. This provides an argument to choose for pairwise instead of stepwise evaluation. In practice, this will mean that the decision makers' scope for policy-making is enlarged. After all, the choice for an alternative is not fixed by impact assessment. This can only be the case when a pairwise analysis results in one alternative dominating all the others.

The problems mentioned can be taken into account while using the currently available multi-criteria evaluation methods. The procedure suggested below is a reliable way to find the dominant ranking order of alternatives.

- Remove all non-discriminatory and nearly non-discriminatory criteria from the analysis. A recommended measure for the degree of discrimination of criteria between alternatives is

    (maximum-minimum)/mean

    When all discrimination factors are equal, or have a value of at least 1.0, the results of multi-criteria analysis are more reliable. Reliability is less when the discrimination factor of one or more criteria is close to zero.
- Make a pairwise analysis, in addition to calculating a complete ranking order of alternatives. This may be time-consuming but can be advantageous, particularly if only two alternatives are involved. In case of n alternatives, $\frac{1}{2}*n*(n-1)$ comparisons need to be made.

The Salomo computer program provides the *dominance check method*, which follows this procedure. To claim an alternative is dominant over all other alternatives is only justified if, after a complete pairwise analysis, this alternative compared to n other alternatives scores a value of n-1.

This chapter began with paraphrasing Buridan the philosopher. According to multi-criteria evaluation the solution to the problem of Buridan's Ass turned out to be incorrect. Increasing the number of alternatives and criteria does not result in valid figures representing the optimal ranking of alternatives. Sometimes the conclusion is limited to two or more alternatives being equally preferable. It might be more profitable to use the dictum of another philosopher of the school of Thomism, William of Ockham. The so-called Ockham's razor states 'Entia non sunt multiplicanda praeter necessitaem', which means 'Remove everything not strictly necessary to get the results and keep the problem as simple as possible.'

8 Leave the decision to the decision makers

Tasks
|
Alternatives
|
Criteria
|
Test scores
|
Importance of criteria
|
Compilation of data
|
Analysis of ranking order
|
Leave decisions to the decision maker

INTRODUCTION

All steps of the tactical approach have been discussed in the previous chapters. Although a large number of issues have been dealt with, some still remain. Given its limitations, decisions about the content of this book needed to be made. In doing so, the main criteria were understanding of the methods, critical reflection and practicability when evaluating reports using these methods.

It has been repeatedly argued that, although theory pays a lot of attention to the possibilities for making well-thought-out decisions, problems may occur in impact assessment practice. Problems may occur in all phases of the model. The way a problem of choice is defined determines to a large extent what the model will look like. There is a significant difference between the question whether aviation facilities should be extended and the question where this extension should be located. The second question implicitly provides an affirmative answer to the first question. In practice, it can be observed quite often that the decision to be taken in a decision-making process changes for strategic reasons. There is no model that could optimize this. Then there are the problems with choosing alternatives and criteria. Which are taken into consideration and which are not? How many are taken into consideration, and are they the most relevant aspects of a problem of choice? Many things can go wrong, also when determining criterion scores, making criterion weights and decision rules explicit, and analysing the ranking order of alternatives.

The conclusion that impact assessments do not have a prescriptive significance cannot be repeated often enough. A decision maker can never base his decision exclusively on such an analysis. There are simply too many choices and pitfalls. Besides, often decision makers turn out to make choices that are decisive to the outcomes, while these choices are not theirs to make and are unjustifiable. This is one of the reasons the final decision should be left to the responsible decision maker. He should determine whether or not to accept the ranking order produced by the model. It is also up to him to determine whether or not to apply this method. Not all people consider it desirable to make the elements of a choice system explicit. Some people claim that policy makers would rather not be informed about the effects of pursued and intended policy. This could undermine their already established opinions and views. For the method to be extensively and successfully used, it should clearly have surplus value, particularly when compared to intuitive decisions. Although this surplus value exists, it does not enable the method to solve such problems as 'fundamental attribution error'. This would require policy makers who have intuitively and effectively developed a programme in the past, and who now claim their personal capacity has led to these results. 'An individual who has succeeded by just plain luck tends to attribute his success to his superb capabilities and repeats his behaviour ... with disastrous results.' (In: Leeuw, 1992: 47)

The many pitfalls of the method can be used as arguments against it. Even when all suggested steps are taken, the method can still lead to suboptimal results. This is the rationality paradox. While the objective of rationality is to optimize the outcomes of policy choices on the basis of an inherently logical and phased method, the same logic leads to a debatable external validity of the method. There is even a multiple paradox as a consequence of influences from the actor system, the choice system and the calculation system. One of the paradoxical influences of the actor system is the commissioning of an impact assessment. Such commissioning may result in objectifying and therefore rationalizing a choice, at the same time having a negative influence on the usefulness of the analysis to the decision maker. The paradoxical influence of the choice system is the adding of alternatives and criteria. This means that not only will more information be incorporated in the analysis, but also that the ranking order could be distorted. The paradoxical influence of the calculation system is the necessity for standardization, which at the same time affects the unambiguous interpretation of the ranking order.

8.1 ADVANTAGES OF IMPACT ASSESSMENT

Yet, all these negative aspects should not lead to throwing out the baby with the bathwater. However, a thorough deliberation of the consequences of decisions will decrease the chance of regrets afterwards about the decision taken. Three advantages of impact assessment are given below.

The first advantage of ex ante evaluation is that results are known before decision-making is concluded. This implies that these results can be incorporated in the decision-making process.

The second advantage of impact assessment is that it is hardly threatening to decision makers, in particular when compared to a summative evaluation afterwards. No choices have been made yet, so it is impossible to judge or condemn someone on that basis. Assessments can be experienced as annoying because they limit the freedom of policy makers.

The third advantage of impact assessment is its contribution to making compromises between actors involved in decision-making. The quality of discussion is ameliorated, and wrongful suppositions can be corrected. The following sections will clarify these advantages.

8.2 USE OF IMPACT ASSESSMENT IN DECISION-MAKING

Evaluation research is often not very user-oriented. The results are delivered too late or are unaccompanied by practical recommendations. The strength of impact assessment is that it results in practical recommendations. It also explicitly puts one or more aspects related to a decision on the agenda, urging the decision maker to at least take these aspects into consideration. In this respect, environmental impact assessments have an exemplary function. Particularly when (policy) decisions have social effects, making aspects explicit and transparent enhances the democratic quality of the decision-making process. Decisions taken in such a way are easier to verify, and the actual deliberations underlying them are clear.

8.3 THREATENING INFORMATION

To the decision maker, receiving information - or even being aware of its existence - can be problematic. In many decision-making processes several decision makers are involved, each having his own interest and his own ideas about what does or does not matter. Conflicts can easily arise under such circumstances. Unequal or illegitimate power distribution are among the causes of such conflicts (Laue & Cormick, 1973). Sometimes this may even result in great anger among the stakeholders. For that reason, companies and government institutions often withhold information (Susskind, 1996) because they fear that people will contest decisions made on the basis of it. In other words, to the decision maker it is threatening to make choices explicit, transparent and verifiable. Analysing such conflicts in their book 'Dealing with Angry People', Susskind and Field (1996) indicate the effectiveness and efficiency of doing just that. First they discuss why people get angry. What in fact is anger? In their own terms 'anger is a response to pain or threat to pain, real or perceived.' Whether anger is rational or irrational is irrelevant. The first three reasons for becoming angry are concerned with the people involved: they are physically or financially affected, they are at risk of becoming negatively affected, or their norms and values are threatened. The second cluster of reasons for becoming angry comprises impotence, the perception of being cheated, and simulated anger based on strategic considerations. The usual way to deal with anger mainly results in negative consequences for the business world. Too often the advice is 'Don't talk to these people. Withhold information. They are extremists that shouldn't be given an official forum. Bring them into disrepute and ignore their demands. In extreme cases, perhaps a little money will silence them.'

The examples given by Susskind and Field indicate that this approach usually fails. Eventually costs will be higher than they would be following their strategy, which is directly inferred from their anger analysis. Their recommendation is: acknowledge the concerns of the other party, encourage joint research of the facts, ensure compensation of known, negative unforeseeable effects, accept responsibility, act credibly and try to establish a long-term relation with the other party.

No matter how naive their approach might seem at first sight, by using practical examples Susskind and Field convincingly succeed in demonstrating that it will almost always result in spending less energy, time and money. Even in cases of conflicting norms and values (the most difficult type of problem), their strategy is more efficient and more effective. Impact assessments which use joint fact-finding - during which the consequences of decisions are explicitly deliberated before they are taken - have a higher chance of accepting inevitable decisions.

8.4 THE STRATEGIC NATURE OF IMPACT ASSESSMENT

Yet, interests may diverge even in cases where the various stakeholders cooperate and have reached agreement about the facts. One group of stakeholders may emphasize the environmental consequences of a decision, while the economic aspects may be the priority of another group. In that case, because weights of criteria and actual criterion scores are equally significant to the determination of a ranking order of alternatives, two completely different ranking orders may be established, thus throwing doubt on the usefulness of impact assessment.

There are two arguments supporting the claim that impact assessment can also be useful under such circumstances. The first concerns the basic idea of decomposing a choice problem into all its constituent components. Finding facts and attributing values to criterion scores and weights are then dealt with separately (cf. Hammond, 1973; Kleindorfer, 1993). 'By decomposing a problem into a set of scientific judgments and a set of value judgments, one may be able to identify a bullet that is acceptable in the view of all parties concerned.' (cf. Kleindorfer, 1993: 227) Hammond and Kleindorfer conclude, according to social judgment theory, that the separation of facts and values is often a good technique when dealing with complex and emotionally charged discussions (idem). A priori this imposes a clear framework that limits people's roles to either value experts or (scientific) fact experts (idem). The tactical approach, which is central to this book, offers such a framework. The decomposition it suggests results in conflicts focusing on those aspects of the choice problem about which conflicts are justifiable and prevents confusion with aspects that should in fact not be part of the discussion. The second idea the tactical approach offers to control conflicts and possibly to arrive at satisfying outcomes, is that agreement may be reached about a second-best solution acceptable to all parties in cases where there are conflicting opinions about the most preferred alternative. An example concerning the organization of a nature reserve (Lauwersmeer) may serve to clarify this. In 1969, this area was cut off from the sea, which raised the question about the use of 7100 hectares of new land and 2000 hectares of fresh-water surface. The Ministry of

Defence took an option to use the area as a military exercise ground. Environmentalist, represented in the Lauwersmeer Study Group, envisaged a nature reserve combined with solely agricultural purposes.

An impact assessment, using six alternatives and five main criteria divided into fifteen subcriteria, led to an investigation of the facts and their appreciation by the parties involved (Kolfoort, 1976). The objective was to understand preferences regarding the use of the Lauwersmeer area and to find a solution acceptable to all parties involved.

	Alternatives					
	1	2	3	4	5	6
Defence criteria						
1.	1000	1000	0	0	0	0
2.	1400	1400	1400	1400	1000	0
3.	48	35	48	35	35	0
4.	10	5	0	5	2	0
Environmental criteria[1]						
1.	1.5	1.5	3.5	3.5	5	6
2.	1.5	1.5	3	4	5	6
3.	1.5	1.5	3.5	3.5	5	6
4.	1	2.5	2.5	4	5	6
Agricultural criteria						
1.	1500	1500	1500	1500	1600	1750
2.	0	0	300	300	300	300
Recreational criteria[1]						
1.	1.5	1.5	4	4	4	6
2.	1	3	2	4	5	6
Economic criteria						
1.	60	60	72	72	76	82
2.	50	50	30	30	20	0
3.[1]	6	5	4	3	2	1

[1] Environmental, recreational criteria and economic criterion 3 are ranking order scores.

Table 8.1 *Scorecard Lauwersmeer*

Six alternatives were investigated:
1. A military exercise ground for 48 weeks of the year and limitation of agricultural land.
2. A military exercise ground of limited size for 35 weeks of the year. No military exercises in the autumn because of the presence of migratory birds.
3. Preserving agricultural land, and limited space for a military exercise ground for 48 weeks of the year.
4. Preserving agricultural land, and limited space and time for a military exercise ground for 35 weeks of the year.
5. Limited space and time for a military exercise ground, and closing the Zoutkamp-Lauwersoog provincial road.
6. No military use of Lauwersmeer, and closing the Zoutkamp-Lauwersoog provincial road.

Five main criteria, divided into fifteen subcriteria, were investigated:

Defence criteria
1. Presence of a shooting practice area for light weapons and military exercises on foot.
2. Presence of a shooting practice area for heavy weapons and military exercises using vehicles.
3. The number of weeks each year that military exercises are allowed.
4. The appropriateness of the military exercise ground.

Environmental criteria
1. Diversity of species with regard to botanical value.
2. Diversity of vegetation types with regard to botanical value.
3. Diversity of species with regard to breeding birds.
4. Diversity of species with regard to migratory birds.

Agricultural criteria
1. Number of hectares of heavy sandy clay.
2. Number of hectares of light sandy clay.

Recreational criteria
1. Noise nuisance caused by military exercises.
2. Attractiveness of the area.

Economic criteria
1 Employment in agriculture.
2 Employment in defence activities.
3 Military spending in the region.

In the scorecard (Table 8.1) the defence and environmental alternatives, respectively 1 and 6, are clearly discernible. The issue now is to determine which criteria are most important. Opinions about this vary from one party to another. Table 8.2 presents the criterion weights attributed by the Ministry of Defence and the set of weights attributed by the environmentalists.

Weights of		Defence	Environment alists
Defence criteria	1	8	5
	2	10	8
	3	10	8
	4	7	3
Environmental criteria	1	5	9
	2	6	10
	3	6	10
	4	7	9
Agricultural criteria	1	5	6
	2	3	6
Recreational criteria	1	8	8
	2	7	4
Economic criteria	1	7	2
	2	8	2
	3	7	2

Table 8.2 *Sets of weights Lauwersmeer*

A simple analysis results in the Ministry of Defence preferring alternative 3, and the environmentalists preferring alternative 5. However, a complete analysis indicates that both parties prefer the same second-best solution, i.e. alternative 4, where agricultural land is preserved and limited time (35 weeks) and space is allocated to a military exercise ground (see Table 8.3). This demonstrates that by using the tactical approach, differences between parties involved can be traced and be made explicit, and also that reaching a compromise is possible.

This implies that impact assessment - notably joint fact-finding and the explication of weights - is able to accelerate negotiations considerably and to clarify where different opinions might meet (a common second-best solution). Joint fact-finding prevents effects from being formulated to fit a desired choice.

Environmentalists ranking order	Department of Defence
Alt 5	Alt 3
Alt 4 <------->	Alt 4
Alt 6	Alt 5
Alt 3	Alt 2
Alt 2	Alt 1
Alt 1	Alt 6

Table 8.3 *Strategic function of impact assessment*

Although this example does not imply that second-best solutions are always acceptable to all parties involved, it does indicate the direction where a solution to the problem might be found. The model serves only as a tool. However, the crucial point of this chapter is that in the end decisions should be left to decision makers.

8.5 CONCLUSION

A final remark about the recommendations made in each chapter of this book. It should be clear that a lot of research still needs to done in order to analyse the appropriateness of these recommendations. The objective of this research should be to create possibilities for analysing policy, linking rationality and politics without one dominating or negatively affecting the other. Such research may result in evaluation methods becoming more than just a tool for determining policy, which is only one phase of the policy process. Instruments with a higher descriptive value may be developed, making the determination of policy more rational because all conditions have been satisfied. At first sight, the model seems simple to apply. However, the great number of conditions that have to be fulfilled brings about the need for reflection in every phase about choices being right and steps being taken at the right time. It is necessary to comply with the recommendations, but certainly not sufficient when prescriptive values are required from an evaluation report using impact assessment. Only when the evaluation methods comply with sufficient requirements will it be possible to rationally deal with politics instead of politically deal with rationality.

References

Arrow, K.J., *Social Choice and Individual Values*, Wiley & Sons, New York, 1951.
Barnes, S.H. & Kaase, M., *Political Action*, London, Sage Publ., 1979.
Bazerman, M.H., *Judgement in Managerial Decision Making*, John Wiley & Sons, New York, 2 ed. 1990.
Ben Zur, H. & Bresnitz, S., The effects of time pressure on risky choice behaviour, *Acta Psychologica*, vol. 47: 89-104, 1981.
Bentham J., *The collected works of Jeremy Bentham*, Oxford UP 1970.
Bernstein, I. & Freeman, H., *Academic and Entrepeneural Research*, Russel Sage, New York, 1975.
Biegel, C., & Smit, V., *Sturend of Gestuurd? Evaluatieonderzoek naar minderhedenbeleid*, Leiden, LISWO, 1991.
Bressers, J.Th.A. & Hoogerwerf, A., (eds.), *Beleidsevaluatie*, Alphen aan den Rijn, Samsom HD Tjeenk Willink, 1991.
Brunt, L., *Anders Bekeken*, Boom Meppel, 1977.
Bryman, A., *Research methods and organization studies*, London, Unwin Hyman, 1989.
Buchanan, J.M. & Tullock, G., The calculus of consent, Logical foundations of constitutional democracy, Ann Arbor, 1965.
Buchanan, J.M., *Cost and Choice: An Inquiry in Economic Theory*, Markham Chicago, 1969.
Buck Consultants International BV, *De aantrekkingskracht van de randstad in internationaal perspectief: Markt en concurrentie analyse*, Nijmegen, 1991.
Burgelman, R.A., Managing the new venture division: Research findings and implications for strategic management, *Strategic Management Journal*, vol 6: 39-54, 1985.
Burgess, R.G., *Studies in Qualitative methodology*, Vol. 1., JAI Press, London, 1988.
Campbell, D.T. & Fiske, W., Convergent and discriminant validation by the multitrait-multimethod matrix, *Psychological bulletin* 56: 81-105, 1959.
Carter, N., R. Klein & Day, P., *How organisations measure success: the use of performance indicators in government*, Routledge, London, 1992.
Chadwick, G., *A systems view of planning; Towards a theory of urban and Regional Planning process*, Oxford, Pergamon press, 1971.

Chaffin, W.W., Individual stability in Delphi studies, *Technological forecasting and social change*, 1980 p. 67-73.

Chen, H.T. & Rossi, P.P., The Multi Goal, Theory Driven Approach to Evaluation: A Model Linking Basic and Applied Social Science, *Evaluation Studies Review Annual* Vol. 6 1981.

Chen, H.T. & Rossi, P.H., Evaluating with sense: The theory driven approach, *Evaluation Review*, Vol 7/3: 283-302, 1980.

Choucri, N.M. (ed.), *Forecasting in International Relations: Theory, methods, problems, prospects*, Freeman, San Francisco Calif., 1978.

Christensen, L.B., *Expermimental Methodology*, Allyn & Bacon, Boston, 1988.

Christensen-Szalanski, J., Problem Solving strategies: A selection mechanism, some implications and some data, *Organizational Behaviour and Human Performance*, vol. 22: 307-323, 1978.

Chu, P.C. & J.J. Elam, *Decison process, task complexity and decison support system effectiveness*, Ohio state university working paper, 1988.

Churchman C.W., *Prediction and optimal decision*, Prentice hall, Englewood cliffs, 1961.

Converse, P.E., The nature of belief systems in mass publics, in: D. Apter (ed.), *Ideology and discontent*, New York, Free Press, 1964.

Cook, T.D. & Campbell, D.T., *Quasi experimentation*, Chicago: Rand MacNally, 1979.

Cook, T.D. & W.R. Shadish Jr, Program Evaluation The worldly science, in: *Annual Review of Psychology* 37: 193-232 1986.

Coombs, C.H., *Psychology and Mathematics*, Michigan Up, 1983.

Cooper, L. Recent themes in visual processing: A selective review, in: R. Nickerson (ed.) *Attention and Performance VIII*, Eilbaum, Hillsdale, New York, 1980.

Cordray D.S., & M.W. Lipsey, Program Evaluation and Program Research, in: *Evaluation Studies Review Annual*, Vol 11: 17-44, 1986.

Crano, W. & M. Brewer, *Principles of research in Social Psychology*, New York, McGrawHill, 1973.

Cronbach L.J., *Designing evaluations of educational and social programs*, Jossey Bass, San Francisco, 1982.

Cronbach L.J. et al., *Toward Reform of Program Evaluation*, Jossey Bass inc, San Francisco, 1980.

Culhane, P.J., H.P. Friesema & J.A. Beecher, *The Content and Predictive Accuracy of Environmental Impact Assessments*, London, Boulder, 1987.

Dasgupta, A.K. & D.W. Pearce, *Cost benefit Analysis: Theory and Practice*, MacMillan, 1972.
Deutsch, K.W., *The nerves of government*, The Free Press, Glencoe 1963.
Dror, Y., *Public policy making reexamined*, Chandler, Scranton, 1968.
Dror, Y., Muddling through, Science or Inertia?, *Public Administration Review* 153-158 1964.
Dror, Y., *Policymaking under Adversity*, Transaction inc., New Brunswick, 1988.
Dunn, W.H., Public policy analysis, Prentice hall, Englewood cliffs, 1981.
Eckstein, H., Casestudy and theory in political science, in: F.L. Greenstein & N. Polsby (eds.), *Handbook of political science*, vol. 7: 79-137, Menlo Park, Addison-Wesley, 1975.
Etzioni, A., *The Active Society: A theory of societal and political processes*, New York, The Free Press, 1968.
Etzioni, A. Mixed scanning: A third approach to decision making, *Public Administration Review*, vol 27, 385-392, 1967.
Etzioni, A., Rationality is anti-entropic, *Journal of Economic Psychology* Vol 7., 1986.
Faludi, A. & H. Voogd, *Evaluation of Complex Policy Problems*, Delfsche Uitgevers Maatschappij BV., 1985.
Feldman, M.S., *Order without design: Information production and policy making*, Stanford UP Californiam, 1989.
Feldman, M.S. & James G. March, Information in Organizations as Signal and Symbol, in: *Administrative Science Quaterly* 26, 171-86, 1981.
Festinger, L., *A theory of cognitive dissonance*, Stanford UP, 1957.
Festinger, L., *Conflict decision and dissonance*, Stanford UP, 1964.
Fisher, R.A., *The design of Experiments*, Hafner Publ. Comp, New York, 1971.
George, A.L., Casestudies and theory development: The method of structured focused comparison, in: P.G. Lauren, *Diplomacy*, New York, 1979.
Gezondheidsraad, *Delphi onderzoek oecologie*, verslag van een commissie van de gezondheidsraad, 1985.
Gill, G.T., *Economics*, Prentice Hall, Englewood Cliffs, 1973.
Glaser, B. & A. Strauss, *The discovery of grounded theory: Strategies for qualitative research*, Chicago Aldline, 1967.
Gordon, G. & E.V. Morse, Evaluation Research, In A. Inkeles et al., *Annual Review of Sociology*, Palo Alto, Calif., 1975.

Guba, E.G. & Y.S. Lincoln, The countenances of fourth generation evaluation: Description, judgment and negotiation, in: *Evaluation Studies Annual Review* vol 11: 70-88, 1986, Sage london.

Guigou, J.C., On French location models for production units, in: *Regional and Urban Economics* 1971, vol 1 no 2.

Harrison, J.R. & J.G. March, Decisionmaking and postdecisional surprise, in: *Administrative Science Quarterly*, Vol. 29: 26-42 1984.

Henderson, P.W. & R.A. Peterson, mental accounting and categorization, in: *Organizational behavior and Human Decision Processes*, 51: 91-117, 1992.

Hersen, M. & D.H. Barlow, *Single Case Experimental Designs*, Oxford Pergamon, 1976.

Herweijer, M., De dynamiek van doelstellend gedrag: Een struikelblok bij evaluatie, in: *Bestuurswetenschappen*, 1981: 348-366.

Holthoon, F.L. van, *The road to Utopia, A study of John Stuart Mill's social thought*, Van Gorcum, Assen, 1971.

Hoogerwerf, A., *Departementale beleidsevaluatie*, in Ringeling & Sorber 1988.

Hoogstraten, Joh (ed.), *De machteloze onderzoeker*, Boom Meppel, 1979.

House, E., *Evaluating with validity*, Sage, Beverly Hills, California, 1980.

Houten, H. van, et al., *Mogelijkheden en dillema's van beleidsgericht Delphi Onderzoek*, Amsterdam UvA, 1988.

Huizenga, F., Interactieregimes in het regionaal bestuur: Een methodologische studie, diss VU, Amsterdam, 1993.

Janis, I.L. *Victims of Groupthink*, Boston, Houghton Mifflin, 1972.

Janis, I.L. & L. Mann, *Decision making: A Psychological Analysis of Conflict, Choice and Commitment*, Free Press, New York, 1977.

Janis, I.L. Groupthink, Psychological studies of policy decisions and fiascoes, Boston, Houghton Mifflin, 1982.

Janssen, R., & Rietveld, P., Multi criteria evaluation in land reallocation plans: A case study., in: *Environment and Planning*, 1653-1668, 1985.

Janssen, R., *De beoordeling van de gevolgen van ruilverkaveling met behulp van een multicriteria analyse*, Wageningen, De Dorschkamp, rapport nr 372, 1984.

Kleindorfer, P.R., H.C. Kunreuther & P.J.H. Schoemaker, *Decision Sciences: An Integrative Perspective*, Cambridge, Cambridge UP 1993.

Klingemann, H.D., *The background of ideological conceptualisation*, in: S.H. Barnes & Kaase, 1979.

Kolfoort, F., *De inrichting van het Lauwersmeergebied -Een multi criteria evaluatie*, doctoraal scriptie, Vrije Universiteit, 1976.

Kratochwill, T.R., *Single-Subject Research*, New York, Academic Press, 1978.

Kuypers, G., *Beginselen van Beleidsontwikkeling*, Deel A, Coutinho Muiderberg, 1980.

Laue, J.H. & G.W. Cormick, *Third party intervention in community conflict: Definitions, perspectives and experience*, Synopsis prepared for the conference on Third Party Intervention in Community Crisis, 1973.

Lebelle, P. & Sj. Muller, *Besluitvorming: Wat weten wij ervan*, Kluwer, deventer 1986.

Leeuw, F.L., *Produktie en effectiviteit van overheidsbeleid*, Vuga, 1992.

Levine R.A. et al. (eds.) *Evaluation Research and Practice: Comparative and International Perspectives*, Sage, London, 1981.

Lindblom, Ch.E. The science of muddling through, *Public Administration Review*, Vol.19, spring 1959.

Lindblom, Ch.E., Still muddling, not yet through, Public Administration Review, 517-526, 1979.

Lindblom, Ch.E., The policy making process, Prentice Hall, Englewood Cliffs, Ney York, 1968.

Lindblom, Ch.E., Ornea J.C., & Stillson, P., *On the optimum solution in operations research*, ORSA 8,5 1960.

Linstone, H.A. & M. Turoff, *The Delphi method: Techniques and applications*, Massachusetts, 1975.

Lipsey M.W. et al., *Evaluation, The State of the Art and the Sorry State of Science*, Jossey Bass Inc, San Francisco, 1985.

Luce, R.D., *Individual Choice Behaviour: A theoretical analysis*, New York Wiley, 1959.

Luce, R.D., The Choice Axiom after twenty Years, in: *Journal of Mathematical Psychology*, 16: 215-233, 1977.

Luce, R.D. et al., *Handbook of Mathematical Psychology*, New York, Wiley 1965.

Luce, R.D. & H. Raiffa, *Games and Decisions*, Wiley & Sons Inc, New York, 1957.

Maasen, P.A.M. & F.A. van Vught, De delphi-methode: Voorspeltechniek en beleidsontwikkelingsinstrument, *Beleidsanalyse*, 2: 9-17, 1984.

Management Consultancy Center, *Scenario onderzoek maaltijdvoorziening Tytsjerksteradiel*, Groningen, 1989.

Manis, J.G., Assessing the seriousness of social problems, *Social Problems* 22: 1-15, 1974.
Mann, H.B. & D.R. Whitney, On a test of whether one or two random variables is stochastically larger than the other, in: *Ann. Math. Statist.* 18: 50-60, 1947.
McCall, G.J. & G.H. Weber, *Social Science and Public Policy: The Roles of Academic Disciplines in Policy Analysis*, Associated Faculty Press, Newe York, 1984.
McFarland, A.S., *Power and Leadership in Pluralist systems*, Stanford UP, 1969.
McGrath, J.E., J. Martin, R.A. Kulka, *Judgement calls in Research*, Beverly Hills, SAGE, 1982.
McNamara R.S. *The essence of security*, Hodder and Stoughton, 1968.
Metselaar M.V., Effecten van crises en de effectiviteit van crisismanagement bij internationale conflicten, in: *Transactie* Jrg 20, 1991 (4) p. 390-401.
Miles, M.B. & A.M. Huberman, *Qualitative Data Analysis*, Beverly Hills, Sage, 1984.
Miller, G.A., The magical number seven, plus or minus two: Some limitations on our capacity for processing information, in: *The psychological review* Vol 63, 81-97 1956,
Mills, J.S., *A selection of his works*, MacMillan, New York, 1966.
Ministerie van Financiën, *Evaluatiemethoden, een introductie*, s'Gravenhage, Sdu, 1988.
Ministerie van Financiën, *Heeft beleid effect?* 's Gravenhage, Sdu, 1990.
Ministerie van Financiën, *Beleidsonderzoek*, 's Gravenhage, Sdu, 1986.
Ministerie van Volkshuisvesting, Ruimtelijke Ordening en Milieu-beheer, Min. van Landbouw en Visserij, *Handleiding Milieu Effect Rapportage*, Kon. Vermande BV 1987.
Misjan, E.J., *Elements of cost-benefit analysis*, George Allen & Unwin, 1978.
Mitchell, J.C., Case and situation analysis, *Sociological Review* 31: 187-211, 1983.
Modderkolk & Janssen, *Evaluatie op decentraal niveau*, in Ringeling en Sorber 1988.
Mol, N.P., *Bedrijseconomie voor de collectieve sector*, Samsom /VUGA, Enschede, 1986.
Mulder, Th. J., *Leiders en Informatie*, Academic Service, Schoonhoven, 1992.

Mulder H.P., G. Walraven et al., Gebruik van Beleidsevaluatie bij de rijksoverheid, Beleidswetenschap 3: 203-227, 1991.
Muller, Sj., *De onberedeneerbaarheid van te nemen beslissingen*, in Lebelle & Muller, 226-246, 1986.
Nederlands Economisch Instituut, *Maatschappelijke Evaluatie van een mogelijke kustuitbreiding tussen Hoek van Holland en Scheveningen*, Rotterdam, 1986.
Newton, T., *Cost-benefit analysis in administration*, George Allen & Unwin, 1972.
Nijkamp, P. et al., Multi criteria analysis and regional decision making in: *Studies in applied regional science* vol. 8 Leiden, Martinus Nijhoff, 1977.
Page, A.N., *Utility Theory: A Book of Readings*, New York, John Wiley & Sons, 1960.
Patton, M.Q., *Practical Evaluation*, Sage London, 1982.
Patton, M.Q., *Utilization Focused Evaluation*, Beverly Hills/London 1978.
Plott, C. & M. Levine, A model of agenda influences on committee decision, *American Economic Review*, Vol. 68: 2-6, 1978.
Polsby, N., *Community power and political theory*, New Haven, Yale UP, 1963.
Prest, A.R. & R. Turvey, Cost-benefit analysis: A Survey, in: *Economic Journal*, vol. 75 no. 300 1965.
Pröpper, I.M.A.M., *Argumentatie en Machtsuitoefening in Onderzoek en Beleid*, Diss, Enschede, 1989.
Pröpper, I.M.A.M., Beleidsevaluatie als argumentatie, *Beleidswetenschap*, 2: 113-136, 1987.
Raad voor Energie onderzoek, *Meerjarenplan voor het energieonderzoek*, Den Haag, 1981.
Reussing, G.H., *Evaluatie van bestuurlijke schaalverandering*, Groningen, publikatiereeks SBN, 1990.
Ridgeway, V.F. Dysfunctional consequences of performance measures, *Administrative Science Quaterly*, 1956.
Rietveld, P., *The use of qualitative information in decisionmaking under uncertainty*, Amsterdam, V.U., 1982.
Ringeling, A.B. & A. Sorber (eds.), *Macht en Onmacht van Bestuurlijke Evaluaties*, Ver. voor Bestuurskunde, Den Haag, 1988.
Rokeach, M., *The nature of human values*, New York, The Free Press, 1973.

Rosenthal, U., *Rampen, rellen, gijzelingen: Crisisbesluitvorming in Nederland*, Amsterdam, 1984.

Rossi, P.H. & W. Williams, *Evaluating Social Programs: Theory, Practice, and Politics*, Seminar Press New York, 1972.

Rossi, P.H. & H.E. Freeman, *Evaluation: A Systematic Approach*, Sage, Beverly Hills, 1982.

Runkel, P.J. & E. McGrath, *Research on Human Behaviour: A Systematic Guide to Method*, New York, Holt, Rineman & Winston, 1972.

Saaty T.L., Scaling methods for Priorities in hierarchical Structures., in: *Journal of Mathematical Psychology*, Vol 15: 234-281, 1977.

Sabatier, P.A., An advocacy coalition framework of policy change and the role of policy-oriented learning therein, *Policy Sciences*, 21:129-168, 1988.

Schellens, P.J.M.C., *Redelijke argumenten: Een onderzoek naar normen voor kritische lezers*, diss R.U.U. 1985.

Schellens, P.J.M.C., Vijf bezwaren tegen het Toulmin model: *Tijdschrift voor Taalbeheersing*, 226-246, 1979.

Schneider, A.L. & R.E. D'arcy, Policy Implications of Using Significance Tests in Evaluation Research, in: *Evaluation Studies Review Annual*, 599-60, 1984

Schuur, W.H. van, *Structure in Political Beliefs*, diss., Groningen 1984.

Scriven M.S., *The logic of Evaluation*, Iverness, CA Edgepress, 1980.

Scriven M.S., New Frontiers in Evaluation, *Evaluation Studies Annual Review*, 109-110, 1986.

Scriven M.S., Pros and cons about goal-free evaluation, in: *Evaluation Comment*, 1-7, 1972.

Scriven M.S., The methodology of evaluation, in: R.E. Stake (ed.) *Curriculum Evaluation*, Rand McNally, Chicago, 1967.

Shannon, C., Mathematical theory of communication, Bell Systems Technical Journal, vol.27: 370-423, july 1948.

Shannon, C. & W. Weaver, The mathematical theory of communication, Un. of Illinois UP, Urbana, 1954.

Smith & May, The artificial Debate, in: McGrey & M.J. Wilson, *Decision making, approaches and analysis*, 1985: 116.

Stufflebeam D.L. & W.J. Webster, An Analysis of Alternative Approaches to Evaluation, in: *Educational Evaluation and Policy Analysis*, 1980: 5-20.

Suchman E., *Evaluation Research*, Russell Sage, New York, 1967.

Susskind, L & P. Field, *Dealing with angry people: the mutual gains approach to resolving disputes*, The Free Press, New York, 1996.

Svenson O., Decision rules and information processing in decision making, in: T. Tyska & J.A. Wise (eds.), *Human decision making*, Bodafors, Sweden: 131-162.

Timmermans, D., *Decision aids for bounded rationalists, An evaluation study of multi attribute decision support in individual and group settings*, Dissertatie, R.U. Groningen, 1991.

Toulmin, S., *Knowing and Acting*, MacMillan, New York, 1976.

Toulmin, S., *The uses of Argument*, Cambridge U.P. Cambridge, 1958.

Turoff, M., The design of a policy Delphi, in: *Technological forecasting and Social change*, no 2. 1970: 149-71.

Tversky, A. & Kahneman, Judgement under uncertainty, heuristics & biases, *Science* 185: 1124-1131, ook in vertaling, in: Lebelle&Muller, 1986.

Tversky, A., Intransitivity of Preference, *Psychological Review* 76: 31-48, 1969.

Tversky, A., P. Slovic & S. Satteh, Contingent Weighting in Judgement and Choice, *Psychological Review*, 95: 371-384, 1979.

Tversky, A., The belief in the 'law of numbers', *Psychological Bulletin*, 87, p. 105-110, 1972.

Tversky, A., Elimination by aspects: A theory of choice, *Psychological Review*, 79: 281-299, 1972.

Tversky, A., & D. Kahneman, The framing of decisions and the psychology of choice, *Science* 211: 453-458, 1981.

Tweede Kamer, vergaderjaar 1985-1986, 43-44 18830.

Veld, D. op 't, et al., *Waar harde data ontbreken*, Scheltema en Holkema, Utrecht, 1983.

Voogd, H., *Multi Criteria Evaluation For Urban and Regional Planning*, PION ltd London., 1983.

Voogd, H., C. Middendorp, B. Udink, A van Setten, *Multikriteria methoden voor ruimtelijk evaluatieonderzoek*, Planologisch Studiecentrum TNO Delft, 1980.

Vries, M.S. de, Interdependence, cooperation and conflict, in: *Journal of Peace Research*, 1991.

Vries, M.S. de, Stepwise Multiple Criteria Evaluation, *Quality & Quantity*, 26 p. 61-76, 1992.

Vries, M.S. de, Prioriteiten (S)Tellen, multi criteria evaluatie in theorie en praktijk, *Beleidswetenschap*, 2: 126-153, 1992.

Vries, M.S. de, *Using Nonparametric Statistics in Evaluation Research*, paper for the international conference 'Social Science Methodology', Trento 1992.

Weisbrod B.A., *Economics of Public Health: Measuring the economic Impact of Deseases*, London, Oxford UP, 1962.

Weiss, C.H. & M.J. Buchuvalas, The challenge of social research to decision making, in: C.H. Weiss, *Using social research in Public Policy Making*, Lexington, 1977.

Weiss, C.H., *Evaluation Research: Methods of Assessing Program effectiveness*, Prentice Hall, Englewood Cliffs, 1972.

Werkgroep'2duizend, *het sociaal leefklimaat in vijf Roermondse wijken*, Amersfoort, 1991.

Werkgroep'2duizend, *Negen naoorlogse wijken in Leeuwarden en hun toekomst*, Amersfoort, 1990. *Het sociaal leefklimaat in vijf Roermondse wijken*, Amersfoort, 1991.

Wheelwright S.C. & S. Makridakis, *Forecasting methods for management,* 4th ed., New York John Wiley & sons Inc, 1985.

White, D.J., *Decision Methodology; A formalization of the O R process*, John Wiley, London 1975.

Wholey J.S., *Using Evaluation to improve Program Performance*, in: R.A. Levine et al., 1981.

Wiener, N., *Cybernetics*, Hermann Paris, 1958.

Wijbouw, G.E.L.A., *Atlantic Canada: A study of its locational profile via qualitative multiple criteria analysis*, diss, Rotterdam, 1983.

Wittman, D., Contrasting economic and psychological analysis of political choice, in: K.R. Monroe (ed.) *The economic approach to politics: A critical assessment of the theory of rational action*, New York, 1991.

Wright, P., The harrased decisionmaker: time pressures, distraction and the use of evidence, Journal of Applied Psychology, vol. 59: 429-443, 1974.

Wright, G., *Behavioural decision theory*, Penguin, 1984.

Yellot jr, J.I., The relationship between Luce's Choice Axiom, Thurstone's Theory of Comparative Judgement and the Double Exponential Distribution, in: *Journal of Mathematical Psychology* 15: 109-144, 1977.

Yin, R.K., *Casestudy research*, Beverly Hills, SAGE, 1984, 1993.

Yin, R.K., The casestudy crisis: Some answers, *Administrative Science Quaterly*, 26: 58-65, 1981.

Yin, R.K., The casestudy method as a tool for doing evaluation, in *Current Sociology*.

Subject Index

accuracy 76, 108, 109, 186
adding of alternatives 176, 180, 192, 196
adding of criteria 176, 183, 184, 192
ambiguous objectives 22, 24
anger 198
anonymity of experts 99
applicability 76-78, 108, 109
argumentation 29, 75, 94-97, 99, 104, 107, 108, 112, 115, 129, 134, 143, 144, 146, 150
assessing data 44
atomized individualism 151
attainability criteria 71
attribute effects 87
attribution of weights 71, 130, 131, 135, 142, 143, 147
availability of data 78
backing 95
balancing 15
barriers 59, 111
belief system 61, 62
bolstering 66, 113, 114, 120, 147
calculating system 12, 35, 37-41, 47, 49, 50, 82
case studies 20, 29, 75, 88, 101-107
case study 101-107, 109, 192, 231
case study database 107
case surveys 101
changed objectives 23
changes of policy objectives 87
choice system 12, 35, 38-41, 47, 83, 147, 196
circularity 135, 174, 192
column duplication 175

comparability of indicators 78
comparative case studies 75, 88, 101, 103, 104
compilation 27, 30, 35, 50, 51, 75, 122, 148, 160, 173, 195
completeness of information 52
complex decisions 6
compromises 197
concordance method 161-166, 182
confidence 9, 42, 44, 58
conjunctive decision rule 44, 69
consumer surplus 14
consumers organization 46
continuity 52, 174, 176
contract research 142
convergence 99, 134
convexity 175, 176
cybernetics 29, 56-59
decision requirements ix, 174
decision rule 14, 15, 38, 39, 44, 45, 50, 69, 139, 148, 153-155, 160
delphi technique 20, 98, 134
dependency structure 67
desirability criteria 71
desirability evaluation 71
disadvantages of ex ante evaluation 83
disaster alternatives 73
discordance method 162-165, 184, 185
discrimination factors 186, 193
discriminatory capacity of criteria 117
dominance check method 193
dominance matrices 167, 168

effectiveness 9, 11, 18, 33, 69, 81, 82, 89-91, 118, 180, 183, 198
efficiency 5, 11, 16, 71, 82, 89-91, 93, 198
environmental impact assessments 1, 4, 5, 9, 107-109, 115-119, 197
evaluative feedback 18
ex ante evaluation 81, 83, 85-87, 142, 197
ex post evaluation 25, 81-85, 87, 149
experimental design 17, 19, 20, 75, 103, 104
experimental research 19, 20, 45, 68, 106
external effect 14
external researchers 4, 147
failing policy 35, 55
feasibility 38, 40, 48, 59, 70, 172, 177, 183
flexibility 59
formative evaluation 16
framing 42, 45, 47, 176
fuzzy gambling 39
goal of case studies 103
goal-attainment 3
group think 46
guidelines for the evaluation 5
hedonistic principle 150
Herzberg 1
ideologues 60-62
impact assessment research 142
impartiality 108, 109
implementation 26, 53, 71-74, 81, 82, 85, 86, 108, 125
imponderabilia 12, 13, 15
importance of prioritizing 146
incrementalism 29, 51, 52, 54, 56, 59, 73
infonates 63
infophiles 63
information theory 29, 56, 58, 59
infozeros 63
integral impact assessment 119
intuitive choice model 45, 50
intuitive choice process 39, 41
intuitive choices 35, 36, 45, 50, 68
irrelevant criteria 57, 135, 184, 185
level of aggregation 68, 70, 71, 77
likert scales 134
linear compensatory decision rule 44, 148, 154, 155, 160
linearity 20, 175, 176
location alternatives 73
magical number seven 68
manipulation 93, 129
meta research 79
methodological requirements 79
micromediation 102
minimizing 69, 120, 139
nonconformity 42
opportunity costs 13
optimizing 69
ordinal level 138, 160, 161, 166
overload 57
overrating 42, 46
pairwise evaluation 186-188, 193
performance indicators 29, 31, 88-94
permutation method 170, 171, 182, 183, 185, 190, 191
pitfalls 3, 4, 33, 121, 196
policy delphi 100, 101
policy makers 1, 6, 16, 17, 21, 28, 31, 36, 38, 46, 59, 64, 74, 85, 122-124, 129, 142,

Subject index

144, 146, 147, 179, 196, 197
polynomic decision rule 154, 155
power structure 67, 129
praxeological requirements 79, 80
preference analysis 133, 134, 177
premise 95, 96
prescriptive significance 196
priorities 8, 23, 28, 29, 31, 32, 48, 72, 101, 122-126, 128-132, 143, 145-147
protocol 106, 107
q sorting technique 133
qualifier 95, 97
qualiflex method 132, 171, 188
qualitative relevance 102
qualitative scorecard 167, 168
quantitative rigour 102
Rand corporation 8, 16, 98
rationalities 45
rationality 4, 8, 41, 45, 46, 50, 52, 64, 97, 185, 196, 203, 204
rationality paradox. 196
recommendations 5, 9, 26, 33, 51, 55, 68, 74, 80, 81, 118, 128, 135, 144, 147, 149, 173, 177, 197, 203, 204
reformulation of objectives 24
regime method 165, 166, 168, 215
reliability 20, 59, 77, 80, 112, 119, 135, 144, 186, 193
reliability of measurement 77
reliable outcomes 185
replication logic 104
research bureaus 142, 146, 147
robustness 59, 192
row adjunction 175, 176
salomo xvii, 75, 157, 186, 193
scenario methodology 20
scenarios 101, 133, 145

scope of evaluation research 25
sector alternatives 72
selection of experts 99
Sen 2
sensitivity 20, 76-78, 108, 109, 176, 177, 180-183, 192
sensitivity of indicators 77, 78
shadow prices 13
side effects 3, 10, 16, 17, 25, 52, 83, 85, 87
sieve evaluation 71
significance and relevance 20
significance tests 20
simplicity 33, 89, 91, 139, 160
special row adjunction 175, 176
stages of case study 106
standardized model 36, 41, 47, 49
stepwise evaluation 68, 69, 186, 193
strength of the conclusion 96
stress 36, 65, 66
strong dominance 174, 176
structural factors 67, 74
structure of evaluation research 80
structure of interests 67
stunet study 9
subjective elements 10, 47
suboptimal results 196
summative evaluation 16, 197
symmetry 174
synoptic 46, 49, 51-55, 59, 65, 67, 73, 74
taboo 47, 64
tactical approach 3, 27-29, 31-34, 36, 40, 45, 46, 50, 195, 199
target alternatives 72
technocratic model 129
time alternatives 73

transitivity 135, 174, 176, 177, 186, 187, 191, 193
transparency 39, 47, 89, 139, 160
transparent 8, 50, 60, 135, 197, 198
triangulation 104, 105, 107
unambiguity 32, 76, 108-113, 137
uncertainty 59, 81, 86, 114, 118
unexpected outcomes 52, 59
unmeasurable objectives 23
utilitarianism 150, 151
utility theory 149

validity 20, 23, 76, 77, 104, 108, 109, 112, 114, 119, 126, 127, 186, 196
validity of an indicator 76, 77
value for money 88
value of human life 13, 14
veto criteria 71, 155
weight of groups 131
weight treatment 157
Weisbrod 12
zero alternatives 72

Author Index

Arrow 174
Barnes 60-62, 125
Bazerman 41
Beecher 108
Ben Zur 58
Bentham 149-152
Bernstein 20
Biegel 145
Bresnitz 58
Bressers 79, 82, 128
Brunt 77
Bryman 102, 104
Buchanan 152
Burgelman 103
Campbell 102, 105
Carter 88, 93
Chadwick 125
Chen 25, 26, 80, 85
Choucri 21
Christensen 58
Chu 69
Converse 60-62, 125
Cook 18, 102
Coombs 177
Cooper 155
Cormick 198
Crano 105
Cronbach 18, 19, 80, 149
Culhane 108
Dasgupta 10
Deutsch 57
Dror 39, 52, 54, 55
Dunn 95, 96
Elam 69
Etzioni 53, 73
Feldman 28, 63
Festinger 120
Friesema 108

Glaser 103
Gordon 20
Guba 24, 25
Guigou 130
Harrison 23
Henderson 43
Herweijer 21, 83, 102
Hoogerwerf 21, 79, 82, 128
Hoogstraten 43
Houten 98, 101
Huberman 103
Huizenga 102
Janis 42, 53, 64-66, 120
Janssen 21
Kaase 60-62, 125
Kahneman 41
Kleindorfer 9, 42, 199
Klingemann 60, 62
Kolfoort 200
Kuypers 21, 129
Laue 198
Lebelle 37
Levine 32, 155
Lindblom 52-54, 56, 73
Lipsey 16, 17, 20
Luce 175-177
Makridakis 21, 39, 41, 42
Manis 127
Mann 42, 53, 120
March 23, 63, 64
McCall 82
McFarland 127
McNamara 172
Metselaar 82
Miles 103
Miller 68
Misjan 14
Mitchell 102, 103

Modderkolk 21, 233
Mol 78, 91, 124, 234
Morse 20, 231
Mulder 37, 62, 63, 80, 234
Muller 232, 234, 236
Newton 10, 234
Nijkamp 135, 234
Patton 21, 23, 24, 80, 234
Plott 155, 234
Polsby 126, 230, 234
Prest 10, 234
Pröpper 94, 96, 97, 129, 234
Reussing 79, 234
Rietveld 133, 134, 231, 234
Ringeling 231, 233, 235
Rokeach 60, 125, 235
Rosenthal 103, 235
Rossi 25, 26, 80, 85, 229, 235
Runkel 105, 235
Saaty 134, 235
Sabatier 25, 235
Schellens 96, 235
Schneider 20, 235
Scriven 16, 19, 20, 25-27, 31, 80, 82, 149, 235
Shannon 56, 235
Smit 145, 228
Smith 56, 59, 92, 235
Sorber 231, 233, 235
Strauss 103, 231
Susskind 198, 236
Timmermans 46, 68, 69, 155, 236
Toulmin 95, 96, 235, 236
Turoff 100, 232, 236
Turvey 10, 234
Tversky 41, 43, 58, 155, 177, 236
Veld 221-223, 236
Voogd 58, 68-70, 128, 131, 132, 230, 236
Weber 82, 233
Webster 149, 236
Weiss 21, 80, 237
Wheelwright 21, 39, 41, 42, 237
White 38, 41, 49, 237
Wholey 31, 237
Wiener 56, 237
Wijbouw 132, 237
Wright 58, 237
Yellot 175, 176, 237
Yin 102-106, 237

DISCARDED